Early childhood studies

A multiprofessional perspective

For Sinéad and Jake

Early childhood studies

A multiprofessional perspective

Liz Jones, Rachel Holmes and John Powell

Open University Press

Open University Press
McGraw-Hill Education
McGraw-Hill House
Shoppenhangers Road
Maidenhead
Berkshire
England
SL6 2QL

email: enquiries@openup.co.uk
world wide web: www.openup.co.uk

and Two Penn Plaza, New York, NY 10121-2289, USA

First published 2005

A catalogue record of this book is available from the British Library

ISBN-13 978 0335 214 853 (pb)   978 0335 214 860 (hb)
ISBN-10 0335 214 851 (pb)   0335 21486X (hb)

Library of Congress Cataloging-in-Publication Data
CIP data applied for

Typeset by RefineCatch Limited, Bungay, Suffolk
Printed in Poland by OZGraf. S.A.
www.polskabook.pl

Contents

List of contributors

Sue Aitken is a Senior Lecturer on a range of multiprofessional degree programmes at Manchester Metropolitan University. She gained both her first degree and her MA with the Open University and has had a successful career in a range of pre-school settings, as well as experience in Further Education. Susan has undertaken research for Cheshire LEA, where she examined multiprofessional liaison between the LEA, Sure Start and Education Action Zone. She has been involved in the evaluation of the DfES pilot arrangements for the Foundation Degree in Early Years.

Ian Barron is Principal Lecturer in Early Childhood Studies at Manchester Metropolitan University, where he is Leader of the Early Years and Childhood Studies Centre. He is a committee member of the national Early Childhood Studies Degrees Network. Ian has had a variety of experiences in the early childhood field, including work in primary schools in inner London and Leeds and the headship of a nursery school in Lancashire and of an infant school in Calderdale. He was a member of the project team that developed *Birth to Three Matters: A Framework to Support Children in their Earliest Years*. His research interests and journal publications are in the areas of training of early childhood workers, constructions of childhood, critical approaches to child development and the construction of ethnic identity in young children. These include:

Barron, I. (2003) 'Towards firmer foundations? An exploration of recent developments in early years education and care', in K. Crawford (ed.) *Contemporary Issues in Education: An Introduction*. London: Peter Francis Publishers.
Barron, I. and Calcutt, C. (2000) Early childhood: too important to get it wrong, *International Journal of Children's Social and Economics Education*, Vol. 4, No. 2.
Barron, I. and Holmes, R. (2004) 'Aspects matter', in L. Abbott and A. Langston (eds) *Birth to Three Matters: Supporting the Framework of Effective Practice*. Maidenhead: Open University Press.
Barron, I. and Powell, J. (2003) Story sacks, children's narratives and social construction of reality, *Citizenship, Social and Economics Education: An International Journal*, 5(3): 129–137.

Jane Bates is a Senior Lecturer in Education at Manchester Metropolitan University. Her first degree and MPhil are in Biology and she has taught

Biology and Health related topics at 'A' Level, on specialist courses at FE level and at degree level. For many years she was Subject Leader for Life Science at MMU Cheshire. More recently, in her role as Associate Leader of Multiprofessional Programmes, she has been involved in curriculum developments within the Childhood Studies degree programmes. She is currently involved in an evaluation of the Time for Children project, run by Volunteer Reading Help for the Who Cares? Trust, and the European Social Funded mentoring project Fempowerment.

Catherine Baxter completed the Early Childhood Studies degree course at Manchester Metropolitan University in June 2001, graduating with first class honours. She developed an interest in the law as an undergraduate and completed the Postgraduate Diploma in Law in 2002, and the Postgraduate Diploma in Legal Practice in 2004, to prepare her for working as a solicitor. Her particular areas of interest are the relationship between children and the law and the treatment of juveniles by the legal system in its broadest sense – police, courts, probation service and legal professionals. During 2006 she hopes to commence practice as a trainee solicitor.

Rosemary Boys is a Senior Lecturer in Education at Manchester Metropolitan University. She presently coordinates the BA (Hons) Primary Education on the Cheshire campus. She gained her Masters in Australia and has spent her career working in both Australia and England. During this time she has worked in mainstream schools and with children with special educational needs (SEN), as a consultant and as an advisory teacher. Her areas of interest are in language and literacy development, the pedagogy of teaching literacy and special educational needs (SEN). She has also done consultancy work for Collins and Heinemann. Her most recent publications have been:

Boys, R. (2002) 'Language, literacy and communication', in I. Keating (ed.) *Teaching the Foundation Stage: Achieving QTS*. Exeter: Learning Matters.
Boys, R. (2003) *Primary English: PGCE professional workbook*. Exeter: Learning Matters.

Caroline Bradbury-Jones is a lecturer in nursing at the University of Wales, Bangor. Her professional background is in nursing, midwifery and health visiting. Prior to her present post, Caroline was a Senior Lecturer within the Department of Health Care Studies at Manchester Metropolitan University. During this time she taught the health module of the BA (Hons) Early Childhood Studies. Caroline gained her first degree and her MA at Manchester Metropolitan University. She is in the process of registering for a PhD and her research interest is in empowerment within nursing.

Karen Browne is a Senior Lecturer in Education at Manchester Metropolitan University. She has been a Lecturer in Childcare and Education in the FE sector and a primary school teacher. She has worked as a behavioural therapist – working with children with autism – and has spent time working with adolescent offenders. Her research has included investigation into the effectiveness of a behavioural modification programme for children within the autistic spectrum. Currently, Karen is engaged in research that examines the relationship between parents and carers of children with Attention Deficit Hyperactivity Disorder and the schools which their children attend.

Elaine Hodson is a member of the Early Years Centre at Manchester Metropolitan University. Previously a nursery school and primary school headteacher, she now teaches on a range of early years courses and has a particular interest in the development of literacy. As a Coordinator for Best Practice Research Scholarships on the Cheshire campus, she is committed to supporting teachers working in school-based research. The area of parental involvement in literacy learning and teaching is one in which she has a keen interest. Her recent publications include:

Keating, I., Hodson, E., Basford, J. and Harnett, A. (2002) Reception teachers responses to the Foundation Stage, *International Journal of Early Years Education*, Vol. 10, No. 3.

Rachel Holmes is a Senior Lecturer at Manchester Metropolitan University, where she teaches on the BA (Hons) Early Childhood Studies and BA (Hons) Primary Education courses. She has a background in teaching in early years, at Key Stage 1 and in the FE sector and has developed an enthusiastic interest in children's creativity, inter-agency working and multiprofessional issues within the early years. Her teaching areas within the university include children's rights, teaching studies and constructions of early childhood. She was a member of the project team that developed *Birth to Three Matters: A Framework to Support Children in their Earliest Years* and is currently involved in a number of early years research projects within the arts. She has an MA Art and Design Education and is currently doing a PhD, her research being focused around her journey as a practitioner-researcher, struggling to find ways through the interrogation of autobiographical narratives, to understand something of the complexity of her teaching 'self', working with under-graduate students. Her recent publications include:

Barron, I. and Holmes, R. (2004) 'Aspects matter', in L. Abbott and A. Langston (eds) *Birth to Three Matters: Supporting the Framework of Effective Practice*. Maidenhead: Open University Press.
Holmes, R. (2004) *An Exploration of Early Years Pedagogy in the Art Gallery*. Report to Manchester Art Gallery and Manchester Sure Start.

Liz Jones is a Senior Lecturer at the Manchester Metropolitan University. Her teaching career spans over 20 years and includes experience in both mainstream education and the special educational needs (SEN) sector. She has published extensively including articles for international academic journals. Her most recent book focused on practitioner research. Outside of the university, Elizabeth has undertaken commissions for various bodies. Currently, for example, she is working with other colleagues from MMU on the National Evaluation of the Primary School/Primary Health Care Links Initiative, as well as evaluating a neighbourhood Sure Start programme. Her recent publications include:

Brown, T. and Jones, L. (2002) *Action Research and Post-Modernism: congruence and critique.* London: Open University Press.

Jones, L. (2001) 'Using videos to investigate speaking and listening', in O. McNamarra (ed.) *Becoming an Evidence Based Practitioner.* London: Routledge and Falmer.

Jones, L. (2001) Trying to break with bad habits in practice by engaging with post structuralist theories, *Early Years,* 21(1).

Jones, L. (2003) Derrida goes to nursery: deconstructing young children's stories, *Contemporary Issues in Early Childhood Education,* 6(4): 228–242.

Jones, L. (2004) 'Observations from the Field', in B. Somekh and C. Lewin (eds) *Research Methods in the Social Sciences.* London: Sage.

Jones, L. and Brown, T. (2001) Reading the nursery classroom: a Foucauldian perspective, *Qualitative Studies in Education,* 14(6): 714–725.

Jones, L. and McNamara, O. (2004) The possibilities and constraints of multimedia as a basis for critical reflection, *Cambridge Journal of Education,* 34(33): 179–296.

Russell Jones is a Senior Lecturer and Programme Leader in Childhood Studies at MMU with particular interests in equal opportunities, children's rights, literacy issues and creative approaches to working with children and young adults. Russell left a primary Deputy Headship to conduct full time PhD study that resulted in the book *Teaching Racism* which was awarded 'book of the week' in the *Times Educational Supplement.* He has completed consultancy work for Dorling Kyndersley and Cheshire LEA and provided University level INSET training on multicultural policies and practices. Russell's recent publications include:

Jones, R (2001) *Learning how to ignore racism: A case study of one white beginning teacher in 'the white highlands' and the two black boys in her care'.* Published by AERA in peer-reviewed online journal.

Jones, R (2004) 'Children's Literature' (chapter) and 'Multilingualism and Race' (chapter) in *Childhood Studies* Wyse, D (Ed) Oxford, London.

Jones, R and Wyse, D (2004) *Creative Approaches to Primary Education* London, David Fulton.

Wyse, D and Jones R (2001) *Teaching English, Language and Literacy* London, Taylor and Francis.

Wyse, D and Jones R (2002) Circular Arguments: Primary School Teachers' Knowledge about Texts in *Changing English* (9)1.

Iris Keating is a Principal Lecturer at Manchester Metropolitan University and a member of the Early Years Centre. At present, she is working with the National College for School Leadership on their Bursar Development Programme. For the three years prior to this she was the Professional Manager of the DfES Best Practice Research Scholarship scheme. She worked for 12 years in primary and nursery education and her interests continue to be in the early years. She is committed to the involvement of families and community in education and in particular to the impact that this involvement can have on mothers. Her doctoral thesis was entitled 'Mothers and their Children's Schools: for whose benefit? The impact on mothers of participation in their children's schools.' Her forthcoming book, based on her research findings about mothers' involvement with their children's schools, explores whether this is a source of empowerment or a means of oppression. Her recent publications include:

Keating, I. (2001) The efficacy of CPD: its impact upon classroom practice, *Professional Development Today*, 4(2).

Keating, I. (ed.) (2002) *Teaching Foundation Stage: Achieving QTS*. Exeter: Learning Matters.

Keating, I. and Roberts, I. (2003) Teachers as researchers: working in higher education partnerships, *Professional Development Today*, 6(3).

Keating, I., Hodson, E., Basford, J. and Harnett, A. (2002) Reception teachers responses to the Foundation Stage, *International Journal of Early Years Education*, 10(3).

Nell Napier is Programme Leader for the Childhood Studies degree at Manchester Metropolitan University. She has been a childcare worker in the voluntary sector, working with children with disabilities, a nurse and a primary school teacher. Her research has included a comparison of nurse and teacher education, perceptions of practitioners in an Early Excellence Centre and the recruitment of under-represented groups into childhood courses. She is currently engaged on an Ed Doc with a focus on multiprofessionalism. She is an experienced external examiner for a Childhood Studies degree. Her publications include:

Leather, N., Hawtin, A., Napier, N., Wyse, D. and Jones, R. (2000) 'The developing child', in D. Wyse and A. Hawtin (eds) *Children: A Multiprofessional Perspective*. London: Arnold.

Napier, N. (2002) 'Roles and responsibilities of other professionals in the lives of young children' in I. Keating (ed.) *Teaching Foundation Stage*. Exeter: Learning Matters.

Napier, N. (2004) 'Overview of children's education and care', in D. Wyse (ed.) *Childhood Studies: An Introduction*. London: Blackwell Publishing.

Napier, N. (2004) 'Toys and games', in D. Wyse (ed.) *Childhood Studies: An Introduction*. London: Blackwell Publishing.

Napier, N. and Sharkey, A. (2004) 'National curricula', in D. Wyse (ed.) *Childhood Studies: An Introduction*. London: Blackwell Publishing.

Napier, N. and Sharkey, A. (2004) 'Play', in D. Wyse (ed.) *Childhood Studies: An Introduction*. London: Blackwell Publishing.

Napier, N., Banton, R. and Medforth, N. (2000) 'Children and assessment', in D. Wyse and A. Hawtin (eds) *Children: A Multiprofessional Perspective*. London: Arnold.

John Powell is a Senior Lecturer in Early Childhood Studies and Multiprofessional Coordinator at Manchester Metropolitan University, with particular interests in equal opportunities, children's rights, multiprofessional issues, professional development and research. John's career in social work spanned more than 20 years, providing him with a rich set of experiences of direct work with families and young children. He has been involved in several areas of research including teenage parents, multiprofessional practice and issues of 'touch'. John has contributed to a number of publications and recent publications include:

Barron, I. and Powell, J. (2003) Story sacks, children's narratives and the social construction of reality, *Citizenship, Social and Economics Education*, 5(3).

Powell, J. (2004) 'Anti-Discriminatory practice matters', in L. Abbott and A. Langston (eds) *Birth to Three Matters: Supporting the Framework of Effective Practice*. Buckingham: Open University Press.

Powell, J. (2004) 'Safety matters', in L. Abbott and A. Langston (eds) *Birth to Three Matters: Supporting the Framework of Effective Practice*. Buckingham: Open University Press.

Foreword

I am delighted to write the Foreword to this book, which I believe to be both a celebration of the tremendous strides made towards the achievement of a multi-professional early years workforce and a challenge to those responsible for training the next generation of professionals. Successful celebrations always involve dedicated planning, and this is no less true in relation to this book, which, although written in a relatively short time, is the result of a journey which started more than a decade ago.

As a member of the 'Rumbold Committee', whose report *Starting with Quality* (DES, 1990) acknowledged that 'working with young children is a demanding and complex task', I, along with well respected names in the early childhood field, argued that appropriate training for that task must be a priority. The kind of training we advocated at that time was one which would seek to break down barriers between professions such as health, care, education and social work; quite revolutionary some 15 years ago!

Whilst debate still continues about the relative merits of the term 'multiprofessional', the question remains as to whether what is needed are multidisciplinary teams or multiprofessional people with the necessary range of knowledge, skills, understanding and experience to meet the needs of young children and families in the twenty-first century.

What was not disputed was the right of young children to highly trained staff of the calibre advocated even further back than Rumbold, and referred to by one of the 'pioneers' of nursery education as 'the elite of an elite profession' (Webb, 1972). The way forward was seen in the development of the Early Childhood Studies degree, which would provide the kinds of opportunities required by professionals training to work in a variety of settings and contexts. I am proud to have been in at the beginning of what is now accepted as the appropriate graduate training for those in positions of leadership in the early childhood field.

This book is written by a team of people who have also been on a journey, one which has involved much debate, discussion, sharing of ideas and, where necessary, breaking down of barriers in order to ensure that the values and principles which underpin the degree are those which are understood, supported and shared by each member of the teaching team irrespective of the discipline they represent.

This is a challenging book and rightly so. Early years practitioners have always been required to defend their practice and this requirement will not diminish as the complexity of the early childhood field increases as new initiatives are introduced. Students and trainers, policy makers and practitioners have a duty to be knowledgeable, to be able to reflect on their beliefs and practice and to articulate concerns, share their views, convey their enthusiasm and act as advocates for young children. This book will help them do just that.

Lesley Abbott OBE
Professor, Early Childhood Education
Manchester Metropolitan University

Preface and acknowledgements

Liz Jones, Rachel Holmes and John Powell

How do you think *seriously* about children and their social worlds? How do you have thoughtful conversations, where critical questions get asked and are wrangled over? This book has provided each of the contributors with an opportunity to stand back and address these questions. We have tried to open up for questioning a number of areas that lie within the terrain of Early Childhood Studies. Additionally, we have tried to illustrate aspects of the students' journey as they struggle to develop a multiprofessional perspective. Moreover, an effort has been made to illuminate the kinds of disturbing that tutors and students undertake as a way of thinking a little differently about children, their childhoods and the services that aim to support these.

The book as a whole can be seen as an exercise in troubling the means by which we order the world. We have put under pressure our own interpretive frameworks, which whilst proving to be a difficult business is nevertheless a necessary step in order to expand the circumference of what we know and how we know it. Overall the book is an effort to engage critically so that there might be a genuine interrogation of Early Childhood Studies. There is a refusal to offer solutions but what we have done we think is contribute towards opening up the field to create what Derrida (1980: 132) refers to as a 'becoming space', where thinking and doing may be less bounded.

It is possible that some readers – like the students who are represented in the book – are beginning a programme of study that centres on Early Childhood Studies. We would suggest that you keep in mind the potential for this book to be revisited as you progress through your own specific journey. Initially, it might be that you will find yourself struggling with certain ideas that are being presented. Our advice would be to try and take what you can from your preliminary readings but not to abandon the tussle that this book obliges. We strongly suspect that with each revisiting you will gain more and more.

We would like to thank all those who have given up their valuable time in order to contribute to the book. We would particularly like to thank those students, past and present, of the Multiprofessional Early Childhood Studies degree at the Manchester Metropolitan University. We are indebted to Kim Edmonds for her thoughtful comments and advice in relation to Chapter 8. We are also grateful to Peter Stubbs of Edinphoto.org.uk for his generous help in sourcing the photo used in Chapter 4 and to Hema Maps of PO Box 4365, Eight Mile Plains, Queensland 4113, Australia for the use of their Upside Down Map in Chapter 14. Finally, grateful thanks to Hafsah Naib for the front cover artwork.

Liz Jones, Rachel Holmes and John Powell
Manchester 2005

Reference

Derrida, J. (1980) *The Archaeology of the Frivolous: Reading Condillac*, Pittsburg, PA: Duquesne University Press.

Introduction

Liz Jones and Ian Barron

Writing the book: a celebration of teaching and learning

This book arises from our collective experiences of teaching the Early Childhood Studies degree course at the Manchester Metropolitan University (MMU). The course, one of the first of its kind in the UK, has been both the inspiration behind and the model for a great number of childhood degrees that have followed its inception. Now in its tenth year it is timely, we believe, to collate the wealth of rich teaching and learning experiences that have been generated so that others might benefit. The contributors to the book come from a diversity of disciplines, with specialized experiences in education, health, social work and law. Whilst offering a theoretically rigorous treatment of issues relating to early childhood studies, the book also provides practical discussion of strategies that could inform multiprofessional practice. A principal task of the book is to demonstrate how students make practical sense of theoretical ideas in a manner that is highly reflective.

Two key principles underpin the Early Childhood Studies course and are as a consequence reflected within this book. The first is that all who contribute to the course share a belief with regard to children, that is, to perceive them as deeply complex, holistic beings. The notion of 'being' is important to us as it captures the fluidity of children and their overall development. There is consequently a resistance to situate young children within a 'stages and ages' paradigm. Rather, notions of the child are premised on the idea that children grow up in complex dynamic societies where variables such as race, class, gender and ethnicity interconnect. Such societies provide the basis for exceedingly diverse experiences and learning on the part of the children, as well as for variations in the way in which adults, including practitioners, establish and activate their relations with them. There is therefore within the book a move away from and an active resistance to universal notions of what constitutes 'the child'. Consequently, a recurring question that is reiterated throughout the book is, 'who is the child?' (cf. Dahlberg et al., 1999).

The second principle is concerned with and centres on the 'self'. There is within the course an embedded expectation that all, students and lecturers alike, will develop and maintain a reflective attitude particularly in relation to young children and their social worlds. The book, whilst drawing on course content, also illustrates our efforts in developing a critical attitude. Here we have found Foucault's (1985) idea concerned with 'care of the self' deeply relevant. That is, the facility to step back from what one habitually and or ordinarily does in order to carefully reconsider it. Having such an attitude means asking hard and pressing questions so that those beliefs, ideas, views and assumptions that are brought to notions of the child are constantly critiqued.

Running throughout the book are extracts of student thinking. Including such thinking has two distinct advantages. First, it further reiterates the diversity that the term 'early childhood' encompasses. In discussions, our students draw extensively on their practical placements. In this way the gap that can sometimes exist between theoretical understandings of multiprofessional ways of working and the realities of actual practice is diminished. Second, by including brief examples of the students' voice there are opportunities for the reader to gain an appreciation of some of the processes that the students undergo. Reflexivity is a key practice that students rehearse during their time on the course, empowering them to develop thoughtful ways of working. It is the way that reflexive practice operates as an insight and awareness raising methodology that connects all the chapters of the book.

Tracking the past ten years

Within the UK nearly all universities including the 'old' and the 'new' now offer an Early Childhood Studies degree. Additionally, there are an increasing number of related books, but looking back ten years this certainly was not the case. As noted previously, one of the original courses was established at MMU. Bearing in mind the multiprofessional and multidisciplinary nature of such degree courses, there is a certain satisfaction to be found in recognizing that the first degrees emerged from university departments of health, social work and education. It would be easy, from these beginnings, to paint a picture of unproblematic multiprofessionalism at the heart of such degree developments. This book, however, seeks to unsettle apparent certainties and to address the challenges that are inherent in developing 'real' multidisciplinary and multiprofessional understandings and practices in relation to children, childhood and childhood provision amongst staff, students and early childhood practitioners.

The development of such degree courses was very much a response to a confused picture of early years provision and training. As David (1990) points out, provision for young children within the UK had traditionally been regulated either by the Department for Education, and had been concerned with 'education', or by the Department for Health and Social Security, and had been concerned with 'care'. Education and training for the early years sector had also reflected this division. Education in the state sector involved a graduate teacher but many had little or no early years education and training and teacher education did not (and, at the time of writing, still does not) address work with children under the age of three. Often there was no graduate involvement in private and voluntary nursery education provision. Education and training for workers in the care sector was even more variable and qualifications were at sub-degree level. Whilst those outside the sector considered being a nursery teacher relatively low status, the status of care work was lower still. This tended to reflect a feeling that care should be seen as a family responsibility and 'any one can work with children'. It also perhaps reflected the lingering legacy of Bowlby's (1969) largely discredited theory that separation from the mother in the first three years was inevitably damaging and to be avoided.

At a policy level, a number of key reports also gave a spur to the development of such degrees, with calls for much better coordination of services for young children and their families and for a multidisciplinary approach to training and education. The Rumbold Report stated: 'We see as essential needs: a closer linkage between the three strands of health, care and education in initial and in-service training . . .' (DES, 1990: 27). Underpinning the development of Early Childhood Studies degrees, therefore, was a belief in the need to break down artificial professional boundaries that work against children and their families. Ball (1994: 28) stated that 'the "seamless web" linking education and care is a key feature of best practice' and the National Commission on Education urged that: 'Consideration should also be given to incorporating a multiprofessional dimension in training, so that both childcare and education are covered' (1993: 133).

The creation of such degrees was moved forward by the work of a group established at the National Children's Bureau to consider the training needs of the early childhood sector. The first Early Childhood Studies degrees reflected the need to provide progression routes for the experienced but non-graduate staff that made up the majority of the early years workforce. They also reflected a belief in the importance of moving towards graduate status for early childhood workers, including for work with children below the age of three. Some of the group saw the degrees as the essential bedrock from which to go on to professional training as a teacher, social worker, lawyer or health professional working with young children; others aspired to a new graduate professional qualification and status along Danish lines, as noted by Fawcett and Calder (1998) and Abbott and Hevey (2001).

The notion of a multiprofessional and multidisciplinary perspective, however, is far from straightforward and different terms abound. Reference is made to multiprofessional, interprofessional, multi-agency, inter-agency, multidisciplinary and interdisciplinary approaches. Although the terms multi-professionalism and interprofessionalism are often used interchangeably, it is debateable whether they mean the same thing. It may be useful to make a distinction between approaches that seek to create a new professional to work with young children who is educated and trained in elements of welfare, care, education and health and those that are more concerned with improving the skills and understanding that the separate professional groups demonstrate in working with each other. Interdisciplinary approaches could be seen to be concerned with different subject disciplines working together to cover the field of early childhood study. Multidisciplinary approaches could be seen to be more about the integration and fusing of those disciplines. Certainly in the case of the MMU Early Childhood Studies degree, the traditional subject disci-plines are experienced as part of an integrated framework rather than via discrete, subject based units of study.

These debates and contradictions run to the very heart of the continued development of Early Childhood Studies degrees. Many of the newer degrees have emerged from university expansion plans rather than from the above policy and practice background, and whilst course teams may show commit-ment to multiprofessional approaches, such concerns may not be well under-stood by those with influence in terms of staffing and course development. At MMU, whilst the original degree was developed and taught by a team that reflected the full range of early childhood disciplines and professions, drawn from across the university, this has proved difficult to sustain and the core early childhood team itself now reflects backgrounds in health, education, social work and social care in order to secure adequate expertise for students. Even then, there are issues about a team that is arguing for multidisciplinary approaches to teaching and practice being made up of tutors whose histories reflect the different professional groupings. All of this also points to further problems in terms of how such degrees should be reviewed by the higher education authorities where content covers psychology, sociology, social work, social policy, education, health and law.

Despite the challenges, there are signs that progress is being made in the UK in developing multiprofessional approaches to education, training and practice. The period since 1997 has seen considerable expansion of provision for young children and also expansion of the early childhood workforce. In the Foreword to *Every Child Matters: Next Steps* (DfES, 2004), the Minister for Children, Young People and Families, Margaret Hodge, refers to '. . . a step change in early years provision, with health, education and social care closely integrated through Sure Start Children's Centres' (2004: 3). Whilst Ball (1994: 29) had held that 'the integration of early education and care . . . does not mean that all staff are (or should be) trained in the same way', many would argue for more consistency in the content of education and training for all of those who work with children:

> Our reforms need to embrace all those who work with children and young people: to set a common core of occupational standards; to build a modular framework to enhance the skills, effectiveness and coherence of the children's workforce; to foster high quality leadership . . .
>
> (DfES, 2004: 31)

As well as concerns to identify common elements of education and training, calls are also made for 'a cultural transformation to create more trusting relationships between frontline professionals' (DfES, 2004: 3).

Whilst a graduate workforce has not yet been achieved, the graduates of Early Childhood Studies degrees are having an impact on policy and practice and there are also signs of growing government interest in European models of provision for children and training for early childhood workers. The UK government's Ten Year Strategy for Childcare notes: 'There is strong international evidence that high quality early education provision and childcare provision gives better outcomes for children . . . Reform of the qualifications, status and experience of the childcare workforce is needed' (HM Treasury/DfES/DWP/DTI, 2004: 25). Importantly, the same document also comments: 'For too long there has been a false distinction between "education" and "care" in early years services that is reflected in different qualifications and regulatory frameworks. For children, such a distinction has no meaning . . . Working with pre-school children should have the same status as working with those of school age' (HM Treasury/DfES/DWP/DTI, 2004: 44). More importantly still, the UK government has stated a commitment to every day-care setting being led by a graduate who may be a teacher or may be 'a new professional combining learning with care, along the lines of the continental pedagogue model . . . there would be the opportunity to develop it to suit the early years framework set out in this strategy, and give "pedagogues" the flexibility to exist alongside teachers in the school system' (HM Treasury/DfES/DWP/DTI, 2004: 46). There are even signs that universities themselves are taking on board the messages in relation to interdisciplinary and interprofessional education and training. There are signs too of Early Childhood Studies being accepted as a subject discipline in its own right, a development called for in one of the first Early Childhood Studies textbooks (Taylor and Woods, 1997).

It would not be in the spirit of this book, however, to consider the development of multiprofessional early childhood study and practice as some form of 'victory narrative'. Subsequently, we seek to explore the complexities and dilemmas that are at the very heart of any post-modern consideration of early childhood.

Mapping the book

The main body of the book is divided into three sections:

Part 1: Power, Politics and Childhood
Part 2: Working Together: Facts, Frameworks and Fantasies
Part 3: Children's Childhoods

Finally in the concluding remarks, as well as summarizing some of the salient features of the book we also look to the future in order to express some of our hopes (and fears) in relation to both the terrain of early years and multiprofessional practice.

Part 1: Power, Politics and Childhood

There are five chapters in this section, which explore ways in which a number of authors draw on their practice in order both to examine and to illustrate the interpellations that circulate between early years, power and politics.

Chapter 1: Researching young children within a multiprofessional perspective

In writing about research and the young child, authors Liz Jones, Karen Browne and Iris Keating concentrate on three issues. The first issue is located around ethics whilst the second is concerned with paradigms. Finally, the third issue situates itself around the question of whose interests are being served when undertaking research. In examining each of the three issues the authors draw upon student experiences when undertaking small-scale research projects within a variety of settings. Additionally, the authors lean on post-structuralist theories so as to examine critically each of their central concerns.

Chapter 2: Exploring tensions within the interplay of rights, duties and responsibilities

Here, Rachel Holmes asks in general, 'What does it mean to have rights?' More specifically, 'What does it mean for the young child to have rights?' If, as Mayall (1994) suggests, children's lives are lived through adult constructions of what it means to be a child then what repercussions does this have in relation to 'children's rights'? In addition to outlining the historical under-pinnings of children's rights, Rachel also draws upon an example of classroom practice where students, through role-play, have to examine and critique a number of positions that relate to the subject. What emerges highlights the complexities between good intentions and the reality of trying to materialize children's rights.

Chapter 3: The politics of play

The notion that play is the young child's work has been in circulation for some time now. In this chapter, however, authors Liz Jones, Elaine Hodson and Nell Napier take this idea several steps further. They highlight how adults can use play as a regulatory tool and how in this sense it becomes a political as well as an educational instrument. Additionally, the authors document how, by deconstructing certain powerful ideas that have historically circulated around play – and still have currency in contemporary practices – it is possible to perceive play as an ideological device aimed at maintaining the social order.

Chapter 4: Exploring families

This chapter, written by Sue Aitken and Liz Jones, details aspects of the journey students undertake when unpacking certain assumptions, ideas and beliefs that are inevitably brought to the idea of the family. By drawing upon post-structuralist theories in general, but particularly aspects of Foucault and Derrida's work, the authors set about destabilizing a number of accounts that are associated with the family.

Chapter 5: Working with parents and carers

The final chapter in this section of the book is centred on working with parents and carers. Currently within the UK, there is a determined drive by government for strong links between the child's home and sites of educare. It is therefore particularly pertinent that the whole issue of working with parents is subjected to close scrutiny. Working collaboratively, the authors Liz Jones, Karen Browne, Sue Aitken, Iris Keating and Elaine Hodson examine a number of questions, including 'what does working with parents mean and what does it look like in practice?'

Part 2: Working Together: Facts, Frameworks and Fantasies

Six chapters constitute this section. The above chapters explore what we perceive as 'facts, frameworks and fantasies' that relate to practices where there is an expectation of multi-agency work. The section will identify issues relating to childhood experiences as they appear to be represented as 'facts' and we will explore the underlying assumptions and outcomes that do not always live up to the hopes that working together has for children.

Chapter 6: Multiprofessional perspectives

In this chapter John Powell highlights the diversity of services for children and their families whilst at the same time alerting the reader to historical, legislative and contemporary political issues which impact upon and help to fashion the different settings that have materialized in early childhood services. John also identifies how students' own personal and developing professional values influence their views of children's needs and their perceptions of children. In foregrounding the importance of inter-agency working, John also highlights some of the tensions when practitioners attempt to cross professional boundaries.

Chapter 7: Anti-discriminatory practice

Russell Jones' starting point in this chapter is 'equality', because as he notes there is no point in attempting to establish anti-discriminatory practice if this does not begin from the position that equality is something worth striving towards. It is his contention that there is no template that will 'resolve' issues of discrimination for children. The chapter therefore avoids offering simplistic responses to complex issues. Rather, examples are drawn from education to highlight three things. First, they illustrate certain types of discriminatory practice. Second, they provide a basis for analysis to explore why such practice occurs and, lastly, they provide a conduit through which Russell explores what some of the repercussions are for children who are subjected to anti-discriminatory practice. Russell's final move is to consider Unicef's plan for 'Building a Protective Environment for Children'. In Russell's view, this provides a strong basis on which anti-discriminatory practices may be established, evaluated and strengthened.

Chapter 8: Legal issues

Catherine Baxter, in this chapter, seeks to explore what makes the law relating to children different from other types of law by exploring the philosophy behind legislation affecting children and their families and by examining the principles upon which it is based. Case studies are used in order to trouble certain assumptions that students might hold in relation to what is right or wrong. Additionally, students consider the role of the state in protecting children who are at risk of harm from their environment and the law's approach to balancing the interests of family members.

Chapter 9: Child protection

In this chapter, John Powell offers us numerous historical reminders about the need for practitioners to work closely together where child protection is an overarching remit. Additionally, he emphasizes areas that are still a cause for concern, including notions such as inter-agency cooperation and communication. John also examines aspects of the Children Act (1989), where the belief that 'the ascertainable wishes and desires of the child should be taken into consideration' is inscribed. Though commendable, this is not free of difficulties. The way that the Act describes the practice of communicating with children is dependent on the skills and abilities of individual practitioners to help children to share what they consider to be their wishes and desires. The apparently robust practices arising from the government's *Working Together to Safeguard Children* (DoH, 1999) document can here be shown to be far more tentative and much more dependent on the insights/actions of practitioners in the field where action is constrained by many difficulties to be as proactive as they may wish. The chapter goes on to argue that a social constructionist methodology can lead to a shift in the ways that child protection policies and practices may be understood so that the language that constitutes policy and informs practice can be seen to be shifting, facilitating a range of insights and understandings. Finally, John suggests that a way forward is for students to develop a critical sense of practice so that they might become more insightful and understanding. As such, they are more likely to develop ways that will make a difference when working with young children.

Chapter 10: Integration, inclusion and diversity

Rosemary Boys situates this chapter around the notion of inclusive schooling as it is played out in the UK. She begins by examining the influences of international human rights legislation on the national recognition of the rights of children with special educational needs (SEN), before moving on to discuss some contemporary understandings of the term 'special educational needs'. A precise historical development of present provision is then provided. This offers an insight into the ways in which children with special educational needs (SEN) were constructed and also allows us to appreciate the progression of contemporary practices. She concludes by considering current progress towards inclusion, as well as reviewing a number of issues that still need to be addressed.

Chapter 11: Health in childhood

Caroline Bradbury-Jones and Jane Bates seek to provide an insight into the issues that they in their capacity as tutors explore with students to facilitate their understanding of health in childhood. They examine the concept of health with particular reference to children's perceptions. The determinants of health are explored in relation to two significant health issues for children in contemporary society: poverty and obesity. In addition to sharing their experiences of teaching students, they also use student narratives in an attempt to capture the essence of classroom discussions. Overall, these indicate some of the movements in thinking that are made by students when commonplace assumptions about factors pertaining to health are displaced.

Part 3: Children's Childhoods

Four chapters constitute this section, at the core of which lies the notion that childhood can be constructed, deconstructed and reframed by many and in a number of ways. Perspectives of children and childhood are examined in terms of their origins and how they relate to historical, geographical and contemporary ways of understanding children.

Chapter 12: Exploring representations of children and childhood in history and film

This chapter is co-authored by Rachel Holmes and Ian Barron. It takes as a starting point those ways in which students tend to view children and childhood. By deconstructing narratives and other symbolic representations of the child, two moves are made. First, students are introduced to the phenomenon of 'othering' and, second, some of the beliefs and firmly held convictions of students in relation to the child and childhood are destabilized. It is in this cleared conceptual space that traditional western 'regimes of truth' (Foucault, 1977) can be challenged.

Chapter 13: Exploring representations of children and childhood in photography and documentary

In this chapter, Rachel Holmes picks up on the theme of 'othering' that was introduced in Chapter 12 and develops it further. Specifically she asks, 'who is other and who is non-other?', particularly as the notion is propagated and provoked through visual narratives. The exploration of these questions is set against the work of a number of theorists, a move that draws attention to the way the term 'other' has shifted in meaning. Rachel then goes on to examine how these 'differentiated interpretations can all impact upon the child'. The overall ambition of this chapter is to interrupt students' 'knowing' of children. By incorporating short extracts of student writing there are opportunities to perceive aspects of this process and to appreciate how habitual conceptualizations are destabilized, thus enabling students to reconsider certain attachments they hold in relation to the young child and childhood.

Chapter 14: International perspectives

This chapter, written by Sue Aitken and John Powell, picks up on and deliberates further notions of 'othering', particularly as it is played out globally. It critically examines the view of the child as victim, using cross-cultural readings of 'work' and 'play' as a mechanism of understanding. Within the international context the chapter highlights how students explore these activities in terms of structure and agency, as well as economic imperatives.

Chapter 15: Understanding development in early childhood

Ian Barron makes clear that students who are destined to work with children should have an understanding of child development. That said, encouraging students to engage *critically* with the study of children's development is not easy. This chapter achieves two things. First, it offers a coherent résumé of historical and contemporary understandings of child development. Second, it details how students are encouraged to think critically, holistically and cross-culturally about their understandings in relation to young children.

Concluding remarks

Here, we summarize certain key features by briefly re-examining the salient points that have been articulated in the preceding chapters. Additionally, we ask a number of critical questions, including:

- What do we consider childhood to mean in the post-modern era?
- How can services capture and support the fragmentation of lived experiences?

References

Abbott, L. and Hevey, D. (2001) 'Training to Work in the Early Years: Developing the Climbing Frame', in G. Pugh (ed.) *Contemporary Issues in the Early Years: Working Collaboratively for Children*. London: Paul Chapman Publishing.

Ball, C. (1994) *Start Right: The Importance of Early Learning*. London: RSA.

Bowlby, J. (1969) *Attachment and Loss, Vol. 1: Attachment*. London: Hogarth Press.

Dahlberg, G., Moss, P. and Pence, A. (1999) *Beyond Quality in Early Childhood Education and Care*. London: Falmer.

David, T. (1990) *Under Five – Under-educated?* Milton Keynes: Open University Press.

DES (1990) *Starting with Quality* (The Rumbold Report). London: HMSO.

DfES (2004) *Every Child Matters: Next Steps*. Nottingham: DfES.

DoH (1999) *Working Together to Safeguard Children: a guide to inter-agency working to safeguard and promote the welfare of children*. London: HMSO.

Fawcett, M. and Calder, P. (1998) 'Early Childhood Studies degrees', in L. Abbott and G. Pugh (eds) *Training to Work in the Early Years*. Buckingham: Open University Press.

Foucault, M. (1977) *Discipline and Punish*. London: Penguin.

Foucault, M. (1985) *The Use of Pleasure*. New York: Pantheon.

HM Treasury/DfES/DWP/DTI (2004) *Choice for Parents, the Best Start for Children: A Ten Year Strategy for Childcare*. London: The Stationery Office.

Mayall, B. (1994) *Children's Childhoods: Observed and Experienced*. London: Falmer.

National Commission on Education (1993) *Learning to Succeed*. London: Heinemann.

Taylor, J. and Woods, M. (eds) (1997) *Early Childhood Studies: An Holistic Introduction*. London: Hodder Arnold.

Unicef's plan for 'Building a Protective Environment for Children'. www.unicef.org/protection

PART 1
Power, Politics and Childhood

1 Researching young children within a multiprofessional perspective

Liz Jones, Karen Browne and Iris Keating

Introduction

The aims of this chapter are, first, to examine the issue of maintaining an ethical stance when undertaking research with young children. Second, we discuss a number of ideas and thoughts that circulate around research paradigms. Finally, the question of whose interests are being served is examined. Before getting to our concerns, we want briefly to detail why we have chosen our foci and in so doing make clear our reasons for certain omissions.

The reasons for our admissions cannot be divorced from the wider macro features in which all social endeavours, including research, are undertaken. Undertaking research is itself part of the Enlightenment project or, as some commentators refer to it, Modernity. The Enlightenment was an intellectual movement that developed in England and Europe during the seventeenth and eighteenth centuries. To explain in detail the philosophical underpinnings of the Enlightenment project is beyond the remit of this chapter. That said, it has been given some attention because it is the foundational underpinning of those beliefs concerning truth, knowledge, power, the self and language that shape western thinking (Flax, 1990).

The Enlightenment would lead society out of the darkness of irrationality and superstition that supposedly characterized the Middle Ages. 'Man' – for the Enlightenment subject espouses an epistemology that is homocentric (Hekman, 1990: 2) – was no longer to be dependent on the guidance of 'another'. Rather, by his own capacities he could progress. These 'capacities' included a faith that rational knowledge of society could be attained and that this knowledge was universal and thus objective. Knowledge that is acquired from the right use of reason is truth, in that it represents something real, unchanging and universal about the human mind and the structure of the natural world. Knowledge can be both neutral (that is, grounded in universal reason, not particular 'interests') and socially beneficial. In other words, rational knowledge, because it is both rational and neutral, can lead to mental liberation and social betterment amongst humanity (McLennan, 1992: 330). Moreover, just as the right use of reason can result in knowledge that represents the real, language can represent objective reality accurately (Flax, 1990).

This belief in rationality, which as we have seen is a legacy of the Enlightenment project, is a central target for post-modern thinking. In general terms, post-modernists propose that the foundationalism and absolutism of modernism is no longer an appropriate way of understanding a world that has witnessed profound changes. These include economic changes (the move from mass production to flexible specialization), political changes (the collapse of the eastern European bloc and a lack of confidence in Marxism) and social changes (the so-called fragmentation of social classes as a consequence of marketing lifestyle niches). Furthermore, these upheavals when combined with the communication explosion, particularly in the visual media of film and television, work at splintering social cohesion and coherence.

These shifts in philosophical underpinnings and social structures have to be acknowledged when supporting students. How we give this support does not mean that we didactically instruct students about the aforementioned complexities. Rather, undertaking research is conceptualized as an arena for engaging in dialogue about the realities of young children's lives where the very question of what constitutes 'the real' is constantly interrogated. There is general consensus that the goals of social research are concerned with establishing facts or principles, collecting information on a subject and/or carrying out investigations into a subject or problematic issue. As tutors, whilst we have to recognize these meanings we also hold on to more ancient conceptualizations. For 'research' stems from sixteenth century Old French 'recerchér', meaning 'to seek' and importantly 'to seek again'. It is this notion of the self who seeks but who is nevertheless dissatisfied with such seeking – who is therefore obliged to seek again – that is a central feature of our work.

The foci of this chapter have been selected because we believe that they centre attention on the conundrum that faces the researcher. That is, the desire to undertake research in order to gain understanding and hence be better placed to enact change, change that might well result in better provision for young children and their families, all of which encapsulates the impetus of Modernity. Meanwhile, our reflexive, post-modern selves work at challenging and thus destabilizing our understanding so that there are opportunities to question why it is we want to interpret phenomena in particular ways and whose interests will be served by doing so.

We begin with 'ethics'. Here we try to illustrate what it is like to behave ethically outside of the checklist mentality that can circumscribe it. So, on the one hand, there are clear and logical procedures initiated by the university that work at ensuring that research endeavours are ethical. However, such rational strategies are limited because they do not capture the relentless activity that is, we believe, incumbent within ethics. Our next move is to place centre stage a question that is inevitably asked by the neophyte researcher, that is, whether to follow a quantitative or qualitative paradigm. Here we evoke the tussles that can occur when, on the one hand, there is the yearning for clarity and comprehension, whilst on the other there is a realization that such objectivity is dependent upon language being able to tell how 'it' really is. In the final section we examine whose interests are served when research is undertaken.

Ethics

As inferred above, our post-modern selves look to post-structuralist theories in order to aid a more thorough self-examination. This examination should be present at each stage of the research, from negotiating access to dissemination of the findings. In all we want to develop what Foucault refers to as a '. . . demanding, prudent, experimental attitude' where '. . . at every moment, step by step, one must confront what one is thinking and saying with what one is doing, with what one is' (Foucault, in Rabinow, 1984: 374). How does one move from Foucault's idealized notions to practice? How, for example, does one behave prudently and experimentally when negotiating access and selecting research methods?

Let us consider this question from the perspective of a student who wants to understand the role of the professional when working with small groups of parents whose children are failing to thrive. The aim of the weekly meetings of the group is to develop parenting skills that will not only inform parents about nutritional content of food but additionally will provide strategies that will improve parent/child relations so that situations such as mealtimes are less fraught. In this instance, neither the parents nor the children have freely chosen to attend sessions. Rather, professionals such as health visitors and paediatricians, as well as child development units, have referred them. The four professionals who coordinate the group are drawn from and resourced by health and social services. Two are health visitors whilst the other two are family support workers. Quite clearly such a group is beset with hierarchical difficulties and contains a number of uneven dyads, including for example professionals/parents as well as adults/children. Given such complexities, how does the neophyte researcher explain her presence to the parents, particularly as such parents already have a realization that they are under surveillance because of a perceived deficit in terms of parenting skills?

When reading student work it is clear that in such sensitive cases as described above a number of students do try to set up face-to-face dialogues, where explanations can be offered and questions answered. This is important because students are then able to take note of other indicators, including the body language of individuals. The readings of such nuances are not one-offs; rather they are attended to throughout the study. In this way the notion of 'consent' can be seen as renegotiable, where at times it will be obvious that an individual is in agreement to be part of the study. At other moments it may become apparent that because of their vulnerability they are merely being acquiescent. By gauging such differences and responding to them, the researcher is coming closer to behaving 'prudently' in relation to ethics.

Similarly, when selecting methodological procedures it is evident that for many of the students this is a tussle between choosing methods that will suit their needs and recognizing the needs of their research participants. Above, we have described a research project that is located around professionals who are trying to support parents who are experiencing a number of parenting difficulties, particularly those that relate to feeding and mealtimes. In examining the role of the practitioner, particularly her effectiveness in undertaking this task, it might seem sensible for the researcher to undertake an interview to gain the parents' perspective. This would clearly suit the needs of the researcher but it is questionable whether it would suit the parents. Expressing opinions, voicing criticisms and perhaps even making judgements all require degrees of self-confidence – a trait that is likely to be absent in those who have been deemed 'deficit'.

If the decision is made not to talk to the parents, how is their perspective gained? In this instance, the student found a questionnaire helpful in fulfilling the need for information whilst giving the respondents a 'protective space'. The anonymity afforded by questionnaires was helpful to the respondents. The parents could take it away with them and respond in their own time. In creating the 'protective space' the student also had to consider the construction of the questionnaire, where ambiguities, jargon and leading questions were identified and eradicated. Additionally, by personally handing out the questionnaire to each parent a conduit was created where the student was able both to explain the purpose of the questionnaire and to underscore her real interest in what they had to say. She was able to appreciate that for some parents the questionnaire caused apprehension and therefore offered to complete the questionnaire with them, basically using it as a structured interview. Overall the student felt that the questionnaire had been significant in reducing coercion and promoting participation. By acting as a scribe to the parents a number of things were achieved. First, clarification of responses could occur and, second, misinterpretations were reduced. Finally, there was an opportunity to be aware of respondents' body language and to probe sensitively, or indeed, not to probe at all.

Similarly, undertaking observations and taking careful notes about the feeding group might well have provided rich insights into the role of the professional. But how would the mothers feel about such obvious scrutiny? With our example, the observations were written up immediately following a group session. This activity, in addition to capturing the basic features of a moment, also became a basis for reflection where the student's own preferred ways of seeing the world were scrutinized, including for example the way that she herself constructed 'parent' and 'parenting'.

So far, scant attention has been paid to the ethical implications of researching children. To address this we offer a brief excerpt from a student's work. In her final dissertation work, Alison Wilkinson, a nursery nurse who was undertaking the course on a part-time basis, began her ethical considerations with the following thoughts:

> *I agree with Fine and Sandstrom's (1988: 46) view that their age (of the children) should not diminish their rights . . . I am aware that in my role as practitioner a central feature of the relationships that I have built up with the children is trust and I therefore aimed to be open and honest in discussing my research with them.*
>
> (Wilkinson, 2003: 24)

Alison then details how the four year old children were talked to on an individual basis and that they granted permission for her to observe and write about their play. She then continues her reflections:

> *. . . however I agree with Morrow and Richards (1996) that possibly the greatest ethical challenge was created by disparities in power between myself in my capacity as both adult and practitioner, and the children. Epstein (1998) discusses the idea of such relationships being bound within the discursive practices of an institution and to some extent I wondered whether the children agreed to my observation of them because their compliance is a feature of the normative school environment . . .*
>
> (Wilkinson, 2003: 24–25)

Alison thus made a determined effort to subject all data that she collected to a reflective gaze. Her efforts at analysing the data was accompanied with the cautious question, 'Why am I choosing to perceive and understand this data in this particular way?' So, whilst she knew that she was not necessarily trying to offer an account from the perspective of the child, she nevertheless was attempting to diminish her own.

Above, attempts have been made to illustrate a number of 'step by step' efforts in behaving in an ethical manner. We recognize that it is not a comprehensive picture. However, the hope is that the accounts given offer some insights into the types of demanding confrontation that are embedded in the notion of behaving ethically.

Paradigmatic issues

What is a 'research paradigm' and in what way does it become problematic? Hughes (2001) perceives a paradigm as a 'framing' mechanism. He writes:

> . . . a paradigm is a way to see the world and organize it into a coher-
> ent whole. Just as a picture frame 'frames' a picture, a paradigm frames
> a research topic; and just as our choice of picture frame influences
> how we see the picture within it, so our choice of paradigm influences
> how we see our research topic . . . Each paradigm is a specific collec-
> tion of beliefs and about our relationship with knowledge, together
> with practices about those beliefs.
>
> (Hughes, 2001: 31–32)

First, let us make it quite clear that when efforts are made to disturb ideas that students hold in relation to research, including quantitative and qualitative paradigms, the intention is not to create what Atkinson *et al.* (1988: 233) refer to as 'fruitless polemic' aimed at defending a particular position. Our students, when they enter the arena of paid employment, have to reside in a world where positivism still has currency. It is evident that here in the UK we live in an audited society (Strathern, 1995), where for example government funded initiatives, including Sure Start projects, Early Excellence Centres and Neigh-bourhood Children's Centres, have to demonstrate both progress and success and in part use statistics to do this. Additionally, they have a duty to categorize their client base in order to indicate that their strategies aimed at targeting specific groups such as teenage mothers or unemployed men are indeed working.

When faced with the prospect of trying to understand, make judgements and as a consequence create knowledge about their placements or about their contexts where they are employed, the students are confronted by situations that are complex. The task of 'making sense' of such situations is daunting, particularly as there is great emphasis within our teaching on 'taking responsibility' – including making responsible choices in relation to method-ological procedures. Effectively, the development of a questioning attitude situates students within what Shotter (1992: 163) refers to as a 'reflexive hoop'. Here it is assumed that nothing is innocent, including those decisions that are made as to which paradigm to adopt in order to 'frame' the research. So, a student might want to understand the notion of 'choice' as it is mani-fested within her place of work, a nursery classroom. Additionally, she is interested in establishing whether any patterns of choice could be related to gender. As a practitioner researcher, she perceives herself to be well placed to undertake various types of observations, as well as interview significant people including the children themselves, the parents and her professional colleagues.

As an initial step the student tries to pre-empt 'her preferred ways of seeing the world in order to document exactly what was happening and refrain from any judgemental or analytical thoughts whilst engaged in observing a specific situation' (Wilkinson, 2003: 30). Borrowing from Sylva *et al.* (1980), she adapts the 'target child' method in order to track the movements of six focus children, including three boys and three girls. She notes all the areas of the room where there are opportunities for different activities and then records the number of visits that are made to each by the target children. Here the classroom is '. . . counted, measured and otherwise catalogued as the prelude to deducing the rules or laws underlying them and giving them coherence' (Hughes, 2001: 53). The numerical information that she had collected as a consequence of the structured observations revealed what she describes as 'useful comparisons that might help in improving the learning environment for all the children'. Additionally, she had found the methodological tool 'easy to implement' and, moreover, it helped her to 'focus and avoid other distractions'. But she also became aware that 'when I watch and choose specific things to write about I am making choices that are guided by my subjectivity' (Wilkinson, 2003: 30). So, whilst the 'innocence of both observable facts and transparent language were assumed' (Lather, 1991: 104), there was nevertheless a loss of confidence in such an assumption. Such a shift caused her to question not just why it was that specific children had been selected as the targeted group but also why others had been left out and, moreover, why some events in the classroom were worthy of being observed whilst others were 'distractions'.

Ill-fitting paradigms

Research, like any other academic pursuit, has been and continues to be a contested terrain. A root cause for the debate circulates around the question, 'Can we study social sciences in the same scientific way in which the natural world is studied?' Two principal arguments emerge:

> . . . epistemologically, the social sciences are no different from the natural sciences and that they should, as a consequence, mimic the methods of the natural sciences; and the argument that, although there are similarities between the social and natural sciences, they require different epistemologies, and, hence, methodologies, because the goal of social sciences – *understanding* – is distinct from that of the natural sciences – *explanation.*
>
> (Hekman, 1990: 3, our emphasis)

As we have seen above, there are moments when we want both explanations and understanding. It is for this reason that experimentation is encouraged. The student cited above did not settle for a particular way of undertaking the project; rather, a hybrid approach was adopted. Hybrid research need not imply an 'anything-goes' abdication of methodological responsibility (Stronach and MacLure, 1997: 109). While we need conceptual frames for purposes of understanding, we nevertheless take note of Lather's cautionary words:

> . . . classifying research and researchers into neatly segregated 'para-digms' or 'traditions' does not reflect the untidy realities of real scholars . . . and may become an end in itself' . . . 'Traditions' must be treated not as clearly defined, real entities but only as loose frameworks for dividing research . . .
>   (Lather, 1991: 108, citing Atkinson *et al.*, 1988: 223)

Methodological responsibility, in our view, means asking, 'Whose interests are being served by the research being undertaken in this particular way?'

Whose interests are being served?

Given that the stated purpose of much practitioner research into early years educare is directed towards improving the lives of young children, it seems only natural to assume that we already have the answer to the question of whose interests are being served. And if the answer to the question is indeed that research is in the interests of young children then all that remains is a dutiful description of how this occurs. Not so, for at this point we move away from a rational perspective, which provides us with a 'common sense' view, and begin to explore some of the complexities where close scrutiny is paid to the notion of contested interests.

We want to locate the discussion concerned with 'interests' around the example given above of the 'feeding group', and as a starting point we want to examine the interests of the student. As noted, the aim of the student's research project was to 'examine the effectiveness of the professional' within the context of the group. To think of the student in terms of being a disinterested observer is naive. Clearly she has a number of vested interests, in that she wants to secure data and she wants this to be detailed enough so that she can gain knowledge about 'professional effectiveness'. Additionally, the student has to ensure that her work is satisfying the interests of the university, where prescribed criteria will to some extent dictate both the process of the research and its outcomes.

Meanwhile, she enters into a sensitive situation. Here, each of the stakeholders, including the professionals, the parents and the children, will have their own notions of what constitutes 'professional effectiveness'. These will to some extent be prescribed by the particular circumstances in which each of the respondents are situated. Additionally, their responses will be governed in part by who is asking the question. In the case of the professional for example, discussing 'professional effectiveness' will in all likelihood be quite a different experience when talking to a university student who is undertaking a small scale research project than when she is having to account for her role within a more bureaucratic context such as writing an official report. In some ways one could imagine the interview situation between the professional and the student as being quite a liberating experience, where there might be an opportunity for the professional to use the situation as an opportunity to reflect and be self-critical about her role. Elsewhere caution might prevail. Describing 'professional effectiveness' within a discourse that is concerned with 'cost effectiveness' and 'value for money', for example, carries with it very different sets of interests than when talking to a university student.

And what about the parents who attend because of difficulties with parenting? They too cannot divorce themselves from the context in which the researcher's questions are being asked. Also, given that they are caught within sets of practices that are aimed at regulating their behaviour in terms of parenting, their opportunities to be 'open' will be curtailed by this. True, steps have been taken to establish confidentiality, but even with such assurances these are vulnerable individuals whose parenting skills have been found so wanting that they are 'obliged' to attend classes. It is from this position of obligation that they have to construct accounts concerned with effectiveness. That is not to say that their views should be discounted or that they should not even be approached to give a view. However, what we are signalling is the impossibility of any individual to be able to respond in completely transparent ways.

Finally, there are the children's interests to consider. Let us for a moment recap on the situation that these pre-school children find themselves in. First, for reasons concerned with the child's health and overall well-being, decisions have been made that they, together with their mothers, should attend weekly sessions at an early years setting. Here, whilst there might be some familiar landmarks such as toys, for the most part every aspect of the context will be strange. For most children making moves from the familiar to the unfamiliar is greatly assisted because of the presence of an attachment figure such as the mother. But in this instance, for a number of reasons, the relationship between mother and child has become so fraught that acceptable levels of care have been jeopardized. This clearly is a vulnerable situation where the researcher must proceed with caution. For example, it might be that in observing the children the student adopts a participant-observer's role that involves playing with the children. Such play bouts might be undertaken on a weekly basis over a relatively substantial amount of time. As experienced practitioners know, playing with or even alongside young children can be a fruitful site for gaining brief insights into the child's own perceptions of their social world. But taking on a play role does imply establishing relationships, where the young child might well begin to develop expectations including perhaps a hope that the student researcher will be a regular visitor to the group. In such a situation the student has to balance her own desire for data whilst being sensitive to the needs of the children.

Concluding remarks

Talking, listening and watching are ordinary everyday practices, but within research they become extraordinary. This is because as research methodological procedures they have the potential to contribute to change in people's lives, and being instrumental in securing change is a deeply serious business. Within the UK the arena of early years educare is dedicated in profound ways to changing lives. It is therefore particularly imperative that we hold on to Foucault's cautionary words, where he urges a relentless caution in relation to how we think and how we act. The above account hopefully goes some way to illustrate efforts in behaving cautiously.

References

Atkinson, P., Delamont, S. and Hammersley, M. (1988) Qualitative research traditions: a response to Jacob, *Review of Educational Research*, 58(2): 231–250.

Epstein, D. (1998) 'Are you a girl or are you a teacher? The "least adult role" in research about gender and sexuality', in G. Walford (ed.) *Doing Research About Education*. London: Falmer Press.

Fine, G. A. and Sandstrom, K. L. (1988) *Knowing Children: Participant Observation with Minors*. London: Sage Publications.

Flax, J. (1990) 'Postmodernism and gender relations in feminist theory', in L. Nicholson (ed.) *Feminism/Postmodernism*. London: Routledge.

Foucault, M. (1984) 'On the genealogy of ethics: an overview of work in progress', in P. Rabinow (ed.) *The Foucault Reader*. Harmondsworth: Penguin.

Hekman, S. (1990) *Gender and Knowledge*. Cambridge: Polity Press.

Hughes, P. (2001) 'Paradigms, methods and knowledge', in G. MacNaughton, S.A. Rolfe and I. Siraj-Blatchford (eds) *Doing Early Childhood Research: International Perspectives on Theory and Practice*. Buckingham: Open University Press.

Lather, P. (1991) *Getting Smart*. London: Routledge.

McLennan, G. (1992) 'The enlightenment project revisited', in S. Hall, D. Held and T. Mcgrew (eds) *Modernity and its Futures*. Cambridge: Polity Press.

Morrow, V. and Richards, M. (1996) The ethics of social research with children: an overview, *Children and Society*, 10(3): 90–105.

Shotter, J. (1992) 'Getting in touch. The meta-methodology of a post-modern science of mental life', in S. Kvale (ed.) *Psychology and Postmodernism*. London: Sage.

Strathern, M. (1995) *Shifting Contexts: Transformations in Anthropological Knowledge*. London: Routledge.

Stronach, I. and MacLure, M. (1997) *Educational Research Undone: the Postmodern Embrace*. Buckingham: Open University Press.

Sylva, K., Roy, C. and Painter, M. (1980) *Childwatching at Playgroup and Nursery School: Oxford Pre-School Project Grant*. London: McIntyre.

Wilkinson, A. (2003) *Deconstructing Choice*, BA (Hons) dissertation, Manchester Metropolitan University.

2 Exploring tensions within the interplay of rights, duties and responsibilities

Rachel Holmes

Introduction

The aims of this chapter are twofold. First, we will consider what it means for the young child to have rights. Second, using a combination of tutor reflections and extracts from students' role-play, the chapter will explore current manifestations of the phenomena of children's rights. It will also examine how the notion of rights is played out in, and determined by, the policies realized within the institutions we provide for children. In an attempt to illustrate how we might unpack some of these dilemmas, we will explore aspects of the students' improvised role-play, in response to a case study of observed practice, offset against students' developing understandings of the rights of children under three.

Children's rights: multiple interpretations and shifting meanings

According to the World Health Organization (2004), the intention to develop international 'standards' for the welfare and protection of children has a long history, which culminated in 1989 in the adoption of the UN Convention on the Rights of the Child (UNCRC) and which was ratified by the UK government in December 1991. Burr (cited in Kehily, 2004) suggests the history of emerging rights began in 1919 with the International Labour Organization (ILO), which pioneered the establishment of international standards on women's work and child labour. The fifth assembly of the League of Nations later adopted the Declaration on Children's Rights (1924), followed by the emergence of what were identified as fundamental human rights, articulated in the Universal Declaration of Human Rights in 1948. Eleven years later, the Declaration on the Rights of the Child, which grew out of the 1924 document, was criticized for not providing a clearly articulated framework of rights, something the 1989 Convention was later to address (2004: 147). This latter document, containing civil and political, social, economic and cultural rights, is an international vehicle that identifies the rights of children and adolescents, considers what is understood as their particular needs for protection and the opportunities they are deemed to require for growth and development. The right to a name and to a nationality (article 7) and the right to freedom of thought, conscience and religion (article 14) are both examples of civil and political rights. The social, economic and cultural rights contained in the Convention include, amongst many others, the right to education (article 28), the right to health and health services (article 24) and the right to an adequate standard of living (article 27). Olejas (2002) suggests the articles of the Convention can be grouped according to particular themes that relate to a child's well-being. The general principles are: article 2 – The principle of non-discrimination; article 3 – The best interests of the child; article 6 – The right to life, survival and development; article 12 – Respect for the views of the child.

All articles encapsulated within the UNCRC have global intentions. They have been ratified by most countries around the world (191 of the world's 193 countries), rendering their manifestations as practices borne out of context-bound interpretations. Our challenge herein is to unpack ideas around how their singularity of intention and outcome becomes polysemous as they travel through languages, cultures, time and lifestyles. It is by deliberating about these complexities that we hope to open up issues throughout this chapter, recognizing that not only are they difficult to contemplate as universal conceptual entities, but that also, even within UK provision, we find interesting dilemmas in their shifting meanings.

A conversation of 'us' with 'us' about 'them': the rights of children under three

We begin by considering a vision of childhood offered by Mayall (1994). He proposes that children's lives are lived through childhoods, constructed for them by adult understandings of childhood and what children are and should be. Conceding to such a strong sense of adult interpretation and powerful intervention, we consider the impact this might have upon the child and the provision made for them in the light of the UNCRC. This chapter provides opportunities for us to explore the construct of social divisions (including for example race, gender, culture, religion) and the ways in which these impact on the young child with reference to their rights. Within this chapter we intend to trace a session undertaken with students. We focused upon cultural practices and found articles 8 and 14 to have some sense of relationship, as well as tension lying within them. We believed they could offer students an interesting context within which to ponder their own initial thoughts around culture and identity.

Article 8

1 States Parties undertake to respect the right of the child to preserve his or her identity, including nationality, name and family relations as recognized by law without lawful interference

Article 14

1 States Parties shall respect the right of the child to freedom of thought, conscience and religion
2 States Parties shall respect the rights and duties of the parents and, when applicable, legal guardians, to provide direction to the child in the exercise of his or her right in a manner consistent with the evolving capacities of the child
3 Freedom to manifest one's religion or beliefs may be subject only to such limitations as are prescribed by law and are necessary to protect public safety, order, health or morals, or the fundamental rights and freedoms of others

(UNCRC, 1989)

We consider a significant theme here to be the child's right to preserve and have preserved a sense of identity, culture and heritage. This seems to present tutors, students and practitioners with notions of duty, responsibility and commitment to finding ways to nurture each child's sense of who they are. However, the articles also create dilemmas in their ambiguity, as we are left to decipher amorphous terminology such as 'evolving capacities', as well as grappling with ways to interpret 'identity' and 'freedom of thought'. We also contemplate whether there are competing discourses at work here, for example the tensions within a child's right to 'freedom of thought, conscience and religion' and her parent's duty 'to provide direction'.

Our intention was to destabilize students' interpretations of the relationship between idealized rhetoric, legislative documentation and early years practice by looking at these articles, positioned against an observation made at a Children's Centre. In an attempt to provide a frame of reference for unpacking the observation, we are also intending to focus the students on *Birth to Three Matters: A Framework to Support Children in their Earliest Years* (DfES and Sure Start, 2002). This framework is gradually assuming status within early years settings in England, informing policies, courses and pedagogical approaches. As the students' studies focus upon the birth-to-eight age range, it seems important that they are able to become familiar with this increasingly significant document. The framework itself is interesting to us, as it builds a picture of the young child in what we consider to be creative and thoughtful ways. In its organization and by utilizing particular language and reframing more traditional understandings of the young child, we believe it offers practitioners the opportunity to explore the context-based work they do by acknowledging the dilemmas that lie within it. Rather than advocating a simplistic and singular view of children and childhood, it seems to position the child as multifaceted, as a co-constructor of the world in which they live, with a strong sense of agency and autonomy. It also seems to position the practitioner as an assiduous questioner, reflective researcher and proactive collaborator with parents and other professionals. For these reasons this document, along with a case study of practice, provided us with an exciting context for exploring the challenges within articles 8 and 14.

In order to capture an aspect of the framework for use within this chapter, we intend to reflect upon the section we feel facilitates disturbances within the case study we are using. The aspect 'A Strong Child' suggests that there is a web of relational processes that embed each child within different contexts. It is through the interactive manifestations of these processes *across* contexts that a child might grow to understand who they are and develop a sense of belonging. Practitioners are urged to contemplate, amongst other things, the interplay of potentially disparate cultural expectations informing these processes that straddle the home and early years settings. For purposes of this discussion we will be focusing upon ways to reinforce a child's right to individuality whilst also nurturing a sense of group belonging. The framework suggests this emerges from the recognition that each child is a member of a family and a community rather than being perceived as an isolated individual. Within 'A Strong Child' it is regarded as central that any early years setting is seen as a system of relations located in a wider social system, within which the child operates, finds meaning and develops a sense of identity. The right to develop a sense of belonging is underpinned by an appreciation of the ways in which family, culture and setting are pivotal to an active partnership in a child's developing self-awareness. The framework goes on to intimate that exchanges of ideas and sharing of different wisdoms between home and setting deem parents as significant co-contributors to the child's holistic learning experience.

We selected the following statement from *Birth to Three Matters*, as we perceived it to raise some interesting dilemmas in relation to the complexities within the UNCRC's articles 8 and 14: 'Children's self-confidence is affected and influenced by the way adults respond to them.' We begin here by asserting that there could be large numbers of 'adults' (parents, carers, practitioners, other family members, friends of family members, the community, etc.) who live and work with each child and who respond to each child's actions, behaviours and different experiences from within their own value systems – in other words, in very different ways. Although understood generally as an enriching experience, there are also struggles that may be perceived within this kaleidoscope of adult influence on a child's developing sense of confidence and identity. In an attempt to explore some of these, we selected the following case study to use with the students. It is one which we understood to lie within the cultural and religious interface straddling familial practices at home and the community of practice operating within an early years setting and one which may also provoke consideration of the aforementioned tensions we perceived within the UN articles.

CASE STUDY

A mixed gendered group of five children were playing outside on a hot day. The practitioner, sensing a rare opportunity, decided to sprinkle them with water and as their clothes became wetter, the children began trying to take items of clothing off, which the practitioner then assisted them with. It was perceived by the practitioner as a source of great enjoyment to all the children as they jumped, ran around and lay down, being consumed by laughter and delight as the water fell over them. After the experience, the practitioner gathered the group together and with help from another practitioner took all the remaining clothes off the children to replace them with dry ones. Later that day, as parents arrived at the Children's Centre to find their children in different clothing and their own wet clothing hanging on their coat peg wrapped in a plastic bag, one parent expressed her concern about what had unfolded earlier that day. She went on to explain how she found it inappropriate that her 32 month old child had undressed amongst a group of other children, as this challenged her daughter's growing awareness of the need for privacy, respect and modesty with regards to her own body, an awareness embedded within her family's cultural beliefs and religious practices. The parent expressed her concern that this awareness needed to begin once the child was mixing with children outside the home setting.

This case study is understood to manifest a relationship with article 14(2) through the unfolding of what we perceived as shared tensions: to facilitate the child's right to 'freedom of thought', set against her perceived 'evolving capacities' and her parent's duty to 'provide direction'. These statements seem to offer an interesting juxtaposition of ideas and struggles within practices. A further complexity was the age of the child, as the silent assumptions within the term 'evolving capacities' set against the Birth to Three framework's claims of a young child's right to autonomy and agency could generate considerable debate. Having given students a copy of articles 8 and 14 and 'A Strong Child' we split them into four groups and each group was asked to consider the case study in the light of the two documents. Working towards a notion of multi-professional perspectives, each group was required to contemplate a different position: group one was to negotiate the standpoint taken by the parent; the second was to consider the practitioner's perspective; the third was to contemplate the child's position; and the fourth was to reflect upon the stance that might be adopted by the UN Convention. Once the groups had explored their respective positions, we created a partially improvised role-play based on each group's discussions, which was intended to bring these differing perspectives together. In order to explore the dilemmas and competing discourses that emerged, we offer an extract below. (Taken from field notes during a discussion.)

> Parent: As a parent having a strong religious background, I want to direct my child within the cultural values and beliefs that we all share at home. Clearly at your Centre, some cultures are not prioritized in the same way that others are. Either there was no knowledge of why undressing might contravene the religious and cultural practices of our community, or there was just a blatant disregard for this. It's very important to us that our child's cultural beliefs aren't contradicted or devalued. It's not enough to provide halal meat and think that's all you need to do. We can't separate our religion from all aspects of our lifestyle and it's hard enough trying to censor what she's surrounded by to make sure she understands what's acceptable, especially being surrounded by billboards, television programmes and magazines that flaunt nudity and other offensive pictures. We expect our child to be protected at nursery as well as at home with us.
>
> Practitioner: The UN Convention on the Rights of the Child as well as the Birth to Three framework have direct implications on our practice and we have obligations as a Children's Centre to ensure our policies reflect these documents, which means constant monitoring and reviewing of our practices. You have to understand that the Centre has an obligation to interpret the Birth to Three framework in a way that respects all religions and cultures by using an anti-bias approach that allows children to make choices based on a range of information.
>
> Child: Yes, I should be able to choose what I do and I did want to get undressed like all my friends, but given that I am nearly three years old, I wonder whether giving me so much choice is realistic? Do I fully understand why I can't do certain things in my religion? I suppose I need to ask whether I do need guidance from my parents or can I trust the adults who look after me at the Children's Centre to do what's best for me? The difficulty here is that the practitioner thought the 'undressing' activity was a valuable learning experience and source of enjoyment for me, whereas my parents think it's a violation of our family's cultural beliefs and religious practices. I don't know what to think, or where I fit into all of this.

Practitioner: We see the Centre as having a vital role in ensuring each child's right to choose a religion and to follow a certain way of life is safeguarded and that each child has the knowledge to make an informed decision. However, children who already believe in one particular religion should also have the right to practice it. Some children are clearly getting mixed messages from home and our setting.

Child: Yes, but what if my parents are pushing me too much, what if their influence is so overpowering that I can't come to my own decision? What if I become an outsider if I can't join in with the other children because my religious beliefs and cultural practices are different from theirs? Will I just be isolated?

UN Convention: We believe that all children have the right to develop their own beliefs without others telling them what to think and follow. This includes parents. Children should have the right to follow their beliefs and choose their religion, to learn about the way other people live so they are able to respect the differences and then no one will feel isolated, just different and that's Okay. But if this child wanted to join in with the other children and didn't see any harm in doing this, the practitioner was right to encourage her involvement. If she felt pressurized to join in when she really didn't want to take her clothes off, then this is a different problem. The parent was imposing her beliefs onto the child when she was perhaps too young to know any different or in fact didn't want to practise parts of her parent's religion if it meant not being able to join in. Perhaps something for you all to think about is whether there is an age at which the parent's duty must override the rights of the child, or whether the child's right should always take priority, or in fact whether you understand parental duty as an aspect of the child's right.

Practitioner: I take your point, but we do believe that the Centre has an obligation to its community by meeting its needs. By empowering children to teach one another about their own religion and involving parents and the community we can try to achieve this. However, we think difficulties arise when parental influence and objections to their child's participation in activities ends up creating a clash of rights and duties between those of the child, the practitioner and the parent, where the adults begin to impinge upon the child's freedom to make choices. Here, the education of the individual child without inter-ference from parents has to be our main concern, otherwise how can children develop their own individual identity? We do recognize that all parents are different and have different levels of tolerance. If a parent feels strongly about something, they need to come in and tell us when they enrol their child. Some parents have high levels of insecurity, which is maybe why this parent feels she cannot allow her child to participate.

This extract seems rich in opportunities to open up ideas relating to the students' understandings of the dialogic relationship between theoretical frameworks and issues arising out of practice. Within the role-play, the child was questioning both the parent and practitioner. The ways in which her 'freedom of choice' seemed to be territory already occupied by adults was articulated, along with her 'evolving capacity' to make her own decision and have a sense of agency within her experiences. The child acknowledges the different significant adults in her life (parent and practitioner), but also recognizes they may have competing agendas, placing her in what she felt was an untenable position – either to work against the cultural expectations of the practitioner or negate her family's cultural practices. Bhatti expresses this concern in her ethnographic study of Asian children at home and at school. In contrast to experiences at the mosque where one child suggests '. . . was where you could be yourself and you could talk in your own language and be normal . . .' (Amina: 13, taped conversation, in Bhatti, 1999: 114), life at school was very different: 'You learn not to have your hands done and not to put coconut oil in your hair on school days even if your mum gets cross' (Pareveen: 8, taped conversation, in Bhatti, 1999: 107).

Although our case study is not located within a school and the child is considerably younger, we believe the Children's Centre could represent one amongst many early contexts where the child finds herself having to negotiate differing, sometimes competing narratives of identity. Somers argues that:

> . . . it is through narratives that we constitute our social identities . . . all of us come to be who we are (however ephemeral, multiple and changing) by being located or locating ourselvs . . . in social narratives rarely of our own making . . .
>
> (Somers, 1994: 606)

Rather than exploring the notion of multiple identities, the students represented these competing narratives as polarizing experiences for the child as she seemed to wrestle with the dichotomy of becoming assimilated within the early years group, set against being ostracized as different. The notion of assimilation leads us to ponder James' thoughts, where the homogenization of groups works to assimilate disparate cultural identities: '. . . a dominant ideology which allows us as adults to attribute to individual children an overarching categorical identity . . . which in turn shapes children's sense of Self' (1993: 75).

Placing Somers' and James' ideas alongside each other in relation to the role-play scenario, the sense of the child's fluid identity, which emerges from differing social narratives constructed around her, could also be interpreted as constraining if in practice there is a tension as the child struggles between hegemonic discourses of culture and a more subtly differentiated sense of self, as Valentine suggests, 'strung out between competing definitions of their "identity" . . .' (2000: 258).

A further interesting idea we located in the role-play was that although the Birth to Three framework considers it important to experience the child as an active agent in co-constructing her understandings of past and present influences, the students' construction of the child seemed to be as the invisible subject of the adults' discussion, a subject perceived, diluted and interpreted through the adult gaze. Although reflecting upon the subjugation of women, we believe Trinh's reflections find resonance with the students' construction of the young child:

> A conversation of 'us' with 'us' about 'them' is a conversation in which 'them' is silenced. 'Them' always standing on the other side of the hill . . . speechless, barely present in its absence. Subject of discussion, 'them' is only admitted among an 'us', the discussing subjects, when accompanied or introduced by an 'us', member, hence the dependency of 'them'.
>
> (Trinh, 1989: 65)

The use of phrases such as 'our child's cultural beliefs . . .' (parent), 'some children are clearly getting mixed messages . . .' (practitioner) and 'too young to know any different . . .' (representative from UNCRC) could be understood to position the child as an object of adult intervention, being permitted into the discussion only as a construction of the adults surrounding her. Her own contributions throughout the role-play were almost rendered soliloquies, prompting no direct responses from the adults, which could be read to mirror a reality of the child's voice, especially those under three. These soliloquies represented her in a state of flux, torn between two competing worlds and grappling with ideas about belonging, whether that be to her family, community and associated cultural practices or to the group constituted by the early years setting. McCraig's (1996) use of the term 'cultural chameleon' creates an interesting perspective, as the child searches for cultural translations between identities at home and in the early years setting. If we return to Mayall's idea, the sometimes disparate adult constructions may well necessitate the child's chameleon-like adaptation to different surroundings. Her reaching out to adults for direction was perhaps the students' interpretation of this young child as having inadequate capacities at this age to understand her rights and be an active agent in the construction of her own life. Perhaps this is an easier way to understand young children, a convenient scapegoat amidst the complexities of this dilemma, or a counterproductive position to take, one which redeems the adult power struggles as reinstatement of the notion of child as 'them' in a landscape of 'us'.

Turning to the parent, the Birth to Three framework suggests that a child's sense of identity and belonging is embedded within her immediate family, rooted within complex cultural, class, religious and racial practices. The role-play constructed the parent as articulate and assertive and she had interpreted article 14(2) by dutifully protecting her young child in the exercise of her rights through necessary parental direction. Within her implication that the Centre had an ethnocentric bias, she suggested that, at best, there was a lack of awareness and, at worse, a deliberate neglect for the significance of the family's lifestyle preferences. Bhatti again identifies this as a concern of some parents in her study:

> Most of the mothers I spoke to . . . expressed considerable unease over cultural differences, 'Well there is this different culture here, different maahol [atmosphere] . . . and I must bring them up so they know what are our ways and . . . what were our elders' ways. And it is hard . . .'
> (Mrs Shaukat: translated from Punjabi, taped conversation, in Bhatti, 1999: 33)

In the role-play she was represented as a parent whose lifestyle is guided by her religious beliefs, manifested through cultural practices, including the parental duty to raise her child in a way consistent with those beliefs. She positioned the practitioner as someone who did not share her beliefs and consequently did not, or even could not, appreciate the detrimental impact of permitting the undressing activity. The parent was constructed as assuming that the practitioner considered the recognition of basic lifestyle differences, such as differentiated meals, to be an adequate gesture in the pursuit of diversity and inclusion, whilst being unaware of other cultural practices, or disregarding them perhaps as inappropriate for young children. Was she suggesting that the practitioner, either through her lack of diverse cultural awareness or hierarchical cultural preference, was 'abnormalizing' some beliefs and practices in the maintenance of norms associated with the freedoms and uncomplicated child-centred and play-based nature of early years practice? As Dyer suggests, 'It has become common for those marginalised by culture to acknowledge the situation from which they speak, but those who occupy positions of cultural hegemony blithely carry on as if what they say is neutral and unsituated . . .' (2002: 4).

The parent's situation was being further articulated in ways that contextualized the undressing activity amongst the plethora of broader societal and political messages she seemed to experience as destructive in her child's developing sense of identity, some of which emerge from the media.

Compounding the ethnocentric practices within the early years setting, the parent identifies television programmes, magazines and billboard images that could be argued present a 'neutral and unsituated' western view of what is regarded as appropriate and often gender-specific behaviours, whilst also positioning 'other' (as in minority cultures, ethnicities, races and religions in Britain) as 'outsiders' in today's multicultural landscape. When taking a particular stance and acknowledging the 'situation from which they speak', are minority ethnic groups being condemned as the unwilling participant in the process of assimilation? Was she making the association between these broader obstacles and the mindset of the Centre, both seeming to exude white, western values, steeped in political correctness, yet a world away from sensitive understandings of a pluralistic society? If so, what was the parent proposing to the setting in relation to the disturbance of assumptions, the destabilization of misconceptions and the challenging of practices that only reinstate the polarities of assimilation or segregation?

Borne out of the political and societal agendas in which it is located, but striving to be representative of the local community it serves, is the institution of the Children's Centre. Here, the need to be 'politically correct' may well have curtailed the expression of the practitioner's personal beliefs about how young children 'should' be cared for and educated. Within the role-play, we believe the practitioner was constructed as resorting to a range of subversive disempowering mechanisms in relation to her exchanges with the parent. The culture of the Children's Centre affected the parent in the choices made available to her child. This seemed to manifest itself in the practitioner's interpretation of the child's undressing experience as a valuable part of belonging to the group and experiencing the sensations attached to what to her seemed like an 'innocent' and pleasurable activity. She was portrayed as justifying her position by referencing the documents that framed her practice and was constructed as finding meaning and relevance within her practices in article 14(1), but perhaps by doing this eclipsing the complex interrelationship between 14(1) and 14(2). It could be argued that the students felt the practitioner needed to assert her sense of equity as an important consideration, interpreted as all children having the opportunity to partake in the same experience at the same time, creating a sense of togetherness and group identity as they all shared in the thrills and excitement of that moment ('. . . respects all religions and cultures by using an anti-bias approach that allows children to make choices'). But this could also be interpreted as the rhetoric of political correctness embedded within educational discourses of equal opportunities and diversity, where the parent's voice becomes disempowered ('You have to understand that . . .'). Did the practitioner seek to position herself as the expert, as the protector of the child's rights, and in doing so make judgements about what was in the best 'educational' interests of the child, even if that served to silence the parent's voice? We ponder whether the practitioner was constructed as standing in judgement of the parent's cultural and religious practices, as having an agenda that raises questions about the realities of the 'multicultural society' in which we are all located. If so, how can we begin to resolve what to the practitioner emerged as a conflict of interests, when retrospectively she conceded to the parent's articulated disapproval, then later retracted the gesture when suggesting a 'clash of rights and duties', citing the parent's influence and objections as the source? It is at the interface of these and other complex dilemmas that the UNCRC and the Birth to Three framework position the practitioner – whose definition of 'a strong child' do we mean, do we use, do we perceive or are willing to negotiate as the 'absolute' in educare terms?

Lost in translation?

By way of bringing these reflections to a close, we return to our initial consideration: what does it mean for the young child to have rights?. We have attempted to explore how the UNCRC's single category 'child', even within the UK, could be read as universalizing and oversimplifying the complexity of young children's forms of identification. It could also suggest an erroneous sense of boundaries around the child's rights as differentiated from the adult's duties. We suggest that the journey undertaken to unpack the concept of children's rights has left us 'lost in translation', in that no single direction has emerged, no fixed point at which we can finally rest. We are left with a kaleidoscope of detours where we are able to explore less familiar contexts and contemplate potential perspectives. Although armed with the universally endorsed UNCRC legislation and more localized *Birth to Three Matters* guidance, we realize the undulating terrain of early years practice is far from easily navigated. Having said this, we believe we *have* travelled somewhere.

By creating a role-play and contributing to follow-up discussions, we experienced students beginning to conceptualize their own learning through the construction and reconstruction of ideas and contemplation of different perspectives from which they could interpret a situation. We observed how they began to consider the implicit power imbalances within relationships that might surround and construct the early life of the child. Cottone suggests that 'We are born of relationship, nurtured in relationship and educated in relationship' (1988: 363) and as students began to challenge each other, reconstitute unfolding complexities and move towards re-conceptualizing taken-for-granted understandings, more oblique perspectives began to emerge. Rather than being satisfied with a more simplistic story about whether or not the child's rights were considered, the students began to examine the details of the case study, which we believe included, for example, what it means for children to live through adult constructions of childhood; the parent's role in supporting a child's sense of cultural belonging; the practitioner's role in preserving whilst building on the child's sense of individuality and interrelational patterns within the group; and the ways in which the practitioner understands the child's own sense of shifting identity and builds self-confidence to be able to express this.

As tutors, we contemplate our own positions in relation to what it means for the young child to have a right to preserve their identity and consider Pahl's observation of ways in which children move between the home and the early years setting: '. . . the transition from home to school and back again preoccupied many of them . . . at home they may well be able to express ideas about the worlds away from the nursery, worlds which are unfamiliar to the nursery workers . . .' (1999: 101). But it must be asked whether at the Children's Centre they were constrained by the world most familiar to the practitioner, rather than having opportunities to seamlessly shift between multiple worlds. Bhatti, after considering the disparate experiences of Asian children at home and at school, concludes that: 'Asian children are not completely like their parents, nor completely like their white peers. They are British Asians . . . in the process of carving out a separate identity for themselves' (1999: 238).

Although this suggests emerging separateness, it could also be seen to advocate a singular and fixed sense of identity. We believe consideration has to be given to how the 32 month old child is constructed by others during this evolving process, how she is affected by gender, ethnicity and class, if she is marginalized, stereotyped, misunderstood or misrepresented. Somers suggests '. . . people are guided to act in certain ways, and not others, on the basis of the projections, expectations and memories derived from a multiplicity but ultimately limited repertoire of available social, public and cultural narratives' (1994: 614).

We would argue that if this process of 'carving out' is embedded within narrative constraints and is interdependent upon the experiences that surround the child, the idea may not be one of separateness in terms of being neither decontextualized nor uncomplicated. It seems to become a process whereby the status quo of discrimination and dominant ideologies could lie unchallenged within institutions and the frames of reference from which the child is able to 'carve out a separate identity' could remain hegemonized, whereby the cultural differences of minority ethnic groups are rendered deferential within prejudiced hierarchical structures. This could eschew practices that are implemented to facilitate the child's right to develop an awareness of, and to preserve, her sense of identity.

References

Bhatti, G. (1999) *Asian Children at Home and at School: An Ethnographic Study*. London: Routledge.

Cottone, R. R. (1988) Epistemological and ontological issues in counselling: implications of social systems theory, *Counselling Psychology Quarterly*, 1(4), 357–365.

DfES and Sure Start (2002) *Birth to Three Matters: A Framework to Support Children in their Earliest Years*. London: DfES.

Dyer, R. (2002) *White*. London: Routledge.

James, A. (1993) *Childhood Identities*. Edinburgh: Edinburgh University Press.

Kehily, M. J. (ed.) (2004) *An Introduction to Childhood Studies*. Buckingham: Open University Press.

McCraig, N. M. (1996) 'Understanding global nomads', in C. D. Smith (ed.) *Strangers at Home: Essays on the Effects of Living Overseas and Coming Home to a Strange Land*. New York: Alethia Publishing.

Mayall, B. (ed.) (1994) *Children's Childhoods: Observed and Experienced*. London: Falmer.

Nutbrown, C. (ed.) (1996) *Children's Rights and Early Education*. London: Paul Chapman Publishing.

Olejas, S. (2002) *Child and Adolescent Rights*. Geneva: Department of Child and Adolescent Health and Development.

Pahl, K. (1999) *Transformations: Meaning Making in Nursery Education*. London: Trentham Books.

Somers, M. (1994) The narrative constitution of identity: a relational and network approach, *Theory and Society*, 23(2), 605–649.

Trinh, T. M. (1989) *Woman, Native, Other: Writing Postcoloniality and Feminism*. Bloomington: Indiana University Press.

United Nations (1959) *The United Nations Declaration on the Rights of the Child*. Geneva: United Nations.

United Nations (1989) *Convention on the Rights of the Child*. New York: United Nations.

Valentine, G. (2000) Exploring children and young people's narratives of identity, *Geoforum*, 31, 257–267.

World Health Organization (2004) Child and Adolescent Health and Development. Retrieved November 2004 from http://www/who.int/child-adolescent-health/RIGHTS/crc_over.htm.

3   The politics of play

Liz Jones, Elaine Hodson and Nell Napier

Introduction

This chapter highlights how play is used as a regulatory tool and how in this sense it becomes a political as well as an educational instrument. Additionally, we document how, by unpacking certain powerful ideas that have historically circulated around play – and still have currency in contemporary practices – it is possible to perceive play as an ideological device aimed at maintaining the social order.

The work of Foucault (1977) has been significant when looking back at the historical landscape of early years education in general and play in particular. Specifically, his work enables us to appreciate how particular discursive practices work at regulating in order to normalize individuals. Walkerdine and Lucey (1989: 34), in following Foucault, make the following point: 'Regulation is not neutral but is about a knowledge which suppresses and silences other knowledges in producing its own vision.'

Subsequently, our efforts are directed at how we, that is tutors and students alike, take a reflexive attitude towards play, where through dialogue we try to engage with play so that any efforts to perceive it as benign are suppressed. As in class, we begin the chapter by considering what we mean by play. Following on from this an historical overview is offered where the relationship between politics and play is made clear. This section is necessary because it both underpins and permeates work that is undertaken with the students in relation to play. In developing a reflexive attitude students, through classroom discussions, personal reading and their own practical experiences within a number of multiprofessional settings, come to appreciate not only the complexities of play but also that these complexities are rooted in various historical contexts. Here, for a number reasons – often described as educational but always carrying a moral and political impetus – play has been hijacked by various social bodies, including for example churches and philanthropists, in order to instil and perpetuate particular notions of what constitutes 'the child'.

In tracing some of the cultural shifts around 'play' we mark out how play cannot be isolated from the micro and macro cultures in which it exists. Attempts are then made to convey the grapplings that students undertake when beginning to disentangle some of the complexities embedded in play. The final part of the chapter offers some further thoughts on the relationship between play, children's identity and politics. We reiterate that institutions for young children have a political responsibility for helping in the formation of the young child's identity. Additionally, we note how play as a set of experiences is not natural; rather, it is produced through discursive practices. We end by remarking on the repercussions – particularly the benefits – of perceiving the young child as always in a state of process. We argue that within this configuration of the child, play can become a means for questioning not only particular ways of being but also those social structures that conspire to keep such ways in place.

Tracing the politics of play: taming the child

A historical narrative about the numerous theories around children and their play would be a lengthy book in itself. Here our concern is to take an albeit relatively swift backward glance in order to identify certain seminal theories that have provided the foundations on which current thinking about play rest.

A quick dive into a handy dictionary provides us with a number of interesting inferences. It can, for example, centre on games, exercise or other activities undertaken for pleasure. Additionally, its function could be to amuse oneself in a game or to occupy oneself in for instance a sport or diversion. Play is also about performing, taking on a role and playing the part of somebody else. It is also bound up with interaction where to 'play with' connotes exploration.

A number of links can be made between the above definitions and, first, the ways in which the child has been conceptualized and, second, the place of play within these conceptions where in a number of guises it has been used to repress, regulate and normalize the young child.

It is worth acknowledging that most theories are relatively recent and that the concept of childhood itself only began to gain currency, in western cultures, at the end of the nineteenth century. It is also interesting to note that initial theories about the interpellation between the child and play centred on biological explanations drawn from the natural sciences. Ethological evidence indicated that young animals played and it was here that the idea of play being 'natural' for young children was established. Bruce (1991) describes Spencer's (1873) view as inspired by developing technology; he proposed that because children were freed from the need to provide for themselves or protect themselves from predators they had surplus energy. Consequently, they required a similar safety valve to a machine. Whilst machinery required the facility to let off steam, so did the developing child. Play was therefore perceived as a conduit for getting rid of biological forces.

However, it was undoubtedly Romantic ideology that crystallized two significant notions that have had considerable effect not only on provision within the context of early years but also on our overall perceptions of children and associated behaviours including play. One of the chief proponents of Romanticism was Rousseau, who proposed the belief that 'man' in his natural surroundings is inherently good – 'the noble savage' – and has therefore the capacity to improve and progress through careful nurturing. Subsequent proponents of this vision undertook further elaborations. Froebel, for instance, conceptualized pre and early schooling as 'gardens' in which the 'godly laws of development' (Hultqvist, 1998: 101) could occur. Given this ideology, where the child is considered as first inherently 'good' and second that this is secured developmentally, what might be some of the consequences? What inferences does it have in terms of play? If the Froebel child is set 'into a moral order in which the goal of human development is perfection' (Hultqvist, 1998: 101–105) then how will play assist in achieving this Utopia?

Play in this instance has to be part of the battle for what is 'good' and 'right' for the child. In brief, play becomes part of the 'nourishment' that will enable the young child to grow, blossom and mature into a godly being. Here within the ideology, the educator's job is one of 'gardener': '. . . (the) educator nourishes the plant and pulls out all the weeds that threaten to invade the garden' (Hultqvist, 1998: 101). To describe and or itemize the many guises that play would have to assume so as to assist the child in his or her moral development would be too lengthy a task but what does need to be emphasized is the place of play in promoting what Foucault describes as sets of discursive practices where the aim is regulation and normalization. Foucault describes a discourse as 'practices that systematically form the objects of which they speak . . . constitute them and in the practice of doing so conceal their own invention' (1977: 49).

Activities such as taking turns, cooperating, sharing and so forth would be part of an array of play-based performances necessary to ensure the correct 'unfolding' of the child along a natural process of development. Such an unfolding cannot however be left to chance. Hence the necessity for training – particularly of mothers – emerges. Once trained, mothers would then have sufficient insight and sensitivity to orchestrate the process whereby good vanquishes evil and, as a consequence, is banished from the garden. Pioneers including Froebel and Margaret McMillan, as well as socialist/democratic movements such as the Fabians, whilst working at different moments and adopting different slants were nevertheless profoundly influenced by the ideology that has been described. It is, as we shall shortly see, an ideology that has reoccurred and continues to hold sway in contemporary early years settings.

With the emergence of compulsory schooling in England in and around 1880, education became a site for intense political struggle. The political impetus underlying the moves towards compulsory schooling perceived education as the solution to the dual problems of crime and pauperism, two social deviations that were caused through 'bad habits'. As Walkerdine notes:

> . . . it was this understanding of bad habits as the cause of crime and pauperism which led to the possibility of seeing popular education as the answer to the nation's ills . . . in this way the problems of poverty, of pauperism and of poor relief were presented as moral issues concerning the habits and life of the poor.
>
> (Walkerdine, 1984: 165)

Initially, monitorial schools were proposed. These pursued endless activities where the central aim was the instilling of 'good' habits aimed at regulation (Jones and Williamson, 1979). Attention was focused on memorizing the 'basics', including reading, writing and arithmetic, and the rote learning of prayers and passages from the Bible. In this way limited skills and appropriate moral values would be instilled. Play in terms of using one's imagination appeared to have little currency within the above model. However, with the demise of monitorial schools an opening occurred in which other forms of pedagogy could be considered. As Walkerdine notes:

> . . . the fate of the monitorial system was sealed by the argument that the civilising goals of elementary education would be realised more successfully if pupils could be taught not merely to memorise their 'lessons' but also to *understand* them . . .
>
> (Walkerdine, 1984: 216, our emphasis)

Understanding, which in this instance would lead to a 'civilised society', was to be premised on a curriculum based on the study of natural phenomena, where the full realization of the potentialities of the child might be achieved. Thus, using their own senses children could explore, understand and as a consequence be freed from the preconceptions of existing society. This movement from memorizing to understanding, where a curriculum was premised on natural phenomena, marks a shift to Rousseauism where first hand experiences are part of the pedagogical repertoire. Here, investigative play including touching would be countenanced and in so doing would help children to understand.

Play and learning as a doctrine is clearly evident in the nursery settings and teacher training colleges that have already been briefly alluded to above. Additionally, other significant events have contributed to further dimensions. For example, the horrors of the two world wars added to the idea that children should be 'free' to play – play thus becoming part of the social apparatus ensuring the 'free citizen' (Walkerdine and Lucey, 1989). Meanwhile, play was also hijacked by other developing movements. Psychoanalysis, for example, used (and continues to use) forms of play to enable children to resolve inner conflicts and anxieties (see, for example, Issacs, 1933; Klein, 1975). However, it is undoubtedly Piaget's child development theories that gave play, particularly in the early years, its distinctive authority as a basis for the evolution of learning. Piaget's theories have been outlined later in the book (Chapter 15). Here our task is to highlight the effects of coupling play with child development generally, but specifically with learning as understood within the discourse of developmental child psychology. Within this discourse, play becomes part of the discursive field that promotes what we understand as normal – that is, the rational being. Additionally, careful observations of play by the practitioner, whether this is the therapist within a medical discourse or the teacher within an educational discourse, become a means of monitoring the child. Thus play has the capacity to produce facts that in turn lead to categorizations of the child. Notions including, for example, 'the cooperative child', 'the independent child' as well as 'the struggling or slow learning child' emerge from and gain their credence as a consequence of the discourse. In brief, play contributes towards our matter of fact, commonsense understandings of the child.

Student grapplings with play

In 1967 the Plowden Report, *Children and their Primary Schools* (DES), was published, a step that saw the government of the time place play at the centre of the primary curriculum within the UK. The report relied heavily on Piagetian theories of children as active learners. However, a rightward drift of successive governments, driven by zeal both to 'raise standards' and to regain competitiveness with the other industrialized countries (Alexander *et al.*, 1992), has led to this being dismantled and reconfigured as the National Curriculum (1988). The legacy of Plowden is, however, not to be underestimated. In our view, its influence has had two significant impacts. First, the current Curriculum Guidance for the Foundation Stage (DfEE/QCA, 2000) continues to support an early years curriculum based on play. Second, traces of its ideology can be found in students' attempts at articulating their views about play and the young child. Play, we are told, can inform us about the child's skills with language, their social and emotional competence as well as their motor capabilities. Often, the student's own pre-university experiences with young children will lend an understandable confidence to these opinions so that sometimes they are couched quite specifically into 'classifications' of play. Hence some might talk about 'solitary play' or play that promotes 'independence' or play that shows the child's 'maturity'. Others, meanwhile, refer to 'free' and 'directed' play, where in the former the child has 'autonomy' whilst in the latter practitioners 'move the children on so that they learn' (first year undergraduate). So whilst students themselves would not in all probability make any links between the Plowden Report and their views, nevertheless it is possible to discern within these opinions and beliefs fragments of its ideology.

At this juncture we want to refer in a more direct way to how we work with students in this area and in so doing continue to explore the play/politics nexus whilst also making clear how as a consequence of reflexivity thinking is shifted. Let us turn immediately to an example of a 'game' that was developed by a student.

Carrie, a first year student, wrote a story. To accompany this Carrie also made a set of characters. These depicted a family, where the parents were of dual heritage, English and African-Caribbean. Meanwhile, one of the two children was a wheelchair user. The story and its accompanying set of characters were intended to be used by parents/carers with their child within the context of the home.

A reflexive reading of Carrie's story

Circulating throughout Carrie's construction are a number of interesting pairings. There are, for example, two parents, which although not explicitly stated we might assume – because of the presence of children – are male and female. Additionally, the parents have dual heritage, where one is English and in all probability is white whilst the other is African-Caribbean and therefore black. Meanwhile, the two children also straddle two polarities where one is able-bodied and the other is disabled. In putting her game together Carrie has incorporated a number of binary oppositions (for example, white/black, able-bodied/disabled). As MacLure (2003) points out: 'Such binary oppositions are one of the key ways in which meaning and knowledge are produced.' She continues that 'one side achieves definition – comes to meaning – through its *difference* with respect to a (constructed) "other" which is always lacking, lesser or derivative in some respect' (2003: 10). In other words, binaries are not neutral; rather, one side – the positive – feeds off and gains strength from the other. However, in developing the pairings in the above game, is Carrie marking out a set of positive and negative differences? Put a little differently, why has Carrie summoned an African-Caribbean parent and a disabled child into her game?

In order to understand some of the significances of Carrie's tale there must be some recognition of what has come to be described as a 'politics of difference' (Weedon, 1999). The necessity of having a politics of difference emerged from the nineteenth century, where discourses such as medicine formed the ideological basis and justifications for a range of social policies towards a number of groups – practices that materially affected their lives. These groups included women and people of colour. So in the case of race, science was used to legitimate both colonialism and slavery. In brief, African people were not only considered biologically suited to slavery but also, like women, they were scientifically categorized as irrational and therefore unsuited for the task of self-government (Stanton, 1960; Brah, 1996). As Weedon notes:

> . . . scientific racism and similar work on gender set the terms of the debates about difference well into the twentieth century. Indeed, the negative qualities consistently attributed to sexual and racial differ-ence from a white, middle class male norm by the institutions of science, medicine, philosophy and the law made it very difficult to see questions of difference in positive terms.
>
> (Weedon, 1999: 9)

The necessity for a 'politics of difference' therefore stems from a need to chal-lenge those social mechanisms that not only *prescribe* certain individuals as different but also simultaneously help maintain notions of 'normality'. Differ-ence in this instance is always a relationship embedded in power relations. As noted, science has been implicated in this process but, as Weedon indicates, other discourses play a part in maintaining hegemonic accounts of what is normal or natural. Given this, in returning to Carrie's story we can begin to have a better inkling as to why certain characters are being played with. It might be that in weaving these characters into the game the student is trying to effect a destabilization of what is ordinarily thought of as being normal whilst simultaneously making visible aspects of society (in this instance 'dis-ability') more visible. But our firmest conviction in relation to the game is that it stems from the liberal strategy of inclusion and acceptance.

To elaborate further, Carrie's game entertains some additional, more dis-crete but significant moves, for this is a game that will be played out in the home with parental help. In positing the home as a site for learning where par-ents/carers take on a pedagogical role, Carrie is tapping into current political discourses that situate both the family and strong family relations as being instrumental in securing social stability (Pugh, 1988; Organisation for Eco-nomic Cooperation and Development, 1998; Pascal and Bertram, 1999; Iglesias and Sen, 1999). Carrie's story, once it is taken into the home, becomes part of a set of discursive practices where the overall ambition is to create responsible parenting that in turn will ensure the evolution of responsible citizens. Other initiatives that are part of the same discursive field include Sure Start projects, Early Excellence Centres and Children's Centres. In brief, Carrie's game, wit-tingly or not, becomes a means for propagating the following political rhetoric:

> Schools, along with families, have a responsibility to ensure that children and young people learn respect for others and for them-

selves. They need to appreciate and understand the moral code on which civilized society is based and to appreciate the culture and background of others. They need to develop the strength of character and attitudes to life and work, such as responsibility, determination, care and generosity, which will enable them to become citizens of a successful democratic society.

(DfEE, 1997:10)

Carrie, in constructing the game and in thinking about its dissemination, has on a practical level become conscious of some of the issues that have been discussed within our analysis of her story. She is learning and will continue to learn throughout the duration of her studies that the construction of the child and childhood occurs within discourse. However, whilst discourses are powerful they are not impervious to change. In a small but nevertheless significant way Carrie herself is doing what we refer to as 'creating openings'. That is, she is evolving as a critical reflexive practitioner and in so doing is able to think a little differently about life and how this is lived. The insertion of the black parent and the disabled child could be read as Carrie's personal efforts at unsettling mainstream consciousness at the very heart of where much of that is moulded – in the home. We would argue that Carrie's practical efforts are a materialization of her own critical thinking. That is, by subjecting her previously held assumptions and preferred ways of seeing she has cleared a conceptual space in which to think out the game.

Concluding remarks: play, politics and identity

Whilst Carrie's story has provided the basis for a number of considerations we are conscious that more could have been said. For instance, we recognize that considerable work has been undertaken about the effectiveness of the home as an arena for learning for young children, particularly in the field of language development (Dunn, 1998; Wood, 1986; Tizard and Hughes, 1984; Wells, 1987). We could have pursued a route driven by Vygotskian theories of learning, where parents and children together are maybe better placed when in the home to capitalize on and exploit the young child's Zone of Proximal Learning (Donaldson, 1978). There are two reasons for our omissions. First, they are being more satisfactorily addressed elsewhere (Chapter 15). Second, our concern has been to grapple with and focus on the politics/power nexus. Thus in the final section of the chapter we want to offer some concluding thoughts around play, politics and identity. Again, it is Foucault's work that provides a basis for the development of our thinking.

As we have seen, much of Foucault's theoretical explorations centred on discourses. Discourses, as has been noted, are inextricably linked to institutions (the law, education, the family and so forth) and to the disciplines or practices that both regularize and normalize the conduct of those who operate within these institutions, including for example psychology and pedagogical practices. Given this, we want now to return yet again to Carrie's game.

To recap, this was a story that featured a family, which had been materialized into a set of moving characters that could be used by the child/family to develop their own narratives within the home. We do not know how Carrie's story might be used when in the home. However, what we can anticipate is that in reading Carrie's story and in creating their own both the child and her family will have to tap into their own discursively produced knowledge of what a family 'is' and how they themselves live this out. Additionally, the presence of a disabled child and the black parent means that discourses that surround race, racism and disability might be drawn on. Finally, because it is an artefact that has been transposed from one institution to another there is a degree of pressure on the parents/carers and perhaps even the child to acknowledge the discourse of educare with its accompanying set of pedagogical practices.

In part, Carrie herself pre-empted the inclination to think of the family in stereotypical ways. Because of the insertion of the black parent and the disabled child, the players of Carrie's game have to think beyond 'the family' that is constructed within, for example, advertising, where there is a heavy reliance on a particular image, where parents are white and children are able-bodied. So what will be the sources for their play? It might well be that the family when playing will capitalize on rituals such as weddings, birthdays or going on a holiday in order to breathe life into their own fantasies. But overshadowing this family and their play is the early years setting. Effectively is this not a family that is 'doing homework' for and on behalf of the setting? The young child immersed as she will be in the 'fabric' – including the rules and rituals of the early years setting – will have already begun to regulate herself. As MacLure (2003: 18) notes, she is learning '. . . how to discipline herself and manage her body – where to sit, when to listen, how to look attentive or surprised' and in this way, so MacLure continues, she will become a 'normal' part of the group.

The child that plays with Carrie's story will in all likelihood draw on this powerful discourse of early educare as well as that of home in order to shape her play. This is not to say that these will be the only discourses. However, what we want to emphasize is that both the discourse of educare and the discourse of the family as conceptualized within government policy have as their ultimate goal the construction of the rational subject. Briefly, to be rational denotes a capacity for individuals to 'reflect on themselves and the world' and in so doing arrive at 'true understanding by the personal application of reason, knowledge and self-consciousness' (Dahlberg *et al.*,

1999: 20). The aspirations that are present within these brief few lines are ones we would aspire to. However, our deep concern centres on the notion of the rational, where efforts to identify who and for what reasons individuals might be considered as rational cannot be divorced from relations of power. As we noted earlier, designating certain members of the population as irrational has far reaching and at times devastating consequences. Quite clearly the discourse of rationality is not the only one that is in circulation within early years settings but it is dominant and it will certainly be the one that will be called upon to both describe and prescribe the child as 'different'.

Our intentions within this chapter have been to highlight the relationship between play and politics. We have demonstrated that play becomes part of particular discourses and that whilst certain discourses including those that seek to promote the rational subject are powerful they are nevertheless subjected to change. As tutors, both when working with students and when pursuing our own research, we struggle with this notion of the self who is essentially determinate, with an enduring rational subjectivity. Our concern then centres on the possibilities for perceiving play as a means whereby children can experience their identities in multiple ways. As Davies (1989: 141) notes: '. . . children need access to imaginary worlds in which new metaphors, new forms of social relations and new patterns of power and desire are explored. They need the freedom to position themselves in multiple ways'. For this to occur, we need practitioners like Carrie who, in our view, is beginning to appreciate how discourses can be interrupted and alternative ways of being can be considered.

References

Alexander, R., Rose, J. and Woodhead, C. (1992) *Curriculum Organisation and Classroom Practice in Primary Schools.* DES.

Brah, A. (1996) *Cartographies of Diaspora: Contesting Identities.* London and New York: Routledge.

Bruce, T. (1991) *Time to Play in Early Childhood Education.* London: Hodder and Stoughton.

Dahlberg, G., Moss, P. and Pence, A. (1999) *Beyond Quality in Early Childhood Education and Care: Postmodern Perspectives.* London: Falmer Press.

Davies, B. (1989) *Frogs and Snails and Feminist Tales: Preschool Children and Gender.* Sydney: Allen and Unwin.

DES (Department of Education and Science) (1967) *Children and their Primary Schools* (The Plowden Report). London: HMSO.

DES (1988) National Curriculum. London: HMSO.

DfEE (1997) *Excellence in Schools.* London: The Stationery Office.

DfEE/QCA (2000) *Curriculum Guidance for the Foundation Stage*. London: Qualifications and Curriculum Authority.

Donaldson, M. (1978) *Children's Minds*. London: Collins/Fontana.

Dunn, J. (1998) 'Young children understanding of other people', in M. Woodhead, D. Faulkner and K. Littleton (eds) *Cultural Worlds of Early Childhood*. London: Routledge.

Foucault, M. (1977) *Discipline and Punish*. London: Penguin.

Hultqvist, K. (1998) 'A history of the present on children's welfare in Sweden: from Froebel to present-day decentralization projects', in T. Popkewitz and M. Brennan (eds) *Foucault's Challenge: Discourse, Knowledge and Power in Education*. New York: Teachers' College Press.

Iglesias, E. V. and Sen, A. K. (1999) 'Investing in early childhood and development, breaking the poverty cycle'. Paper presented at the Inter-American Development Bank Conference, Paris, March 1999.

Issacs, S. (1933) *Social Development in the Young Child*. London: Routledge.

Jones, K. and Williamson, K. (1979) The birth of the schoolroom, *Ideology and Consciousness*, 6: 59–110.

Klein, M. (1975) *Love, Guilt and Reparation and Other Works, 1946–1963*. London: Hogarth Press.

MacLure, M. (2003) *Discourse in Educational and Social Research*. Buckingham: Open University Press.

McMillan, M. (1860–1931) in T. Bruce (1991) *Time to Play in Early Childhood Education*. London: Hodder and Stoughton.

Organisation for Economic Cooperation and Development (1998) *Early Childhood Education and Care Policy: Proposal for a Thematic Review*. Paris: Organisation for Economic Cooperation and Development.

Pascal, C. and Bertram, T. (1999) *Research to Inform the Evaluation of the Early Excellence Centres Pilot Programme*. University College, Worcester: Centre for Research in Early Childhood.

Pugh, G. (1988) *Services for Under Fives: Developing a Coordinated Approach*. London: National Children's Bureau.

Spencer (1873) in T. Bruce (1991) *Time to Play in Early Childhood Education*. London: Hodder and Stoughton.

Stanton, W. (1960) *The Leopard's Spots: Scientific Attitudes Towards Race in America 1815–59*. Chicago: University of Chicago Press.

Tizard, B. and Hughes, M. (1984) *Young Children Learning: Talking and Learning at Home and at School*. London: Fontana.

Walkerdine, V. (1984) 'Developmental psychology and the child-centred pedagogy', in J. Henriques, W. Holloway, C. Urwin and V. Walkerdine (eds) *Changing the Subject: Psychology, Social Regulation and Subjectivity*. London: Methuen.

Walkerdine, V. and Lucey, H. (1989) *Democracy in the Kitchen: Regulating Mothers and Socialising Daughters*. London: Virago.

Weedon, C. (1999) *Feminism, Theory and the Politics of Difference*. Oxford: Blackwell.

Wells, C. G. (1987) *The Meaning Makers: Children Learning Language and Using Language to Learn*. London: Hodder and Stoughton.

Woodhead, M., Faulkner, D. and Littleton, K. (1998) *Cultural Worlds of Early Childhood*. London: Routledge.

Wood, D. (1986) 'Aspects of teaching and learning', in M. Woodhead, D. Faulkner and K. Littleton (eds) *Cultural Worlds of Early Childhood*. London: Routledge.

4 Exploring families

Sue Aitken and Liz Jones

Introduction

> When looked at in detail, family lives are enormously varied and diverse. When you begin to consider this, it is clear that the nuclear family does not exist except as a powerful image in the minds of most people.
>
> (Bernardes, 1997: 13)

The aim of this chapter is to mimic aspects of the journey that our students embark on when 'exploring families'. There are a number of underlying reasons for taking such a journey. First, a child's experiences of family life is a significant part of their overall early experiences and within discourses of early childhood there is a deep belief that early experiences play a major part in determining the life of individuals (Cannella, 2002). Second, our students in a variety of ways and in a number of different contexts will be working with and on behalf of a large number of families. As a consequence, this chapter attempts to reflect how we give students a reflective space where a questioning attitude towards the notion of 'the family' might be developed. Subsequently, we illustrate how certain assumptions and commonsense understandings about 'the family' are unsettled so that the stability of particular constructs such as the 'normal' or 'nuclear' family are destabilized. What follows are our efforts in 'looking in detail' (Bernardes, 1997).

Playing with images

At various junctures in the students' studies a range of stimulants are used in order to trigger dialogue. One example is shown in Figure 4.1.

As an activity, the students both respond to and create their own questions about the photograph. For example, are the adults married? Were the children

Figure 4.1   A family: an anonymous photograph taken between 1890 and 1911.

conceived after marriage? If married, where would the marriage have taken place? What might be the social consequences for this family if they were unmarried, or indeed, if they were married in a non-Christian ceremony or that the children were illegitimate?

By unpacking the photograph in this way students make a number of decisions including:

*   This is a couple married within a Christian church, whose children are legitimate and baptized.

- To not have undertaken any of the above actions would have been considered unacceptable and might well have resulted in social exclusion for both the adults and the children.
- The father is the breadwinner.
- The mother has responsibility for the management of the household and the care of the children.
- The children would be strictly disciplined (seen and not heard).
- Both parents, but especially the father as head of the household, would be obeyed and respected.

Having knitted together this family, the students are asked to consider what some of the consequences might be in terms of this family being a suitable environment for the bringing up of children. In responding students forge links between their own experiences of family life and that with the family that has been conjured from the photograph. So, for example, those students who were themselves brought up in homes where religion was a prevalent feature have sympathy for and empathize with notions that circulate around 'obedience' and an understanding of a moral order where children can identify between right and wrong. Others recognize this as a family where children would have familiar routines and clear boundaries, practices that in their view provide children with stability. However, there is in general unanimous agreement that a primary strength of this family is the mother, where the consistency of her care would ensure that the children not only would experience stable relationships as children but also would themselves mature into secure adults.

In brief, the photograph becomes a mechanism whereby certain assumptions concerning the needs of young children and the place of the family in satisfying these can be articulated. What also begins to emerge is the relationship between family life and society, where the social structures that exist within the family are both a reflection and an embodiment of those that exist within society as a whole. Effectively, the students reiterate a functionalist account of the family as evoked in the work of, for example, Durkheim (1984) and Parsons (1937). Here the family is universal and ubiquitous, where each generation prepares the next to uphold the functions, structures and moral standing of society. That it is the shared and perpetuated morals and values of society that the family transmits in order to create the greater good for all. And that stability within the family is a necessary precursor of stability within society (Parsons, 1951).

Clearly, there is much that resonates between this account and current political discourses that are in evidence both here in the UK and in the USA where the family is very much being perceived as the foundations for and the perpetuation of civil society. However, before pursuing this line of enquiry we want to undertake further play with the photograph.

Normalization and regulatory power: 'breadwinners' and 'childcarers'

In this section we want to highlight other trains of thought that are pursued by tutors and students alike and which again have at their centre the above image. Our first strategy is to focus on the gender of the individuals, whilst our second is to engage with practices of deconstruction in order to unpick the manner in which the family has been 'fabricated' (Foucault, 1979) by the students. Why we are pursuing these lines of enquiry will, we believe, become clear as the analysis develops.

The decision to fix on gender as opposed to, for example, social class is because in many ways 'the body' is a relatively obvious and determinable signifier. Weedon makes the point that the body is the primary referent 'in visually grounded categorizations of the body' (1999: 99). She continues that '. . . the gender and racial characteristics popularly ascribed to bodies still bear traces of nineteenth-century theories of sexual and racial difference which were used to justify social inequalities based on both male and white supremacy' (1999: 99).

Additionally, the students have undertaken further categorizations with the man being perceived as 'the breadwinner' whilst the woman is the 'childcarer'. Walkerdine and Lucey (1989) offer a highly accessible account where these two positions are subjected to a Marxist critique. Here, however, our own preference is to offer an analysis that is underpinned by post-structuralist theories in general but particularly the work of Foucault and Derrida. Previously in Chapter 3, attempts have been made to elaborate on Foucault's exploration of 'discourse'. Here we continue the clarification. Within a Foucauldian approach, discourses:

> . . . are inextricably linked to institutions (the law, education, the family, etc.) and to the disciplines that regularize and normalize the conduct of those who are brought within the ambit of those institutions – psychology, medicine, science, psychotherapy, pedagogy, and so on.
>
> (MacLure, 2003: 176)

Thus the mother of our imaginary family, for example, would have been immersed in a number of discursive practices that worked together in defining her femininity. As Weedon notes:

> . . . dominant nineteenth-century discourses of femininity . . . had material implications for their physical, intellectual and emotional development, shaping bodies, minds and emotions in particular ways

which were thought to be conducive to women's apparently natural roles as wives and mothers.

(Weedon, 1999: 103)

And what of the father? Here the concept of hegemonic masculinity (Connell, 1995, 1996; Davis, 1996) is helpful in understanding the father's position within the household and men's position within nineteenth century society. Within this concept, numerous discursive practices, again with an institutional base (the law, church, education and so forth) worked at positioning men more powerfully than women. The circulation of such discourses produced commonsense or taken-for-granted notions of 'the right ways to think, feel and behave' (Gee, 1990: xx). Through discursive power, understandings about 'what counts as normal (and deviant) sorts of human beings, as well as what counts as normal (and deviant) relationships between them' (Gee, 1990: 175) would be prescribed. As a consequence, for the father to be the breadwinner whilst the mother centred her attention on the children and the home would therefore be considered unproblematic and moreover *natural*. Davies offers us this neat summary:

> The male–female dualism is an *idea* with material force through which males are allocated positions in which they can act as if they are powerful. They thus become powerful both through developing a subjectivity which is organised around power and through the discursive practices which establish male power as real and legitimate. Females are allocated positions of weakness, complementary to and supportive of that power.
>
> (Davies, 1989: 109, author's own emphasis)

The students, when making decisions about the individuals in the photograph, do so because of their own current immersion in particular discursive practices that are concerned with the family and with gender relations, as well as historical knowledge of nineteenth century social life.

Clearly, discourses are powerful but they can nevertheless be subjected to change and reversals. As Foucault asserts:

> . . . we must not imagine a world of discourse divided between accepted discourse and excluded discourse, or between the dominant discourse and the dominated one; but as a multiplicity of discursive elements that can come into play in various strategies.
>
> (Foucault, 1981: 101)

This is borne out when one considers discursive practices around a phenomenon such as discipline and the young child. It is quite likely that the children in the photograph when learning what was right or wrong experienced corporal punishment so that certain lessons were pressed home. Currently, numerous discourses including the law and those centring on children's rights are used in order to protect children from being physically chastised by adults, including their parents. That said, there are various factions here in the UK, including religious fundamentalists, who seek redress through the law to have the right to use corporal punishment. Here the maxim 'spare the rod and ruin the child' is given overtones of a religious/moral nature in order to vindicate the use of corporal punishment.

Clearly, aspects of the students' response have been governed by the fact that they are working within the parameters of the image where the presence of a man and a woman is going to direct their responses in particular ways, where the heterosexual nuclear family will overshadow other conceptualizations of the family. So the act of looking at and discussing the photograph might well give the students an appreciation of how discursive power functions, but the question of whether specific notions regarding the family including the nuclear family have been destabilized still remains. In order to do this our approach is to return once again to the image and to the students' thinking concerning the family.

It is at this juncture that we engage with practices of deconstruction. Following Jacques Derrida (1976), tutor and student efforts at deconstructing are aimed at what Spivak (1976) refers to as 'mind-set', where ingrained habits and assumptions work at legitimating authoritarian 'fictions' (Brown and Jones, 2001). As Spivak notes:

> . . . a certain view of the world, of *consciousness*, and of language has been accepted as the correct one, and, if the minute particulars of that view are examined, a rather different picture emerges. That examination involves an enquiry into the 'operation' of our most familiar gestures.
>
> (Spivak in Derrida, 1976: xiii; author's emphasis)

'Consciousness' concerns the way we think about things, and our thinking is underpinned or made secure by logic. In looking at the photograph the students have used reason in order to offer interpretations and impose meaning. Effectively, if we want to destabilize a notion such as the nuclear family we have to think seriously about how we think. Destabilizing thinking is a tricky business and this is where we have found the work of Derrida helpful. Much of Derrida's work centres on a sustained attack on what he considers to be the authoritarianism of western thought and in particular its commitment to essentialism. A vivid example of essentialism in western thought is the practice or phenomenon of 'logocentricity': the belief that words are representations of meanings already present in the speaker's mind (Sim, 1992: 429). That is, there is a direct correlation between thinking and language, where the latter is transparent. In order to illuminate this point Derrida offers a critique of the speech/writing couplet where in the western world writing has been viewed as subordinate to speech. Thus speech, because it issues directly from the speaker, has been considered as direct, authentic and uncontaminated.

For Derrida, the relationship between speech and transparency of meaning is the heritage of logocentrism and phonocentrism, which he explains as the 'absolute proximity of voice and being, of voice and the meaning of being, of voice and the ideality of meaning' (1976: 12). Writing, on the other hand, has traditionally been perceived as 'lacking the transparent integrity of representation that speech commands owing to its temporal and spatial remoteness from the act of its creation and from the presence of the semantic and interpretive guarantee of its author' (Parker, 1997: 76). If speech is perceived as authentic presence, by contrast writing is language's 'bastard' (Kearney, 1986: 118). So, by examining the speech/writing couplet we can begin to appreciate how speech is perceived positively where presence, transparency of language and thus mastery of meaning can be assured. Writing, meanwhile, because it is open to interpretations, cannot offer us certainty and thus is second rate, the negative other to speech. However, in deconstructing the speech/writing couplet Derrida is not attempting to reverse the binaries so that writing is then positively valorized over speech. Rather, it is a 'turning back' in order to question why, for example, we choose to fix particular categories in specific ways. So, by engaging with deconstruction we are not merely playing with words because, as MacLure emphasizes, deconstruction carries 'an ethical and a political charge' (2003: 179). Likewise, Shapiro notes that deconstruction has the power to show how '. . . every social order rests on a forgetting of the exclusion practices through which one set of meanings has been institutionalised and various other possibilities have been marginalized' (Shapiro, 2001: 321).

Thus, in returning to the students' thoughts our primary task is to identify the binary structuring around which their thinking has been organized. The following polarities can be established:

+	−
father	mother
bread winner	childcarer
work	home
legitimate	illegitimate
married	not married
social inclusion	social exclusion
head of house	subordinate

Derrida (1981) emphasizes that the binaries that we use to organize our thinking are not peaceful partnerships but function as a consequence of domination. He writes:

> . . . we are not dealing with the peaceful co-existence of a *vis–a vie*, but rather with a violent hierarchy. One term governs the other (axiologically, logically, etc.), or has the upper hand, occupies the commanding position.
>
> (Derrida, 1981: 41)

In looking at the image neither students nor tutors can look at it 'objectively'; rather, as we have seen, particular assumptions or 'truths' about the world are called upon. Categories are summoned and status is awarded. To do this, the students resort to an essentialist notion of the family in order to make judgements, where individual identity is fixed and stable. Thus men *are* breadwinners whilst women *are* carers. So what happens to notions of difference within this process? What happens to all those 'others' who are situated within the negative polarity? That is, the illegitimate child, the unbaptized, the man who for whatever reasons cannot be a breadwinner, the barren woman and so forth? As the students themselves have inferred, people who do not comply whether in terms of attendance at church and/or failing to undertake particular rituals such as baptizing a child or marrying in established ways fall outside of the status quo and are as a consequence in danger of being socially excluded and marginalized.

Ostensibly, our efforts have been channelled at destabilizing our own interpretive frames that serve as structuring or ordering mechanisms. Moreover, we are developing a growing appreciation of how these are tied in with and relate to the social order (Lather, 1991). It is evident that the social order has changed in very many significant ways since the taking of the photograph. As a word, 'family' is being stretched to cover multiple configurations (Silva and Smart, 1999). The students' own experiences of family life reflect this diversity. Family life for the students included parenting by divorced parents where mother was the main carer whilst the father was visited on a regular basis, divorced parenting where the father was completely absent and divorced parenting where the father was the central carer. Additionally, the students' experiences included adoption, step parenting as well as being cared for by grandparents. Moreover, students on a practical basis work with children who live with foster parents and others who are in children's homes. But whilst we might have diversity in the ways in which families are structured, it is our contention that present day discourses that relate to early years education and care have at their core an *ideal* family. Again, work is undertaken to explore this notion. At this juncture, we want to recall the positive strengths of the 'fabricated' family. These included the following:

- The children would learn to be obedient and have a clear sense of what was right and wrong.
- Familiar routines and clear boundaries would assist them in developing into stable individuals.
- Consistent care from the mother would ensure stability both as children and as adults.

Such assumptions are part of our collective common sense both about children's needs and how these should be met. In brief, they are part of our 'familiar gestures' (Spivak, 1976). So what's *wrong* with these views? Again, to situate a question within the right/wrong polarity is, we believe, unproductive. Better perhaps to ask why an adherence to these notions persists. Cannella captures our concerns:

> In our rush to make the world better for younger human beings, we have not, however questioned the values underlying the concept of early experience, the ways that a societal focus on the early years conflicts with the lived experiences of various groups of people, or the ways that focusing on early experience may disempower people and even ultimately limit human possibility.
>
> (Cannella, 2002: 65)

As has been remarked upon elsewhere in this book, we are living in times that are characterized by rapid change where many structures, including for example religion and social class, have fragmented and as a consequence no longer lend an air of fixed certainty to people's lives. In the initial analysis that was undertaken by the students it is, we believe, possible to see how the students identified a family that by comparison lived in more secure times. Stability within social contexts impact on what Dahlberg *et al.* (1999) refer to as 'children's biographies'. They write that 'in a more stable society the children's biography and knowledge were almost predetermined (Asplund, 1983) much the same as their parents'. The family would therefore assist in enabling the children to assume their true/essential identity whilst the children themselves would reproduce knowledge and cultural values. In not too dissimilar ways both here in the UK and in the USA, the family is being conceptualized as pivotal in strengthening civil bonds where cultural values can be promoted and maintained. Strong family ties with responsible parenting are being perceived as a means of countering a number of social ills, including unemployment, crime and drug abuse (Deutsch, 1998). To this effect, policies have been developed and funding released so that young children and their families can be supported in such a way as to provide a 'firm foundation' from which civil society can evolve. Such steps are surely positive.

Whilst welcoming the spotlight that is currently being trained on children and their families we nevertheless feel that there is cause for reflection in our search to 'get things right'. Above, the students identified that via a particular form of parenting the children would learn to distinguish between 'good' and 'bad'. In order to decide what is 'good' or 'bad' we have to make judgements. We can perhaps make the assumption that the family that has been central to our enquiry might have appealed to some fixed point outside of themselves, including for example religion, in order to decide what was a good/bad or indeed right/wrong and so forth. By appealing to this outside point, judgements can be determined so that they know with certainty what is right, wrong, good or bad. In a similar vein current policies and practices, including for example initiatives such as the Sure Start programme, seek to promote 'good parenting', where again judgements have to be made against some normalizing standard of what constitutes 'good parenting'. Categorizing – as we have seen – is not a benign act. Rather, it can work so that 'others' are marginalized and pathologized, where 'those whose views of early life experience (most often the poor and minority groups) are not the same as the accepted standard' (Cannella, 2002: 89). And what of mothering? What constitutes 'good mothering' in our present times, where care will be consistent? In making judgements about this to what do we appeal? What yardstick do we employ to make such a decision? Are we tied to some universal understanding of what constitutes the 'good mother', where the task is to regulate (through parenting classes) those who are not good mothers? And if we are, what are some of the consequences of this?

Overall, our work with the photograph aims to displace our thinking and to 'continuously demystify the realities we create, to fight the tendency for our categories to congeal' (Caputo, 1987: 236). In brief, by playing with and unravelling ideas, thoughts and conjectures that were prompted by the image we have made ourselves confront some of the repercussions of our everyday, habitual thinking. As Lather would put it, we have been trying to be reflexive 'where we are learning to attend to the politics of what we do and do not do at a practical level' (1991: 68).

Conclusion

As we noted previously, these explorations that are concerned with the family are promoted by both an ethical and political imperative. In exploring families we have indicated how discourses function and that whilst 'discourses may or may not be bad, all are dangerous, especially without *examination*' (Cannella, 2002: 89, our emphasis). We have also tried to illustrate the awkward business of examining the logic that circumscribes thinking so that those ways in which we construct aspects of our social world can be closely examined. We end with some cautionary words from Derrida. We have found these to be difficult words that resist a too speedy reading; they have to be brooded over. That said, we believe them to be particularly salutary for those of us who wish to behave as *responsible* early years professionals:

> Once you know or you think you know in a determinant judgement what your responsibility is, there is no responsibility. For a responsibility to be a responsibility, you must, you should, know whatever you can know; you have to try to know the maximum, but the moment of responsibility or decision is a moment of non-knowledge, a moment beyond the programme. A responsibility must be infinite, and beyond any theoretical certainty or determination.
>
> (Derrida in Brannigan *et al.*, 1996: 223–224)

References

Asplund, J. (1983) *Time, Space and Collective*. Stockholm: Liber.

Bernardes, J. (1997) *Family Studies: An Introduction*. London: Routledge.

Brannigan, J., Robbins, R. and Wolfreys, J. (1996) *Applying: To Derrida*. Basingstoke: Macmillan.

Brown, T. and Jones, L. (2001) *Action Research and Postmodernism: Congruence and Critique*. Buckingham: Open University Press.

Cannella, G. S. (2002) *Deconstructing Early Childhood Education: Social Justice and Revolution*. New York: Peter Lang Publishing.

Caputo, J. (1987) *Radical Hermeneutics: Repetition, Deconstruction and the Hermeneutic Project*. Bloomington: University of Indiana Press.

Connell, R. W. (1995) *Masculinities*. St Leonards, NSW: Allen and Unwin.

Connell, R. W. (1996) Teaching the boys: new research on masculinity, and gender strategies for schools, *Teachers College Record*, 98(2): 206–235.

Dahlberg, G., Moss, P. and Pence, A. (1999) *Beyond Quality in Early Childhood Education and Care: Post-modern Perspectives*. London: Falmer Press.

Davis, B. (1996) Power knowledge desire: changing school organisation and management practices. Canberra, Act. DEETYA.

Derrida, J. (1976) *Of Grammatology* (translation by G. Spivak). Baltimore, MD: John Hopkins University Press.

Derrida, J. (1981) 'Positions: interview with J.L. Houdebine and G. Scarpetta' (translation by A. Bass), in J. Derrida *Positions*. Chicago: University of Chicago Press.

Deutsch, R. (1998) *How Early Childhood Interventions Can Reduce Inequality: An Overview of Recent Findings*. Washington DC: Inter-American Bank, Sustainable Development Dept., Poverty and Inequality Advisory Unit.

Durkheim, E (1984) *Divisions of Labour in Society*. Basingstoke: Palgrave MacMillan.

Foucault, M. (1979) *Discipline and Punish: The Birth of the Prison* (translated by A. Sheridan). Harmondsworth: Penguin.

Foucault, M. (1981) *The History of Sexuality 1: An Introduction*. London: Allen Lane.

Gee, J. P. (1990) *Social Linguistics and Literacies: Ideology in Discourses*. London: Falmer.

Kearney, R. (1986) *Modern Movements in European Philosophy*. Manchester: Manchester University Press.

Lather, P. (1991) *Getting Smart*. London: Routledge.

MacLure, M. (2003) *Discourse in Educational and Social Research*. Buckingham: Open University Press.

Parker, S. (1997) *Reflective Teaching in the Postmodern World*. Buckingham: Open University Press.

Parsons, T. (1937) *The Structure of Social Action*. New York: McGraw-Hill.

Parsons, T. (1951) 'The social structure of the family', in R. N. Ashen (ed.) *The Family: its Functions and Destiny*. New York: Harper and Row.

Shapiro, M. (2001) 'Textualizing global politics', in M. Wetherell, S. Taylor and S. J. Yates (eds) *Discourse Theory and Practice: A Reader*. London: Sage.

Silva, E. B. and Smart, C. (1999) *The New Family*. London: Sage Publications.

Sim, S. (1992) 'Structuralism and poststructuralism', in O. Hanfling (ed.) *Philosophical Aesthetics: An Introduction*. Milton Keynes: Open University Press.

Spivak, G. C. (1976) Preface, in J. Derrida, *Of Grammatology* (translated by G.C. Spivak). Baltimore, MD: John Hopkins University Press.

Walkerdine, V. and Lucey, H. (1989) *Democracy in the Kitchen: Regulating Mothers and Socialising Daughters*. London: Virago.

Weedon, C. (1999) *Feminism, Theory and the Politics of Difference*. Oxford: Blackwell.

5 Working with parents and carers

Liz Jones, Karen Browne, Sue Aitken, Iris Keating and Elaine Hodson

Introduction

> *The parents around here are too busy trying to survive to worry about attending parenting classes or becoming involved with their child's school or nursery. They need a way out of depressing poverty before they can begin to think about those things.*
>
> (Part-time student, early years practitioner)

As we write, there is within the UK a determined drive by government for strong links between the child's home and sites of education. This impetus is particularly prevalent within early childhood institutions where successful working between the institution and the parent is conceptualized as the making of a 'firm foundation' for stable civilized society (Rose, 1999; Wagner, 1994). It is therefore particularly pertinent that the issue of working with parents is carefully considered. Our feeling is that working with parents and carers is so deeply entrenched in our thinking that we rarely stop to question from where our ideas emerge and the implications these have upon our actions.

The overall aim of this chapter is to problematize the notion of working with parents and carers so as to disturb the taken-for-granted, commonsense ideas that have become the cornerstone of practice. In order to do this the intention is to frame our discussion around the quotation that is offered above. We believe that the statement captures and tentatively refers to some of the hopes, dilemmas and difficulties that circulate around the aspiration of working with carers. We begin by thinking about the notion of 'parents'. This is followed by a discussion that is located around 'parenting classes'. We then tussle with a number of ideas that circulate around 'involvement' before moving on to consider some of the implications of what it means to have 'busy lives', particularly where 'poverty' is a feature.

Parents/carers: who are they?

The care and upbringing of a child is primarily undertaken by adults. However, there are an increasing number of young people who for a variety of reasons take on the responsibility of caring for family members (Becker, 1998). Moreover, the expression 'hard to reach' has been coined here in the UK to describe parents and carers who for diverse reasons are reluctant to access services that are aimed at supporting vulnerable families. This includes those who stand outside 'a normalized view of self and family that supports the status quo' (Cannella, 2002: 88), such as the parent with mental health difficulties or the ones who are confronting drug dependency and/or alcohol related issues. It also includes single parents (male and female) as well as refugees, travellers and others drawn from minority groups. So whilst parenting as a function might be understood in a singular way, efforts are made to prevent thinking about parents as a homogenized group.

An initial step that is taken by students when beginning their explorations within 'working with parents and carers' is to recognize the 'stretching' that has to be undertaken by the term in order to accommodate the diversity that exists within the phenomenon of parent/carer, as well as considering the invisibility of certain parents. As a word, 'accommodate' means 'to make fit' or 'to bring into harmony', as well as 'to adjust or become adjusted'. Subsequently, we note how early years institutions both historically and in current times have been and continue to be implicated in processes of accommodation, where the ambition is to bring individuals into harmony or make fit. As Cannella (2002) notes: 'the discourse of early experience emerged out of a fear and the need to control the behaviour of diverse and less powerful others'. She continues:

> The poor have been created as those who are dangerous, whose behaviour must be governed through standardization and regulation. Surveillance and intervention into private lives is legitimised because the 'danger' must be controlled.
>
> (Cannella, 2002: 88)

Parenting classes

In general terms we attend classes in order to learn. So what is it that parents will learn when attending 'parenting classes', and why are such lessons considered important? First, let us begin by considering the context in which such classes are being held. Here in the UK, under the auspices of the current Labour government, a wide range of resources have been devoted to early childhood services. As an example, £500 million has been invested in the Sure Start programme (2004). The overall ambition of this is to increase opportunities for adults to return to work and to promote the well-being of children, families and communities. It is possible to discern within this initiative what Popkewitz and Bloch (2001) refer to as a discourse of salvation or redemption, where the parent is 'rescued' in order to secure the 'safety' of the child that will in turn ensure stable society.

The correlation between sound parenting and stable society has been supported by a number of discourses. For example, the early and middle periods of the twentieth century witnessed the emergence of a number of powerful medical and psychological discourses that located the ideal carer as being the mother. It is from the work of such luminaries as Freud, Harlow and Bowlby that the idea of 'proper' mothering emerged. So, for example, the psychoanalytical divining of Freud placed great emphasis on the relationship between the child and its mother, where the nature of this was said to result in an adult who was either adjusted to the demands of civilized society or maladapted (Eyer, 1992). Meanwhile, Harlow's (1959, 1973) experimental studies with monkeys identified that baby monkeys' 'normal' behaviours were affected by 'abnormal mothering'. Moreover, work by Bowlby (1951) also identified the mother/child dyad as being instrumental in securing normal development. Maternal deprivation, where there is an absence of love and care between the child and its mother, was in Bowlby's view as serious as dangerous diseases. 'Deprived children, whether in their homes or out of them, are a source of social infection as real or serious as are the carriers of diphtheria or typhoid' (Bowlby, 1951: 157).

Clearly, these discourses have in more recent times been modified, abridged and adapted. For example, Klaus and Kennell's (1976) work on bonding between the newly born child and its mother has had a huge impact. So, whilst being found to be flawed and wanting by the scientific community in terms of research rigour, their ideas nevertheless spawned a number of initiatives – including bonding rooms in hospitals – as well as becoming a central ideology within natural child birth organizations. Eyer has described how the construction of bonding coincided with the need in '. . . the psychological and medical professions to secure women and children as patients, and to find pathology in this clientele, which they could then treat' (1992: 1).

A brief examination of early years initiatives that are being undertaken within the UK reveals that they have been profoundly influenced by the medical and psychological discourses referred to above. The Sure Start initiative has, for example, four key national objectives, with the first being identified as '. . . improving social and emotional development' (Sure Start, 2004). Here the aim of the Sure Start initiative is to '. . . support early bonding between parents and their children, help families to function, and, through early identification support children with emotional and behavioural difficulties' (Sure Start, 2004).

Thus across the UK in a great number of Sure Start programmes activities such as baby massage and bonding classes are being undertaken. Often health practitioners including health visitors run these. It is important to note however that Sure Start has been conceptualized by government as a strategic project that targets vulnerable families. Put simply, Sure Start initiatives are only to be found in areas where indices levels, including those that measure ill-health, unemployment, drug misuse, teenage pregnancies and so forth, are high. Given this, we begin to appreciate that from a governmental perspective at least not all parents are thought to be in need of classes. Given some insights into the discourses that surround proper mothering we can now appreciate how and why parenting classes are conceptualized as mechanisms of rescue or remedy.

Similarly, Hughes (2003) highlights how parenting classes can be an apparatus where parents, aided by practitioners, learn to conform. That is, the practitioner, including for example the health visitor who runs the baby massage class, will be '. . . teaching the parents how to observe and understand their child's development' (Hirschey, 1999: 270). The belief is '. . . that parents will learn how to behave appropriately with their children once they know what the educator knows . . .' (Hughes, 2003: 256). Furthermore: 'Conforming "approaches" to educator-parent relationships generally means educators teaching parents who are working class and from culturally diverse backgrounds to conform to white, middle class norms of child rearing' (Hughes, 2003: 256).

We began this section by asking what it is that parents will learn when attending 'parenting classes' and why such lessons are considered important. It would seem that they could well be classes in conforming aimed at securing a normalized notion of what it means to be a parent. Subsequently, we consider not only the repercussions when centres work with parents in this way but also alternative conceptualizations of working with parents.

Becoming involved

Of course, a great number of parents become involved in their children's educare in ways other than parenting classes. That said, even this assumingly benign statement needs thinking about. For as Reay (1998) notes, within the context of education the predominant figure in home/school relations is the female. Yet the term 'parent' is randomly used and can be seen as shorthand: for 'parent' read 'mother'. Additionally, Cameron *et al.* (1999) indicate how early childhood educare has been largely the domain of women, where a central feature is that it is gendered:

> . . . not just because the workforce is nearly always women, but because the way the work is thought about by parents, workers,

government policies, colleges who train workers, managers and policy makers and not least, wider society.

(Cameron *et al.*, 1999: ix)

This raises a set of perplexing questions in relation to men becoming involved in early years settings. On a simplistic level it might be argued that men will feel out of place in settings where women are prevalent. However, more significantly the overall status of work that is aligned with the care of young children is low (Farrell, 1998). Perhaps for some men, particularly those who experience themselves as 'marginalized', to become involved with early years institutions would in itself be another form of denigration.

So, given the caution that we have attached to 'parents', let us now examine what 'getting involved' can mean. Whilst there seems to be consensus that parental involvement is a 'good thing', what constitutes involvement is vague. As Smith notes: '. . . it is defined and attempted in a hundred different ways' (1980: 8). Undoubtedly the pioneering work of the Head Start programme in the USA (Weikart and Schweinhart, 1987) has had enormous impact on our thinking in terms of parental involvement and children's learning, particularly for children who are from impoverished backgrounds. This 'reforming' approach to parental involvement reflects the view that children's educational opportunities are enhanced when parents are involved in it (Hughes, 2003).

If we cast our eyes back over the terrain of education within the UK during the last 20 years or so, it is possible to perceive planned attempts to involve parents in educational activities with their children where reading was a central focus (Tizard *et al.*, 1981; Heath, 1983; Minns, 1990; Nutbrown, 1994; Hannon, 1995). Here there appear to be two strands of thinking at work. One centres on the idea that in order to become literate the child needs to be involved in literacy practices both at home and at school (Baker *et al.*, 1996; Bryant *et al.*, 2000). The other is concerned with national standards, where parental support in reading and indeed in other areas of the curriculum will go some way to improve these (Cairney, 1997). To this effect, a great number of schools have introduced home/school agreements where parents sign up their commitment to supporting the child (Crozier, 1998).

Meanwhile, first-hand accounts from our students indicate that a considerable number of early years institutions are extremely successful in engaging with parents as well as getting them involved. By pooling student thoughts it would appear that parents (invariably mothers) assist in early years settings, including playgroups, nurseries, nursery and foundation stage classrooms, as an additional 'pair of hands', where they play alongside children, help with art and craft activities, assist when the children are baking or when they are gardening. Additionally, parental help is used to accompany the children on walks and other trips out as well as lend support when special events occur such as a concert. Moreover, there are occasions when family members who have a specific skill or expertise give talks to the children, show photographs, let them handle artefacts and so forth. These activities, particularly in a school context, are done under the guidance of either a teacher or a manager. Moyles (1989) describes these parents as being accepting of and entering into the school's ethos. Arguably these are positive steps, but what happens when the parents' efforts in offering support are out of kilter with the early years institution? Where, for example, the parent's help in supporting the young child's early writing skills is 'inappropriate' when matched against what happens in the nursery class (Walkerdine and Lucey, 1989). Here it would appear there is a conflict between expert professional knowledge where the parents' function is to supplement such knowledge but – so it would seem – are ill equipped for the task. Foot *et al.* (2002: 7) talk of parental involvement being 'shaped' and 'harnessed' by the institution, leaving us to wonder about those who, for whatever reasons, are unable to be shackled in such ways.

An increasing number of theorists do however offer an alternative slant to working with parents, where both the early years institution and the carers are perceived as being part of a 'learning community'. Premised on democratic ideals, a learning community works hard at destabilizing hierarchical relationships where, for example, expert knowledge is privileged over other forms of knowledge, including anecdotal parental knowledge (Fiddler, 1995; Dahlberg *et al.*, 1999; Hughes, 2003). So, for example, within an early years institution that perceives itself as part of a learning community the teacher would avoid the use of overtly technical language that might work at excluding the parent from participating more fully in dialogue, dialogue that might well serve the interests of the child. Additionally, practices aimed at conforming where parents are educated into 'good' practice (cf. Dahlberg *et al.*, 1999) would be shunned. Rather, as Hughes makes clear, a learning community is one that takes a 'transforming' approach to relationships. He writes:

> A transforming approach to relationships between educators and parents promotes democratic citizenship by inviting parents and others to form policies, manage resources and evaluate services; and by devolving decisions about what and how children should learn.
>
> (Hughes, 2003: 269)

Again it is evident from student discussions that there are early years institutions that are attempting to practise 'transforming approaches' when working with parents and carers. Some of our part-time students, for example, describe their own settings where parents are members of various 'sub-groups'. One example was a 'Landscape Task Group'. This it seems is a body that is made up of a mix of parents – including males – who in conjunction with centre practitioners are extending and developing the institute grounds so as to include a 'wild plants' section and a climbing area. It would appear that parental involvement was included at each stage of planning. Indeed, the original idea came from the local community who felt that their children would gain an immense amount from 'growing things and watching them grow' as well as 'having somewhere safe and exciting in which to play'. Embodied within this project are a number of key principles that underpin a transforming approach. These include:

- listening to parents;
- respecting parents' views concerning children and their learning;
- avoiding hierarchies by establishing equitable partnerships;
- including parents at all stages of planning.

Too busy

Having tried to unpack certain ideas, beliefs and theories that circulate around 'working with parents', let us refer back to the quotation that was used to open the chapter. It may be recalled that here the reason given for non-parental involvement was that 'parents were too busy trying to survive' and that 'they need a way out of depressing poverty before they can begin to think about those things', which in this instance refers to 'parenting classes' or 'getting involved with their child's school or nursery'. The irony here is that many of the current government funded early years initiatives are perceived as a means of supporting parents so that they can have the chance to '. . . take up work, education or training' (DfEE, 1998, para. 1.29) and in so doing move out of the trap of poverty. Yet despite the unparalleled attention and resources that have been devoted to early childhood services it would appear that for some parents becoming involved is still beset with difficulties. Moss (1999) in following the Italian historian Ginsburg (1989), makes the point that '. . . the Minority World lives in a culture where we are constantly being offered solutions before we have asked the critical questions' (1999: 234). So what critical questions might aid us when thinking about parental involvement? These, as one insightful student noted, cannot be divorced from the context. Thus each institution will have questions that are specific to the needs of both the early years institution and the community that it serves. Below we offer an extract of a student's thoughts:

> *The way we communicate to parents can send all kinds of messages. On the one hand we don't want to use jargon but on the other we don't want to patronize the parents. We also have to think about things like letters home, the posters that we put up advertising classes. Do we include parents when*

designing these? What translation services are available so that all parents have access including ethnic minority families? Are we communicating or are we just giving information? Isn't dialogue more than telling people things? We know that parent knowledge of the child is important but not all people will feel comfortable talking about themselves or their family. Is my own knowledge about different cultures sufficient enough? If I don't know about different traditions, customs and practices how can I be sensitive to them? If parents are going to be involved in making decisions about the curriculum or about classes that suit their needs then not only do the times of the meetings have to be really thought about but also the language that is used within the meeting has to be inclusive. You also have to think about physical aspects. Could you get a wheelchair in the room? Can we be 'open' and yet have settings that are safe? Some parents might have had negative experiences at school so how will these parents feel attending classes? How will they feel about negotiating buzzer systems in order to access a building? You cannot have a 'one size fits all' system. You also have to have time so that the shy parent, the one who does not have confidence, can just spend time in the early years setting.

As early years practitioners, when we work with parents and carers we share with them what Farrell (1998: 107) refers to as a 'privileged responsibility', where together we strive in order to provide children with a basis for a good life. Whilst consensus about what constitutes a good life may differ (Dahlberg *et al.*, 1999), nevertheless it is a persistent idea and one that lies beneath the notion of working with parents. In sum, we have taken the notion of 'working with parents and carers' and subjected it to what Foucault refers to as a 'flushing out', where the assumption that it is 'a good thing' has been critiqued and in so doing cleared a conceptual space where our thinking might be a little different: 'As soon as one no longer thinks things as one formerly thought them, transformation becomes very urgent, very difficult and quite possible' (Foucault, 1988: 155).

References

Baker, L., Allen, J. and Shockley, B. (1996) 'Connecting school and home: constructing partnerships to foster reading development', in L. Baker, P. Afflerbach and D. Reinking (eds) *Developing Engaged Readers in School and Home Communities*. New Mahwah, NJ: Lawrence Erlbaum Associates.

Becker, S. (1998) *Young Carers and their Families*. London: Blackwell.

Bowlby, J. (1951) *Maternal Care and Mental Health*. Geneva: World Health Organization.

Bryant, D., Peisner-Feinberg, E. and Miller-Johnson, S. (2000) Head Start parents' roles in the educational lives of their children. Paper presented at the Annual Conference of the *American Educational Research Association*, New Orleans, LA.

Cairney, R. (1997) Parents and literacy learning: new perspectives, *Every Child*, 3(2): 4–5.

Cameron, C., Moss, P. and Owen, C. (1999) *Men in the Nursery: Gender and Caring Work*. London: Paul Chapman.

Cannella, G. S. (2002) *Deconstructing Early Childhood Education: Social Justice and Revolution*. New York: PeterLang.

Crozier, G. (1998) Parents and schools; partnership or surveillance? *Journal of Educational Policy*, 13(4): 125–136.

Dahlberg, G., Moss, P. and Pence, P. (1999) *Beyond Quality in Early Childhood Education and Care: Postmodern Perspectives*. London: Falmer Press.

Department for Education and Employment (DfEE) (1998) *Meeting the Childcare Strategy*. London: HMSO.

Eyer, D. E. (1992) *Mother-infant Bonding: A Scientific Fiction*. New Haven: Yale University Press.

Farrell, A. (1998) 'Gendered settings and human rights in early childhood', in N. Yelland (ed.) *Gender in Early Childhood*. London: Routledge.

Fiddler, M. (1995) Building a learning community, *Association Management*, 47(5): 40–7.

Foot, H., Howe, C., Cheyne, B., Terras, M. and Rattray, C. (2002) Parental participation and partnership in preschool provision, *International Journal of Early Years Education*, 10(1): 5–20.

Foucault, M. (1988) *Politics, Philosophy, Culture: Interviews and Other Writings, 1977–1984*. L. Kritzman (ed.). New York: Routledge.

Gandini, L. (1993) Fundamentals of the Reggio Emilia approach to early childhood education, *Young Children*, 11: 4–8.

Hannon, P. (1995) *Literacy, Home and School: Research and Practice in Teaching Literacy with Parents*. London: Falmer Press.

Harlow, H. F. (1959) Love in infant monkeys, *Scientific American* 200 (June 1959): 68, 70, 72–73, 74.

Harlow, H. (1973) 'Love in infant monkeys', in T. Greennough (ed.) *The Nature and Nurture of Behaviour: Developmental Psychobiology*. San Francisco: Freeman. (Original work published in Scientific American in July, 1959.)

Heath, S. B. (1983) *Ways with Words: Language, Life and Work in Communities and Classrooms*. Cambridge: Cambridge University Press.

Hirschey, S. (1999) Developing partnerships with parents. Paper presented to the *Association for Childhood Education International*, San Antonio, Texas, April.

Hughes, P. (2003) 'Curriculum contexts: parents and communities', in G. MacNaughton (ed.) *Shaping Early Childhood: Learners, Curriculum and Contexts*. Berkshire: Open University Press.

Izzo, C., Weissberg, R., Kasprow, W. and Fendrich, M. (1999) A longitudinal assessment of teacher perceptions of parent involvement in children's education and school performance, *American Journal of Community Psychology*, 27(6): 817–39.

Klaus, M. and Kennell, J. (1976) *Mother-Infant Bonding*. New York: Wiley.

Minns, H. (1990) *Read it to me now!* London: Virago.

Moss, P. (1999) Renewed hopes and lost opportunities: early childhood in the early years of the Labour Government, *Cambridge Journal of Education*, Vol. 29(2): 229–238.

Moyles, J. (1989) *Just Playing: The Role and Status of Play in Early Childhood Education*. Buckingham: Open University Press.

Nutbrown, C. (1994) *Threads of Thinking: Young children learning and the role of early education*. London: Paul Chapman Publishing.

Popkewitz, T. S. and Bloch, M. N. (2001) 'Administering freedom: a history of the present', in K. Hultqvist and G. Dahlberg (eds) *Governing the Child in the New Millennium*. New York: Routledge Falmer.

Reay, D. (1998) *Class Work: Mothers Involvement in their Children's Primary Schools*. London: UCL Press.

Rose, N. (1999) *Governing the Soul: The Shaping of the Private Self*, 2nd edn. London: Free Association Press.

Smith, T. (1980) *Parents and Pre-School*. London: Grant McIntyre.

Tizard, B. (1974) *Pre-School Education in Great Britain: Research Review*. London: SSRC.

Tizard, B., Mortimore, J. and Burchell, B. (1981) *Involving Parents in Nursery and Infant Schools*. London: Grant McIntyre.

Wagner, P. (1994) *The Sociology of Modernity*. New York: Routledge.

Walkerdine, V. and Lucey, H. (1989) *Democracy in the Kitchen: Regulating Mothers and Socializing Daughters*. London: Virago.

Weikart, D. and Schweinhart, L. (1987) 'The High/Scope cognitively orientated curriculum in early childhood', in J. Roopnaarina (ed.) *Approaches to Early Childhood Curriculum*. Columbia, OH: Merrill Publishing Company.

PART 2
Working Together: Facts, Frameworks and Fantasies

6 Multiprofessional perspectives

John Powell

Introduction

The government's green paper *Every Child Matters* (The Stationery Office, 2003) set out wide-ranging policy changes for the development of a more effective service working for children:

> . . . We want to move to a system locally and nationally where there is:
> - Clear overall accountability for services for children, young people and families
> - Integration of key services around the needs of children, in particular, education, social care, health, youth justice and Connexions.
>
> (TSU, 2003: 69)

This statement in a key government report signals an apparent major shift from an earlier situation where contact between individual agencies often appeared to take place haphazardly, to a 'new' state of affairs where closely linked working relations that consistently cross multi-agency boundaries are the 'norm'. The above quotation suggests that a raft of policy and practice modifications will lead to a coherent national system that will integrate child-care and result in service providers effectively communicating with each other. In other words, effectively dealing with the 'gross failure of the system and the widespread organisational malaise' highlighted in the Laming Report (HMSO, 2003: 4).

This chapter will explore some of the above claims, which are impacting powerfully and informing the apparent construction of a 'stronger' multipro-fessional set of perspectives as well as the direction in which they seem to be heading. There will also be discussion about the experience of students as they develop a sense of critique to engage with their developing sense of multipro-fessional perspectives.

It is important to identify early in the discussion what a term such as 'multiprofessional perspective' might mean. The *Collins English Dictionary* (2000) offers the following meanings:

Multi –   (1) many or much (2) more than one.

Professional –   (1) relating to, suitable for, or engaged in as a profession
                  (2) engaging in an activity for gain or as a means of livelihood
                  (3) extremely competent in job, etc.
                  (4) a person who engages in an activity with great competence
                  (5) an expert player who gives instruction.

Perspective –   (1) a way of regarding situations, facts etc and judging their relative importance
                  (2) the proper or accurate point of view or the ability to see it
                  (3) theory or art of suggesting three dimensions on a two dimensional surface in order to re-create the appearance and spatial relationships that objects or a scene in recession present to the eye
                  (4) to inspect carefully.

Both in this chapter and when working with students, the term multiprofessional is favoured as it indicates a degree of inter-agency and interdisciplinary cooperation. Having a multiprofessional perspective suggests an environment in which different professional practitioners may ideally share their views in order to agree action in relation to a child or a family. There is therefore a need for a sense of shared cultural belonging where meanings, values and understandings can be jointly developed. This particular assertion, however, is one that would need to be explored on a fairly continuous basis to counter practitioner dynamics becoming based on the status of particular 'expert' practitioners and potentially leading to an institutional set of responses based on power.

Making sense of multiprofessional perspectives

The attempt to understand multiprofessional perspectives is a key consideration for students and practitioners who are affected by the introduction of the biggest reform of children's services for 30 years (Carvel, 2004). Referring to the dictionary can be a useful way of immediately beginning to appreciate the complex meanings implied within the use of the term 'multiprofessional'. However, the additional element of 'perspective' opens up potential insights into ways in which a range of practitioners from different institutional organizations and with different outlooks, roles, expectations and belief systems may construct children as well as their parents and carers. The development of critical ways of thinking is usefully supported by applying a social constructionist approach, which requires the suspension of assumptions about the ways things seem to be and what appear to be the causes of power in a social structure (for a more extensive discussion see Stainton Rogers R. and W., 1992 and James *et al.*, 1998).

> Constructionism welcomes both the voices of tradition and critique into dialogue, while granting neither an ultimate privilege. Commitments do not require rigidity, nor critique eradication of the past. More importantly, the constructionist dialogues contain enormous potential; they open new spans of possibility for creating the future. This is so in the intellectual/scientific world, in the world of professional practice, and in our daily lives.
>
> (Gergen, 1999: 5)

The dictionary definition suggests that a 'professional' possesses a sense of competence or expertness with the ability of developing a perspective that contains a 'proper or accurate point of view or the ability to see it' (CED, 2000). The process of assessing any multiprofessional situation is highly dependent on professional interaction and therefore multiple perspectives. Students, however – particularly in accounts based on their placement activities and contact with practitioner views – highlight that communication may appear incompatible and even unworkable in an atmosphere totally dominated by more powerful 'expert' views. This line of argument also raises questions for students concerning whether or not all 'expert' positions would be given the same credibility with apparently less expert viewpoints that may be shared in a practitioner peer group, or whether there would tend to be a developing hierarchy with some views being held in greater esteem than others. Indeed, during teaching and learning sessions the students often discuss how difficult it may be for some practitioners to develop perspectives that can challenge more highly considered 'expert' positions, which again suggests that the possibility for multiprofessional agreement is likely to be tied to power dynamics and financial budgets. Far from cooperative and coordinated practices being achieved, it may instead be less likely for agreement to be reached where there are disputed outcomes.

It may also be problematic for the development of a multiprofessional group perspective(s) if each practitioner perceives their status and relevance as related to the perceptions of other colleagues representing different professional disciplines. Similarly, students who come with relatively fixed views in relation to professional identity and status, and where, for example, they perceive themselves as emergent practitioners, will recognize that some perspectives tend to be privileged over others, thus swaying the emphasis of any group perspective towards a particular single agency viewpoint such as that of health, social work or education. These power issues could impact on practice by making it less likely for a multiprofessional perspective to agree a holistic set of priorities for a child. Students, through their discussions and by participating in role-play, begin to appreciate that there appear to be connections between the ways that practitioners see their standing in the professional community and the ways that perspectives may be constructed. Students begin to consider whether practitioners are equally valued and respected by others in any given professional community and how this can affect the relationship that they may have with each other and how they refer to each other.

There are therefore several issues likely to arise for students about practitioners viewing themselves as more or less 'expert' participants in the development of a multiprofessional perspective. Students begin to appreciate that a set of perspectives might develop amongst practitioners that may present a view that seems difficult to challenge. Alternatively, some professional voices may not be easily heard, thus representing real barriers to communicating alternative ways of constructing children or their needs. It becomes clearer as the students' studies progress that such a hierarchy based on 'competence' and 'expertness' may lack a sense of democracy amongst a multiprofessional practitioner group. This is an important concern as it suggests that it may undermine one of the main aims identified in *Every Child Matters: Next Steps*, that:

> . . . all professions share a common language and core of training, and encourage professionals to work together to share professional insights, while retaining and enhancing the specialist skills that health professionals bring.
>
> (DfES, 2004: 40)

There can therefore be considerable barriers to clear and open communication due to the coming together of several perspectives, which may lead to divergent and ineffective practices rather than those informed by a convergent perspective.

Developing a multiprofessional perspective

This section will look at how the study of multiprofessional perspectives develops over the duration of the students' studies and how tutors focus the attention of students on three key areas. First, individual services that are available in the community are considered; second, there is an examination of the ways in which different practitioners tend to use 'technical' language; and, finally, the issues arising from multiprofessional practices are considered.

This 'layering' over the three years of the students' studies is to facilitate the developing ability of students to critique multiprofessional practice in all its complexities. When students first begin their studies they are often unaware of service provision and the array of service personnel who staff them. The focus initially is on developing a familiarity with the services that exist within local neighbourhoods. This type of investigation is undertaken in order to develop their understanding of the wide range of services that might be accessible, either through families choosing to access them or because they are required by practitioners to do so due to concerns that have been identified.

This characteristic of multiprofessional perspectives as an area of study represents concerns to develop insights into the ways that practitioners may perceive the children they are working for and with, in the many and varied contexts in which they meet them. This is an important consideration since it establishes a sense of there not only being extensive networks of practitioners working in professional communities that are linked to each other. It also highlights the different ways practitioners will have of understanding the children with whom they are involved and the ways children and their families may appear as different to different practitioners such as a nursery teacher, a community health visitor or a social worker. For example, most students will have had a placement and noted the ways that practitioners view the children in their care and will have compared these practitioner constructions together in sessions.

There is understandably a belief, particularly at the beginning of students' studies, that multiprofessional practices can be viewed as a comparatively uncomplicated, shared practitioner construction of children and their families. At this point, student constructions of multiprofessional perspectives are typified by the view that there are clear objectives and communications between practitioners which seem coherent. In order to unsettle this notion, students in year two concentrate on the communication that is likely to take place between practitioners, and the possibilities for misunderstandings and barriers to communication are far more noticeable. All of which means that when students are in the final stages of their studies they are likely to be far more questioning and concerned about the ways that practices operate. They are likely to explore the dynamics of power relations existing between practitioners, as well as attempting to offer ways of overcoming these barriers.

Multiprofessional practices as a recent phenomenon

To most students, multiprofessional perspectives as an area of academic interest appears to be an extremely recent development that arose from concerns for the well-being of children in notorious child protection cases. However, this section sets out to consider how over time it has come into sharper focus, to currently appear to symbolize a real need to create coordinated professional services for children and their families.

The development of multiprofessional work is seen by the current government to be a priority. This construction is strongly argued in *Every Child Matters* (TSO, 2003), which preceded the Children Act 2004 and which arose itself from the Laming Report (2003) into the death of Victoria Climbiè. In the green paper, Paul Boateng as the Chief Secretary to the Treasury comments that:

> We will be called upon to make common cause across professional boundaries and with reformed structures and services to create the means by which the needs, interests and welfare of children can be better protected and advanced.
>
> (TSO, 2003: 4)

This has begun to impact through a range of measures that build on existing services in some cases and radically recreate others. *Every Child Matters* therefore maps out the government's response to the shortfalls in the child protection system identified by Lord Laming. The strategies suggested recognize that there are socio-environmental factors such as poverty that may lead to some children becoming vulnerable. As Holland points out:

> . . . it is likely that those living in poverty are more likely to require support than others. It is known that living in poverty provokes stress, due to factors such as overcrowding, lack of play facilities, fewer leisure opportunities and the lack of means to purchase respite from caring responsibilities.
>
> (Holland, 2004: 90)

Whilst the government has pledged to eradicate poverty, it sees the 'community' as a focal point in achieving this aim through developing support for struggling families and vulnerable children. At the heart of each community *Every Child Matters* sees Sure Start Children's Centres located, which will '. . . play a key role in communities alongside schools and general practitioners as a focus for parents and children to access services' (TSO, 2003: 26).

This, it may be argued, should allow for the development of more meaningful relationships between local communities, which will also provide the Children's Centres with service users, and a range of professional practitioners who should be more accessible to them. The Sure Start initiative is accompanied by other multiprofessional developments such as Full Service Extended Schools, which are also discussed in *Every Child Matters*:

> The Government wants to integrate Education, Health and Social Care Services around the needs of children. To achieve this, we want all

schools to become extended schools – acting as the hub for services for children, families and other members of the community. Extended schools offer a range of services (such as childcare, adult learning, health and community facilities) that go beyond their core educational function.

(TSO, 2003: 29)

Although the development of services described in *Every Child Matters* is linked very clearly to the Laming Inquiry into the death of Victoria Climbiè, it may also be argued that the development of integrated service provision with a strong community presence forms part of a historical political discourse, where the ultimate goal is to overcome poverty. It may therefore be argued that a significant part of wider governmental responses relate to concerns that go back several years and are related to dealing with 'extensive poverty still present in the UK' (Hill, 2004: 261). These are concerns that were initially identified in the 1960s (see Abel-Smith and Townsend, 1965) and suggested: '. . . the welfare state was neither markedly redistributive nor particularly effective at eradicating poverty' (Hill, 2004: 262).

Hill argues that there has been an attempt by successive governments to advance more effective service provision, with the development of the Social Exclusion Unit at the central level:

> . . . to try to secure co-ordinated action on problems like street homelessness, deprived housing estates and truancy. At the local level there is the idea of the development of zones in disadvantaged areas where, with help from some cash from the centre, policy innovation and inter agency coordination may be enhanced . . .
>
> (Hill, 2004: 266)

The government is clearly targeting deprivation through innovations such as the Education Action Zones and Employment Zones, which focus on the most deprived areas to attempt to alleviate the problems of schools and chronic unemployment (Glennerster, 2000). The part that education might play in bringing about significant change in society, by making it a fairer and more equal place for developing opportunity, is an idea that has been around since the 1960s and found expression in the Plowden Report, which proposed positive discrimination through Education Priority Areas:

> . . . The ideological basis of this outlook lay in human capital theory, then widely accepted. Investment in human capital – that is, in education – was the key to economic, and so to social advance. Wealth creation through this means gave the opportunity for a relatively painless redistribution, and so for the construction of

> a more equal society in which class and other social divisions might
> be overcome. Education in this interpretation was *the* tool for social
> change . . .
>
> (Simon, 1988: 5, author's emphasis)

This resonates with Tony Blair's 'five necessary characteristics of a modern
welfare state' (Blair, cited in Hill, 2004: 264), which involves the welfare state
in tackling exclusion and the need to develop new ways to deliver welfare,
including partnerships between the public, private and voluntary sectors.
Over the last few years of the New Labour government, a raft of white papers,
green papers and legislation have been set in motion:

> The 1997 White Paper *The New NHS: Modern, Dependable* (DH 1997)
> repeatedly urged NHS and local authority organisations to work more
> closely together. This was formalised in the 'duty of partnership'
> imposed by the 1999 Health Act on all NHS organisations and sup-
> ported by a number of other policy and funding initiatives. Con-
> versely, the Local Government Act 2000 empowers local authorities to
> work in partnership with other local agencies to improve economic,
> social and environmental wellbeing.
>
> (Glendinning *et al.*, 2001: 137)

The message from the government emphasizes the importance of partnerships
as a potentially effective way of developing new joint working practices that
are constructed along recognizable and clear lines, which include pooling
budgets, delegating responsibilities to a 'lead' organization and integrating
front-line health and social services staff into a single organization (Hudson
et al., 2001 cited in Glendinning *et al.*, 2001). This practice is repeated across a
number of key areas of provision including childcare through the Sure Start
strategy, which is pledged to provide Children's Centres where they are
needed most – in the most disadvantaged areas – to offer families early education, childcare and health and family support, with advice on employment
opportunities. Children's Centres will link up Sure Start local programmes,
Neighbourhood Nurseries and Early Excellence Centres to extend their success
(from Sure Start website, 2004). The Sure Start Children's Centres will be home
to a number of community services aimed at supporting service users and their
children, who should be able to access the services that they need without fuss
or difficulty.

   The picture that is emerging, and with which the students have to get to
grips, is of a sea change in the ways that health, social care and education
provision is being organized and structured. The sense of isolated and arbitrary
professional responses to community needs is being targeted and claims are
being made that suggest that long-term problems such as deprivation and

poverty will be able to be dealt with in a more successful manner through the innovation of partnership interventions. These interventions, it is claimed, will challenge the stereotypical barriers that have existed between professional practitioners and will therefore lead to a stronger sense of cooperative practice. Indeed, the whole project of improving intervention in child protection cases, as well as attempting to deal effectively with poverty, relies on successful multiprofessional practices. Such tumultuous change leaves our students asking, 'What's my role in all of this?'

Moves from policy to a shared multiprofessional perspective

A central concern has to be addressed: the concept of a 'multiprofessional perspective' or 'set of perspectives' needs to be realized as part of the development of multiprofessional practices. This concern relates to developing ways that professional practitioners with different backgrounds and roles will actively engage with each other to construct a joint/multiple set of perspectives that will be workable. Before considering any constructive action to support the development of the infant multiprofessional discourse, it is important to look at the possible issues both our students and practitioners face when attempting to work together in multiprofessional relationships.

In class, it is quickly identified that there are likely to be types of communications that characterize interactions between practitioners and may also represent barriers between them. For example, students note that there is concern that practitioners will clearly appreciate what their roles comprise of and how they relate to other practitioners from different service traditions and backgrounds. Students also become aware that this concern is particularly relevant when several practitioners are involved with one area of work, and this raises questions about coordination as well as the importance of understanding the power dynamics that are present when different practitioners meet.

Morrow and Malin discuss the issues arising from working in partnership with parents and note the impact on professional roles in a variety of contexts including the staffroom:

> Within Sure Start, parents and professionals had more direct, more informal, contact with each other than previously. The extent to which this relationship had changed varied according to professionals' previous background and experience together with the demands of their current role.
>
> (Morrow and Malin, 2004: 169)

In a recent class discussion concerning the above findings, students raised issues arising from direct and close working practices, including confidentiality and the sense that with close professional contact the barriers and distance between professionals can often be reduced. Some of the students were concerned that moments of contact in the staffroom could also lead to more discussions taking place on an ad hoc basis relating to service users, suggesting an ease of communication that might sacrifice clearly defined ethical understandings of when and about what it was acceptable to talk. Students felt that the informal context for practitioner contact may produce a shared perspective that might confirm stereotypes and prejudices rather than ease a professional discourse.

Our students, when in placement, are able to observe how practitioners in their daily work view children and their families through their own particular ways of seeing and understanding, and these ways are strongly linked to situations such as the training they have received and whether it was completed in multiprofessional contexts or not. Stevenson (1989) argues that there are several potential barriers to inter-agency cooperation, which include the different structures and organizational systems that practitioners come from. In addition, practitioners from different professional organizations will tend to be working to different standards and have different historical backgrounds and cultures to inform their practice. Training that has been conducted in unitary agency contexts will tend to reinforce for the individual that agency's values and belief systems, whilst conversely multiprofessional training should allow for a cross-fertilization of agency constructs. This chapter recognizes this and provides continued opportunities for the reader to understand children and their families through a range of different professional perspectives, constructed by a team of tutors with experience of working professionally in health, education, social services, law and management settings.

Students do not only notice differences but may also appreciate common concerns between professional perspectives. They appreciate that this may result in a child being viewed by a group of practitioners representing different disciplines and professional perspectives as having multiple constructions, which appear connected through a combined construction of perceived 'concern'. The health visitor may chiefly view a child as a medical construction living within a social context, whilst a teacher may view the same child as an educational construction operating within several social systems such as their peers and family. However, students are able to see that there will be moments when a child may appear to a teacher as more a construct of health than of education, and vice versa. It becomes clearer to students that within a practitioner's gaze there are likely to be moments when the view relating to a child is refined and adjusted to reflect insights into different states of being that help explain some of the concerns that have been identified.

Students become aware that the work that takes place in multiprofessional contexts can be, and indeed often is, importantly concerned with the well-being of a child. This is emphasized in the Children Bill (2004) (now enacted), which has a strong focus on child protection and children identified as being in need:

> Each person or body with functions under any enactment of conducting assessments of children's services must for the purposes of those assessments co-operate with other persons or bodies with such functions.
>
> (Children Bill [HL], 19th July 2004: 14)

This small extract from the Bill relates to the ways that practitioners are expected to cooperate when involved in assessing the needs of children that come to their attention. As students can recognize, the value of all practitioners pooling their perceptions of a child in a context where some concern is noticed helps views to be voiced, considerations to be shared and actions to be coordinated.

Students are aware that it is usually assumed that when a referral is made from one professional group to others there will be a sense of acknowledgement of the perceptions and insights offered. This assumption, however, as students learn, may be a false one and a multiprofessional group meeting to discuss a particular child may have a range of constraints that influence their thinking, such as inadequate staffing resources, differing values and attitudes in relation to children than other practitioners, and different priorities when considering allocation to a practitioner with a view to them becoming involved.

The points made above, and those often made by students, have resonance with the recent results recorded by the Joseph Rowntree Foundation, which made the following findings in research concerned with Connexions staff. First, staff in partner agencies were confused about the variety of different roles played by Connexions Personal Advisers (PAs) and unclear about PAs' legitimate roles, responsibilities and authority. There was lack of clarity, particularly in schools, resulting in a continuing suspicion that Connexions had not brought the radical changes some had hoped it would. However, PAs found some providers difficult to work with because of conflicting priorities and working practices. Despite some progress, there was little systematic or effective information sharing. This was most likely to occur within multidisciplinary teams working from the same base. Failure to share information sometimes resulted in an incomplete assessment of needs and inappropriate patterns of support (Coles *et al.*, 2004).

The sense of a 'united' multiprofessional perspective requires access to a common discourse. In this respect, Wenger reminds students and practitioners alike that: 'A perspective is not a recipe; it does not tell you just what to do. Rather, it acts as a guide about what to pay attention to, what difficulties to expect, and how to approach problems' (1998: 9).

Students have the opportunity to actively and constantly critique situations concerning the changing world currently being experienced by professional practitioners. This sense of active engagement at a critical moment in multiprofessional development offers students a unique set of opportunities to work together and rehearse and debate issues to develop insights into the world of practice that they may later wish to enter through postgraduate training. They should begin to recognize the early glimmerings of a common language referred to in *Every Child Matters* and the Children Act (2004), or its absence as multiprofessional perspectives continue to be a goal that all professional practitioners aim for.

References

Abel-Smith, B. and Townsend, P. (1965) *The Poor and the Poorest*. London: Bell.

Carvel, J. (2004) Children's services shake-up biggest in 30 years. London: *The Guardian*. John Carvel, Social Affairs Editor, Friday March 5, 2004.

Chief Secretary to the Treasury (2003) *Every Child Matters*. London: TSO.

Children Act (2004). London: The Stationery Office Ltd.

Children Bill (2004).

Coles, R., Britton, E. and Hicks, L. (2004) *Building Better Connections: Interagency Work and the Connexions Service*. London: Policy Press.

Collins English Dictionary (2000) (5th edition). Glasgow: HarperCollins.

DfES (2004) *Every Child Matters: Next Steps*. Nottingham: DfES.

DoH (1997) *The New NHS: Modern, Dependable*, Cm 3807. London: HMSO.

Gergen, K. J. (1999) *An Invitation to Social Construction*. London: Thousand Oaks.

Glendinning, C., Abbott, S. and Coleman, A. (2001) 'Bridging The Gap': New Relationships between Primary Care Groups and Local Authorities, *Social Policy and Administration*, 35(4), September: 411–425.

Glennerster, H. (2000) *British Social Policy Since 1945* (2nd edition). Oxford: Blackwell.

Hill, M. (2004) *Understanding Social Policy* (7th edition). Oxford: Blackwell.

Holland, S. (2004) *Child and Family Assessment in Social Work Practice*. London: Sage.

Hudson, B., Young, R., Hardy, B. and Glendinning, C. (2001) National Evaluation of Notifications for Use of the Section 31 Partnership Flexibilities of the Health Act 1999: Interim Report. Leeds: Nuffield Institute for Health; and Manchester: National Primary Care Research and Development Centre, cited in Glendinning, C., Abbott, S. and Coleman, A. (2001) 'Bridging The Gap': New Relationships between Primary Care Groups and Local Authorities, *Social Policy and Administration*, 35(4), September: 411–425.

James, A., Jenks, C. and Prout, A. (1998) *Theorizing Childhood.* Cambridge and Oxford: Polity Press.

Lord Laming (2003) *The Victoria Climbiè Inquiry: Summary and Recommendations.* London: HMSO.

Morrow, G. and Malin, N. (2004) Parents and professionals working together: turning rhetoric into reality, *Early Years,* 24(2): 112–126.

Prout, A. and Prout, A. (1997) *Constructing and Reconstructing Childhood: Contemporary Issues in the Sociological Study of Childhood.* London and Washington DC: Falmer Press.

Simon, B. (1988) *Does Education Matter?* London: Lawrence and Wishart.

Stainton Rogers, R. and Stainton Rogers, W. (1992) *Stories of Childhood; Shifting Agendas of Child Concern.* New York and London: Harvester Wheatsheaf.

Stevenson, O. (1989) *Child Abuse: Professional Practice and Public Policy.* Hemel Hempstead: Harvester Wheatsheaf.

Sure Start (2004) http://surestart.gov.uk/

Wenger, E. (1998) *Communities of Practice: Learning, Meaning and Identity.* Cambridge: Cambridge University Press.

7 Anti-discriminatory practice

Russell Jones

Introduction

In order to understand the underlying principles of anti-discriminatory practice, it is first important to deal with issues of equality. Notions such as discrimination and equality are problematic from the outset, because there is little or no point in attempting to establish anti-discriminatory practice if this does not begin from the position that equality is something worth striving for. Equality of opportunity, provision and experience are easy words to use but difficult concepts to grasp and even more difficult to establish in terms of practice in childhood settings. It is important for our students to begin by realizing that there can be no template that will 'resolve' issues of discrimination for children, and that it can only be counterproductive to offer simplistic responses to incredibly complex issues. In recognition of these complications, we will begin by clarifying these terms and relationships. The chapter will then focus initially on one area of childhood to enable contextualized discussion to take place. By looking at anti-discriminatory practice in education as a form of 'case study', it is then intended that anti-discriminatory practices and principles can be applied to multiprofessional settings.

It needs to be established that equality does not mean aspiring to a bland world where everything is 'equal', everyone's experiences are 'the same' and all children's experiences in life are somehow tempered by this process. Equality is not about restricting broad, sweeping opportunity for some in order to make everyone 'equal'. Neither is it about establishing opportunities 'for everyone' without also considering whether 'everyone' is able to access those opportunities at all. Equality is concerned with acknowledging that disadvantage exists in modern society and that the way in which power is allocated and deployed sometimes means that those who are disadvantaged initially become further disadvantaged.

Discrimination forms part of the power system by which social inequalities persist over time, so put simply, anti-discriminatory practices seek to redress this balance. Anti-discriminatory practices set out to acknowledge from the start the ways in which inequality and disadvantage can have negative effects on people's lives, and instead try to establish working practices that make these power relationships more visible and bring about a 'fairer' construct.

It is important to acknowledge and understand that not everyone would want to subscribe to these notions of equality, discrimination and anti-discriminatory practice. Some would argue that society is improved by removing these aspirations completely and simply allowing individual 'freedom' to dominate the way in which policies and practices are established. This thinking would support the idea that talent will succeed regardless of any perceived disadvantage; that success is rewarded with power and status and that the 'cream will always rise to the top'. At the same time, this position would hold that those who do not succeed are less worthy of holding power and status, and that disadvantage has little part to play in this process. This position puts the blame for lack of success firmly on the shoulders of the individual who has not succeeded in surmounting social disadvantage in order to achieve his or her full potential.

Conversely, it would be argued that disadvantage and inequality are precisely the reasons why those who do *not* experience these to begin with end up with powerful positions and high status. This position would claim that it is because some people begin from a privileged, advantaged position that they succeed so easily. It would be further claimed that institutional policies and practices are established to ensure that precisely this group of people succeed at the cost of others, and that unless this process is made highly visible then we are doomed to a cycle of deprivation and disadvantage that will never be broken.

Of course, it is easy to see why this argument is so important when it comes to looking at children and their experiences in the early twenty-first century. We might well like to believe, for example, that we live in a meritocratic system where, right from the very beginning of a child's life, there is a level playing field that ensures that everyone experiences the 'same' education system, so that those who succeed will be those who are worthy of success. We have a universally applied National Curriculum for all children and sweeping initiatives such as the Literacy and Numeracy strategies that apply all over the country, creating the perception of educational equality for all pupils. If, however, we begin to look at this differently and suggest that not all children experience education (or health, or housing, or law) equally, then we can begin to see the explicit need for anti-discriminatory practices. Anecdotally, we may suggest that a child's background has significant links with educational attainment, but statistically it is difficult to deny the relationship between poverty and attainment:

Children from disadvantaged homes face greater barriers to achieving their potential at school. About one in twelve school leavers have no GCSE passes and the gap between the highest and lowest achievers has grown. Up to 75 per cent of the difference can be explained by factors affecting pupil intake, including low income. Low income, as indicated by eligibility for free school meals, could account for 66 per cent of the difference in GCSE attainment at local authority in 2000, nine per cent (or 170,000) of English 16–17 year olds were not in education, employment or training, a rise of 10,000 on the previous year. These young people were more likely to have disadvantages associated with poverty, such as having neither parent in work or parents in manual occupations.

(NCH, 2002: 50)

So, we begin to see that we have two sides of the same coin: we want to believe that all children are entitled to and receive the same education and yet we are continually reminded that there are significant groups of children for whom this does not seem to be a route to success and that these groups are clearly identifiable. If we can look at an education system that delivers the same curriculum to all children but then say it is not delivered or experienced equally, perhaps we will begin to see the point here. To take the position that policies of anti-discrimination are unnecessary, we must first believe that all schools offer equal opportunities to pupils in terms of physical resources, parental support, quality of teaching staff, condition of the school buildings and so on. We would have to believe that a school in a wealthy, suburban area that attracts children who live in large expensive houses and who have highly qualified and powerful parents is equally likely to succeed as a school in an area of mass unemployment, where significant numbers of parents experience long-term sickness and poverty and are unable to break their cycle of deprivation.

This dilemma is precisely the one faced by the Ofsted inspection regime as they set about the business of comparing every school in the country in order to establish league tables, which were 'fair' indicators of a school's progress with its pupils. Initially, Ofsted inspectors were told to make 'no allowances' whatsoever and that their inspection criteria could be applied equally to all schools, all teachers and all pupils. It soon became obvious that this process resulted in inspection results that confirmed the successful status of those establishments who benefited from all the advantages mentioned previously and systematically ignored enormous successes made by schools in areas of significant disadvantage, instead decrying them for having not reached the desired levels and targets. This process has recently begun to change significantly, and inspections are beginning to acknowledge 'value added' performance by schools whose pupils do not perhaps start their educational careers from a position of strength.

If it is accepted that it is necessary to establish practices that ensure children have a more productive start in life, then we now understand the need for anti-discriminatory guidance that shapes and informs those practices. This is not about ensuring everyone has 'the same' (in the way that every child will 'receive' an education based on the National Curriculum), it is more about working to ensure that as adults, we establish practices that do not confirm and compound any disadvantage or inequality the child may bring to that setting.

There is legislation that establishes the framework for equality of opportunity in Britain, but anti-discriminatory practice goes further than this. Initially, the Sex Discrimination Act (1975) and the Race Relations Act (1976) established statutory frameworks to ensure that anti-discriminatory practices related to race and sex are required by law, but in practice this legislation refers largely to adults and often to the workplace. In terms of the application of these regulations, it is not difficult to see that their application and monitoring are easier processes in the workplace and that children are likely to experience anti-discriminatory practice in a very different way. Since the inception of this legislation, however, children have been given further support as outlined in the UN Convention on the Rights of the Child (UNCRC, 1989). Yet it is noticeable that again children experience adults who often 'act in the child's best interests' and in so doing actually disregard the rights and needs of individual children. Often, as we will see later, this is not through reasons of malice or disregard for children's rights but because many adults simply do not see legislation applying equally (or, indeed, especially) in the case of children. Subsequently, they can overlook or disregard significant issues related to class, gender, race, ethnicity or ability. For all these reasons, anti-discriminatory practices are not only necessary but they are essential in child-focused settings, as they establish clear rights and entitlements for all children and create an environment where adults working in the setting are required to work actively to support the agreed practices and principles to the benefit of all children in their care.

In the terms laid out by the UNCRC, non-discrimination means that no child should be injured, privileged or punished by, or deprived of, any right: on the grounds of his or her race, colour or gender; on the basis of his or her language or religion, or national, social or ethnic origin; on the grounds of any political or other opinion; on the basis of caste, property or birth status; or on the basis of a disability. In practice, this should mean that every child is able to enjoy the same rights regardless of, for example, birth circumstances such as wealth or privilege, geographical location or minority group membership. The Convention recognizes and supports basic human rights, such as the freedom to worship, the right to an identity and the right to freedom of thought and speech, and it upholds these rights as they are applied to children's lives.

Anti-discriminatory practice is therefore a centrally important element to many working for, with and on behalf of children today. It would be easy to assume that this is a simple concept to understand and that practitioners in a range of fields understand and subscribe to notions of anti-discriminatory practice, but the reality is somewhat more complicated. We could begin by looking at simple definitions and state that anti-discriminatory practice aims to develop working practices that are beneficial to all children regardless of race, class, gender and ability issues, but this disguises many problems and misconceptions in this area. If we are genuinely to understand these issues and if our equally genuine intention is to develop practices that work in every child's best interests, then we have to look beneath this surface rhetoric. We need to understand how discrimination works, how its subtleties are experienced by young people and what we can do at institutional and personal levels to overcome this to ensure that all children receive the best that we can offer, equally.

It is often difficult to initiate, develop and promote anti-discriminatory practices in childcare and education settings because workers in these areas like to feel that they are in 'caring' professions and that they are not discriminatory in any way. This is completely understandable, and it is difficult to imagine people who enter childcare and education settings with the express purpose of discriminating against certain groups of children. However, the reality is that unless these adults have opportunities to explore their own beliefs, practices, language and stereotypes, it is likely that discriminatory practice will occur.

In class, students are offered a number of examples of practice as a basis for discussion, and at this point it might be useful to look at a couple of case studies to see how emergent discussions might help to inform anti-discriminatory practice. Initially, students would be asked to discuss the role and responsibility of a midday supervisor in a Key Stage 1 setting. Typically, their responses would include references to notions of 'supervision', health and safety, child protection and perhaps a mild form of surveillance. It is less likely to receive responses related to cultural transmission or anti-discriminatory practice, and yet workers in these positions are often able to demonstrate behaviour and language use that is highly influential.

Students are then offered a scenario where a school's midday assistant notices that some children are not using their knives and forks correctly. These children are openly criticized for being ill-mannered and for not eating in the normal way. When asked to comment on this, student reactions typically range from:

> *Well, they are just doing their job.*

> *If the children aren't taught to have any manners at home then the school has to take the responsibility.*

If the midday assistant doesn't show them how to eat properly then who will?

to:

It seems harsh that the children have to be told off in public, shouldn't this be done away from the other children?

Doesn't this just make the child feel isolated from their peers?

Of course, on the surface this is a simple story: a child was not using the 'correct' eating utensils properly, was ill-mannered and the midday supervisor felt it was her job to reprimand him. The resolution came once the knife and fork were used in the same, 'normal', way as the other children around the table. At this point, students are typically happy with this example of practice (although some see it as 'harsh'). We then explain that this child had no experience of using knives and forks prior to entering the school's reception and had been taught to use his fingers to eat at home as part of his cultural upbringing. This is not uncommon, and many cultures have conventions where certain foods are eaten with the fingers rather than utensils.

Once students have this broader picture their responses to the scenario change dramatically and they begin to realize that what has happened is clearly discriminatory. Their responses become much more concerned about the child who was corrected and how it feels to have the culture of the school and the culture of the home clash so visibly. Questions are then usually raised about how the midday assistant should have responded, about what she could have been expected to know, about the potential for such 'innocent' acts to be replicated in a literacy class, in a PE lesson or during a piece of drama. Suddenly, students need more information in order to establish anti-discriminatory practices that are going to support both the child in question and the midday supervisor, and it is at this point that the 'real' discussions can begin to take place. It soon becomes obvious to all that successful anti-discriminatory practice is an issue for all staff in a child-based setting. It becomes equally obvious who teaching staff who are heavily committed to anti-discriminatory practice can have their work negated by caretakers, cleaners and midday assistants who have simply not been invited to training sessions, have no ownership over agreed policies and may not share the same views. Students at this point tend to defend the midday assistant's stance, raising questions of ownership, inclusive practices and elitism as they begin to realize that unless all staff take part in the process then the policies are unlikely to succeed.

A second case study used with students again highlights practices that can be unintentionally problematic. Students are invited to comment on the ways in which they try to ensure that every pupil is 'treated the same' in their classes. Research evidence is used where young teachers sought to adopt a 'colour-blind' approach in their classrooms to ensure that every child is treated 'equally'. Students recognize this appeal to egalitarianism as something worthy, something caring and something that is certainly desirable in their developing practice in the classroom, as it ensures fairness and equality for all. Transcriptional data is offered as discussion points for the students:

> As far as I am concerned they are all children, they're not girls and boys . . . a child is a child, it doesn't matter what sex they are or what colour they are, what religion.

> I think it is better to have relationships with the children in your class because they are individuals, they are not Tommy who's black, Billy who's in a wheelchair, they are Tommy and Billy and the wheelchair and the colour bit doesn't even come close. It's more about what is going on here (indicates her heart) that I am interested in, and I get very cross with people who start treating them in different ways because of that, whether they mean to or not. It makes me very angry.

> They are individuals. I don't look at them as brown or white, or boys and girls, it's how they are as a class. Their personalities.
>
> (Jones, 1999: 44)

Initially, students respond with familiarity and recognize these statements as ones they too have made as they enter the profession. They then begin to see that perhaps this is not as simplistic as they imagined. Typically, one student will look at the third quote and suggest that this is confused; the teacher is trying to see the child as an individual as well as a class member. Somebody usually points out that a wheelchair in a classroom they taught in would have been very noticeable indeed, and that to try to see all children in the same way would not serve the needs of the child whose mobility was restricted. References are usually made to the small amount of computer space, and it is realized that if everyone had been 'treated the same' then the child in the wheelchair would never have used the computer. Another student typically suggests that actually it does matter if the child is a boy or a girl, while another might point out that, 'Shouldn't we be using a different word than "brown" to describe children?'

This subject continues to open up all kinds of concerns, and again we enter a different kind of understanding where it is realized that effective anti-discriminatory practice is not about treating everyone the same or about adopting a 'colour-blind' approach. The whole issue is far more complicated than this would lead us to believe. The session usually concludes with the realization that when inexperienced (and sometimes experienced) teachers ignore issues of race and ethnicity in their classrooms, they typically do so because they believe that this is a 'good' thing to do, often claiming that it 'helps' the solitary black or Asian child feel as though they are 'just like everyone else'. In practice, however, all this achieves is a sense of isolation or lack of worth, as institutional and professional practices merely serve to remind some children that they need to work harder to establish their own identities, needs and concerns.

Tony Sewell's (Sewell, 1999) work has further illustrated that many children leave the compulsory state education system feeling as though no teacher actually recognized or acknowledged their ethnic identities. While the teachers felt they were doing the 'right' thing, the child's experience was of being treated as 'honorary white pupils'. At the time of writing, we were aware of a rural primary school where every child is white except for one Hindu boy who has been at the school for a year. School assemblies are exclusively Christian by nature and his parents have the dilemma of either encouraging him to take part in a religious service to which he has no affiliation or removal and complete daily isolation from the rest of the school because of his religious beliefs. In this instance, the boy leaves his religious and cultural identity at the door of the school hall for 20 minutes every day in order to be a 'normal' member of the school 'family'. In real terms, this is discriminatory practice at an institutional level; only one child in the school has to negotiate issues of identity and belief in order to experience the 'normal' school day, and in this example it is the Hindu child. Thirty years ago, the Bullock Report stated that, 'No child shall be expected to cast off the language and culture of the home as he [sic] passes the school threshold' (1975: 50), and yet, in twenty-first century Britain, this is precisely the experience of this single child. The Convention on the Rights of the Child stated clearly that:

> Parties shall respect and ensure the rights set forth in the present Convention to each child within their jurisdiction without discrimination of any kind, irrespective of the child's or his or her parent's or legal guardian's race, colour, sex, language, religion, political or other opinion, national, ethnic or social origin, property, disability, birth or other status.
>
> (UNCRC, 1989, article 2)

And yet this child's fundamental rights are ignored for the convenience of the institution. Whilst these two examples may be seen as 'merely' anecdotal, it is important to understand that this is the way in which most discriminatory practice happens; it is not malicious or deliberate, it happens for 'practical' reasons of 'common sense' or for convenience. It is therefore important that anti-discriminatory practice is not about policies that are kept in cupboards and trawled out at times of inspection or surveillance. If anti-discriminatory practice is to mean anything then it has to be about education, continual monitoring and a willingness to listen to children's voices and put them before the interests of bureaucracy and institutionalized practices.

If the evidence of these children's stories is to be seen as merely anecdotal, then it is important that we explore them further to see how anti-discriminatory practices would enhance these children's lives. A clear indicator of discrimination in practice and an area of current concern is that of exclusion from school. At a time when more than 9000 children are excluded from school every year and up to 1000 are 'lost' through truancy (Slater, 2004: 2), it is important that we begin to see how children respond to discriminatory practices that are left unchallenged. If we suggest that discriminatory practice is disadvantageous to children in any setting, then the worst possible outcome of these flawed practices would be exclusion from school – the denial of the child's right to education. Of course, there can be many reasons for exclusion and there is a separate debate to be had about the purpose and value of exclusion *per se*, but in the context of this chapter we need to think about exclusion as the final exertion of power in a child-based setting, and the suggestion that discrimination and exclusion figures could be linked.

Two highly significant publications have highlighted the ways in which children who are members of particular groups in society experience exclusion differently. First, the work of Tony Sewell has identified the reasons why black boys are up to 15 times more likely to be excluded than their white peers for the same offences (Sewell, 1999). In the time since Sewell's work this issue has not been resolved and is still of significant concern. Second, the work of Wright *et al.* (2000) has further identified the case that children are disproportionately excluded from school in relation to issues of race, class and gender. As Wright *et al.* point out:

> The most striking aspect of this trend in exclusion is the apparent relationship between gender, ethnicity, culture and social disadvantage. Central to an understanding of the reason why certain ethnic minority groups feature disproportionately in exclusion statistics is an examination of the school processes, which lead to exclusion.
>
> (Wright *et al.*, 2000: 8)

Both Sewell and Wright *et al.* explore in detail notions of discrimination in practice, linking them through to exclusion statistics. They find that the practices of adults in the researched settings were performing discriminatory roles in the way in which they handled children from minority groups in general and policies of exclusion in particular. Again, what often came to the forefront of the findings was that these adults were unaware of the consequences of their actions and were not knowledgeable about the cultural differences of the pupils (for example, issues of 'respect' were often misinterpreted as issues of conflict and aggression). Subsequently, children who were initially disadvantaged became double disadvantaged when anti-discriminatory practices were not evident. It is important to acknowledge that anti-discriminatory practices have begun to change this tide of events since the publication of these reports. There is significant evidence that mentoring programmes aimed at helping both pupils and teachers understand the way in which problem escalation begins with a lack of understanding have begun to impact positively on exclusion figures. The placing of 'emotional literacy' at the heart of the educational agenda (Hutchins, 2004) has further helped adults understand the way in which discrimination impacts disproportionately on children in minority groups.

Having agreed that there is value and purpose in establishing notions of equality and having established that children are protected under relevant legislation, it is necessary that practitioners look at their settings and then work hard to establish anti-discriminatory policies and practices that will benefit the lives of all children in their care. This is much easier said than done since it is not a paper policy nor (as we have already seen) legislation that will necessarily bring about the required changes to working practices that challenge discrimination and set out to ensure that all children experience discrimination-free provision.

In trying to apply some anti-discriminatory principles to multiprofessional settings it is helpful to look at Unicef's plan for 'Building a Protective Environment for Children'. Working within the definitions of discrimination set out in the UN Convention, Unicef outlines the following points for action that are applicable in all settings related to children:

- Attitudes need to change. In societies where attitudes or traditions facilitate discrimination, children's protection will always be undermined;
- Governments need to be committed to combating discrimination. This includes ensuring not only that policies and legislation are non-discriminatory, but also that there are proactive plans in place to address all forms of discrimination;
- Discrimination needs to be discussed and condemned openly and publicly. At the most immediate level, children suffering discrimination need to be free to speak up about their concerns. At the national level, media attention and civil society engagement against discrimination can play an important role;
- Laws against discrimination need to be in place and enforced. An adequate legislative framework, its consistent implementation, accountability and a lack of impunity are essential to fighting discrimination;

- Health workers, teachers, police, social workers and many others who deal with children need to understand and know how to address discrimination. Families and communities also need to understand how to protect, and be supported in protecting, their children from discrimination;
- Children need to be aware of their right not to be discriminated against. They should also be supported and enabled to act as advocates against discrimination;
- Discrimination must be monitored and reported on. An effective monitoring system is required that records the incidence and nature of discrimination and allows for informed and strategic responses. Such systems should normally be participatory and locally based;
- Children who have suffered discrimination are entitled to care and non-discriminatory access to basic social services.

(Unicef, 2004)

For those working in childhood settings this list presents a strong starting point through which anti-discriminatory practices may be established, evaluated and strengthened. We can see that it is every worker's responsibility to ensure that children experience their right to a protected environment, and that it is the individual's responsibility to act on behalf of the child when discrimination occurs. Furthermore, practitioners are challenged with the professional responsibility of knowing and understanding the subtle ways in which discrimination can be experienced by young people. Similarly, it is the responsibility of all those working in multiprofessional settings to monitor discrimination to ensure that practices are not merely based on paper policies, but rather that they reflect an explicit commitment to anti-discrimination that sends a visible message of support to children.

References

Department of Education and Science (1975) *A Language for Life* (The Bullock Report). London: HMSO.

Hutchins, L. (2004) Where feelings run high, *Times Educational Supplement*, 15th October.

Jones, R. (1999) *Teaching Racism*. Stoke-on-Trent: Trentham Books.

Millam, R. (1996) *Anti-discriminatory Practice*. London: Cassell.

NCH (2002) *Factfile: Facts and figures about children in the UK*. London: NCH.

Sewell (1997) *Black Masculinities and Schooling*. Stoke-on-Trent: Trentham.

Slater, J. (2004) Councils Lose Children, *Times Educational Supplement*, 10th December: 2.

Thompson, B. (2003) *Promoting Equality: Challenging Discrimination and Oppression*. Basingstoke: Palgrave Macmillan.

TES (1998) Blacks 15 times more likely to be excluded, *Times Educational Supplement*, 11th December: 1.

Unicef (2004) www.unicef.org/protection/files/discrimination

United Nations (1989) *UN Convention on the Rights of the Child*. Geneva: United Nations.

Wright, C., Weeks, D. and McLaughlin, A. (2000) *Race, Class and Gender in Exclusion from School*. London: Falmer.

8 Legal issues

Catherine Baxter

Introduction

This chapter seeks to explore what makes the law relating to children different from other types of law by exploring the philosophy behind legislation affecting children and their families and by examining the principles upon which it is based. Case studies are used in order to trouble certain assumptions that students might hold in relation to what is right or wrong. Additionally, students consider the role of the state in protecting children who are at risk of harm from their environment and the law's approach to balancing the interests of family members.

Whenever a dispute occurs regarding a child's upbringing, various people may have an interest in, or views about, what should happen to the child. Usually disagreements are best resolved through discussion and compromise. Agencies and systems exist which encourage conciliatory methods of resolving such situations. However, where such methods fail, inevitably the responsibility falls on the law courts to decide what is best for the child. The objective of this chapter is to illustrate the processes that students circumnavigate as they develop insights into the workings of the legal system. Such insights are necessary for practitioners who will be working with children and families, some of whom may seek redress from the legal system in order to stabilize aspects of family life.

Law and morality

Initial discussions with students often centre on trying to get to grips with 'lawful behaviour' and behaviour that is 'morally correct'. At the beginning of such dialogues there is sometimes a blurring between the two, where each more or less means the same. However, although law-abiding citizens use the law to regulate their conduct, it is not always the case that what the law prescribes is morally right. Consider the following two situations.

Example 1

Teuta is a Kosovan asylum seeker who was brought to England by the British government during the war in Kosovo. Her husband Agrim was separated from her in the fighting. With the stress of moving plus the birth of a child she succumbed to a serious mental breakdown. Three months later, the Red Cross traced her husband. The British government refused Agrim permission to travel to the UK to be with Teuta. Eventually Agrim was able to obtain enough money to pay a smuggler to help him travel across Europe to be with his wife.

Example 2

Sarah is relaxing in her deck chair watching her neighbour's two year old playing in her paddling pool. The toddler splashes enthusiastically for a moment and then slips on the floor of the pool and falls into the water. From her deck chair in the neighbouring garden Sarah can see the child drowning. The girl struggles for another couple of minutes and finally dies. Sarah eventually wanders in to her house.

Students are understandably shocked when it is explained that Agrim has committed a serious offence, a crime for which he could potentially go to jail for 14 years (ref AIA 92). Meanwhile, Sarah has not committed any offence by omitting to act and is entirely innocent. But in moral terms who was right/ wrong?

The legal positivist position is that the law is a set of rules and as such the right thing for a citizen to do is to obey the law because it is the law. In brief, the legal framework is a strategy for settling disputes and provides a set of rational rules, which enable large numbers of disparate people to live together (Llewellyn, 1941). But should an individual always obey the law?

When faced with a family law type decision such as which parent a child should live with following a divorce, the temptation for the decision maker is to do what is right in the sense of what appeals to their own sense of what is right or wrong. Judges, however, are not allowed to do this. They must apply the rules that make up the law at the time of making a decision. The procedures that judges go through is referred to as 'statutory interpretation', and it is this process that we try to recreate in the classroom.

Parental responsibility

'Parental responsibility' is woven into the Children Act (1989) and is a key principle and a crucial concept of child law. Parental responsibility is defined in section 3(1) to mean:

> All the rights, duties, powers, responsibility and authority, which by law a parent of a child, has in relation to the child and his property.

The law recognizes that very young children lack the capacity to make decisions about their own upbringing. Older children, whilst they may have better understanding than younger children, may not be mature enough to make decisions which take into account all the relevant factors of their circumstances in order to judge what is in their long-term best interests. There is no list detailing 'rights, duties, powers, responsibility and authority'. In essence, these are the aspects of parenthood that are required to enable parents to perform their duty properly. Clearly, parents will interpret them in different ways because of the highly subjective nature of both what is best for their child and their individual interpretations of what rights, duties, powers, responsibility and authority encompasses. They allow parents the freedom, for example, to make choices regarding a child's religious upbringing, to make decisions about their education and to have the authority to consent to medical treatments.

The thinking behind parental responsibility is that the state, recognizing that children are vulnerable, has responded by devising a legal concept to protect them by identifying specified individuals and imposing responsibility on them until the child attains adulthood. However, the powers conferred on individuals with parental responsibility are limited and cannot be exercised in a way that infringes the rights of others. Recognizing that certain individuals have certain rights to control various aspects of a child's upbringing and make decisions on his or her behalf does not imply that it is a static situation. Parental rights are derived from parental duty and exist only as long as they are necessary for the protection of a child. Thus, where a parent acts in clear violation of this principle, then parental responsibility can be challenged and removed, for example, where a parent has been proven to abuse a child.

Who is the 'parent'?

The title 'parent' initially seems to be uncomplicated, but within the law this is not the case. Herring (2001) describes how amongst lawyers the following understandings of the term parent have been discussed:

- The biological or genetic parent. This usually refers to the genetic component, although this in itself is further complicated when considering children born as a result of fertility treatment in circumstances where the male, female or both genetic components of the child are not those of one or both of the parents who will care for the child.
- The social parents. Here it is those who carry out the job of parenting, such as feeding, cleaning, washing and clothing a child. Often the genetic and social parent is the same person but not always. If a woman becomes pregnant by her husband and then divorces him during pregnancy and her new partner moves in with her, the new partner will become the social parent, although the husband is the genetic parent.
- The psychological parent. This is a concept that has been influenced by Bowlby's (1951) attachment theory. The psychological parent will provide for and support the child's 'emotional demands for affection, companionship and stimulating intimacy' (Goldstein et al., 1996: 146). The person may or may not be a blood relation to a child. There are two significant consequences that result from this view: first, a child should not be removed from the psychological parent by the state unless there are compelling reasons for doing so: second, on divorce or separation the child should reside with the psychological parent and contact with anyone else should not be at a level that undermines the child's relationship with the psychological parent.
- Licensed parents. These are people who are appointed or approved by the state to be parents to a child, the most common example being adoptive parents.

Barton and Douglas (1995) have argued that the law as it stands relies primarily on the intention to be a parent as key to the notion of parenthood. That is, that people who have acted in a way that shows that they have voluntarily undertaken the obligations and status of a parent are regarded as the child's parents. They suggest that a person should not be held responsible for a child unless he or she has explicitly or implicitly undertaken those responsibilities as a parent.

Thus the law in England and Wales treats separately the questions of 'who is the parent?' and 'who acquires the legal rights and responsibilities as parents?' The law acknowledges that people who are not parents can acquire the legal rights and responsibilities that attach to parenthood and that some people who are parents should not acquire parental responsibility.

So, who has parental responsibility for the child?

The law automatically confers parental responsibility on the mother of a child when he or she is born. The situation as regards fathers is more complex. A father who is married to a child's mother at the time of his or her birth has automatic parental responsibility. Similarly, a father who is registered as the child's father on the birth certificate now has automatic parental responsibility. This is an area of the law which has recently altered and many commentators would argue that this change supports the view that the law evolves in response to the dominant values of society at the time it is created and so gradually begins to reflect those values.

Alternatively, parental responsibility can be acquired if the father makes a parental responsibility agreement with the mother or if he obtains a parental responsibility order from the court. Clearly, this leaves the unmarried father who is not registered as the father on the birth certificate of a child in a much weaker position as regards his power to influence decisions about the child's upbringing. This distinction has been the subject of much controversy and many commentators argue that in this area of family law there is strong evidence of discrimination against men. Additionally, a guardian with a residence order in his or her favour, parents of an adopted child or indeed any individual with a residence order in his or her favour acquire parental responsibility automatically. Finally, a local authority is also given parental responsibility for a child if they are awarded a care order or an emergency protection order for a child.

Working with the welfare checklist

There is a list of factors provided in the Children Act (1989) in section 1(3) which the judge should consider when deciding what is in the child's best interests. These are referred to as the welfare checklist and are listed below:

(a) the ascertainable wishes and feelings of the child concerned (considering in the light of his/her age and understanding);
(b) his/her physical, emotional and educational needs;
(c) the likely effect on him/her of any change in his/her circumstances;
(d) his/her age, sex, background and any characteristics of which the court considers relevant;
(e) any harm which he/she has suffered or is at risk of suffering;
(f) how capable each of his/her parents, and any other person in relation to whom the court considers the question to be relevant, is of meeting his/her needs.

The checklist has been devised in response to research findings that have shown that children are at risk of suffering disadvantage in a variety of ways, including economically, in terms of health and behaviour, and regarding the development and maintenance of future relationships, when there is a disagreement about their upbringing. In the enactment of the checklist, the law recognizes that children are vulnerable and need protection; their inception was an attempt to address this. The interpretation and application of the welfare checklist is highly subjective and judges are given wide discretion to weigh up the different factors when making their decision. It is therefore difficult to predict how a judge might decide a particular case.

The following case study provides students with a basis for using the checklist in order to make decisions in relation to the welfare of young children.

CASE STUDY

Stephen and Fiona have been married for eight years and have two children, Abigail aged 6 and Jacob aged 4 years. Stephen works from home and has spent a lot of time caring for the children. Following a career break Fiona returned to work two years ago as a journalist. She travels extensively in her work. Fiona recently met and moved in with Ryan, a younger man who she works with, taking Abigail and Jacob with her. Ryan is also a successful journalist; he works long hours, is extremely ambitious and has recently been offered a lucrative offer to work in the USA. Abigail dislikes Ryan, but Jacob is ambivalent towards him. Stephen thinks the children should live with him because he is at home more of the time. Fiona thinks that the children should stay with her because she is their mother and because childcare is not a problem for her as she is in the process of employing a nanny.

Students begin the debate by considering the issue of ascertaining the wishes of the children. Here the students struggle with the ages of the children in relation to their ability to make their views known. So, on the one hand, they believe firmly that the children's views should be listened to. However, they question whether the children have the capacity to 'hold all the bits of the picture together so as to make an informed judgement' (student comment). Meanwhile, another student makes a staunch plea for professionals to *listen* carefully so that the children can express their feelings, including any worries. As this student notes, 'It is only by listening to Abigail that we might then appreciate why she dislikes Ryan.' The students also wondered whether the children would feel guilty about choosing between one or other of the parents.

In considering the physical, emotional and educational needs of the children, students emphasize the need for stability. So at first there is general consensus that Abigail and Jacob should remain in Stephen's home because 'they are familiar with it, they might well have developed friendships with other children in the neighbourhood and they might well be settled at school'. However, they also recognize that the emotional and physical needs of the children will not remain static. As one student noted, 'How will Stephen address Abigail's needs when she is an adolescent and she starts her periods?' In discussing 'change in the children's circumstances', much of the debate centres on what young children can 'cope' with and what systems are in place to help them cope. So, because Stephen works from home they perceive him as being able to care consistently for the children. He will, for example, be able to take and collect the children from school and he is perhaps better placed to accommodate any out of school activities that the children might participate in. However, they also note that a nanny could fulfil these functions. Concerns are expressed about Ryan and the fact that he is ambitious: 'Will this necessitate moving jobs that might well entail moving house?' Meanwhile, the notion of 'background' triggers a number of complexities because it is here that students begin to discuss issues to do with the children's immediate culture. As one student asked, 'Have these children got cultural or religious affiliations that we need to know about?' Another wanted to know about the strength of kinship relations, where it might be that the children have developed strong ties with relatives such as grandparents, aunts, uncles or cousins.

Attention is then directed towards notions of 'harm' and the 'risk of suffering'. Perhaps not too surprisingly, it is the relationship between Ryan and Abigail that the students struggle with when contemplating this aspect of the checklist. As one student remarked:

> I would want more insight into this relationship. After all this is a young man who might not have had any previous experiences of being with young children. It might be that he is nervous about his relationship with Abigail. It seems that things are slightly easier with Jacob. Maybe this is because he is able to relate more easily with him, share common interests . . .

Finally, the issue of which parent or parents are capable of meeting the children's needs is considered. Again, the students tussle with this. Some will question who the children have 'bonded' with, where they wonder if Stephen might be the significant attachment figure. They recall that Fiona would have been absent for periods of time in the early stages of the children's lives. Would this have impacted on the children? But they also recognize that Fiona and Ryan are likely to be more affluent and therefore able to offer the children much more in material terms.

Whilst the students can wrangle with this case they are clearly unable to make any sound judgements, because unlike a judge they do not have access to, for example, the Children and Family Court Advisory and Support Service and any reports. Additionally, they are unable to undertake observations of either parent or the children. Neither are they able to interview any of the individuals who are involved. That said, the process that they have been through broadens their overall perspective. It gives them some awareness of the law as it relates to family breakdown. In brief, it adds to their overall practical wisdom.

So, what might the judge decide?

Since Stephen and Fiona were married, they both have parental responsibility for their children: section 2(1) Children Act (1989). Both will continue to have parental responsibility even if they divorce, as the Children Act (1989) emphasizes the continuity of parental care; the emphasis is on the obligation of the parents to meet the needs of the child rather than the archaic idea of parental rights. There are two issues that need to be resolved, namely, where Abigail and Jacob live and the extent of the non-resident parent's contact. As a parent, Stephen could apply for either a residence order to decide where the children should live or a contact order dealing with the arrangements for contact or visits as a right under s 8 of the Children Act (1989).

In determining Stephen's application for a s 8 order, the welfare of each child must be the court's paramount consideration. The court will consider what is in Abigail and Jacob's *best interests*, not what both parties want. In dealing with the application for a s 8 order, the court must have regard for the non-interventionist policy in s 1(5) of the Act. This provides that the court should not make an order unless it is preferable to not making one. This policy was devised to encourage resolution wherever possible. Having become involved the court must recognize that delay will often prejudice the welfare of the children and so must have a strict timetable for resolution of the proceedings. The judge then uses the statutory checklist of factors in s 1(3) of the Act to consider what is in the best interests of the child or children.

The first factor is the ascertainable wishes of the child in the light of their age and understanding. Both Abigail and Jacob are very young and are well below the age where their opinions would be viewed as decisive. Most children of six and four years will want to have contact with both their parents, but may be unable to grasp the wider implications or long-term significance of a choice of residence.

It has generally been thought that it is more appropriate for a mother to care for very young children than a father: Brixley v Lynas [1996] 2FLR 499, [1997] 1 FCR 220. This would have in the past favoured Fiona, but in Re H

(A Minor) (1983) it was emphasized that times had changed and that many fathers are as capable of looking after small children. There are obvious advantages to young girls being with their mothers through puberty. However, these children have been used to their mother being away from home for a significant amount of time. Prior to the separation the children have been cared for predominantly by their father and there is nothing to suggest that he has been unable to meet their needs, so it cannot be assumed that the children will remain with their mother in the long term.

As the students noted, Stephen would be able to provide stability. Fiona, in contrast, has a busy career, which involves extensive travel. If there were a strong possibility of Fiona and Ryan relocating abroad, this would be viewed with caution by a judge who would see this as having potentially detrimental effects on the relationships between Stephen and his children. The lack of a stable home base could also have possible educational disadvantages and may well count against Fiona. May v May (1986) illustrates the importance attached to good education.

The court would want Abigail and Jacob to remain together, as siblings derive considerable support from each other: Adams v Adams (1984). It would be extremely unlikely for the children to be separated just because Abigail does not seem to like Ryan. The courts have a tendency to preserve the status quo to avoid unnecessary disruption: J v C (1970). If the children are used to their home with Fiona and Ryan and are settled at school, then the court will try to avoid uprooting them, as this would be viewed as detrimental to their welfare. Alternatively, if the children are obviously missing their former home and returning them to their father would not necessitate them changing schools and would provide them with more stability in the long term, the judge might favour granting a residence order to Stephen with provision for generous contact with Fiona. Stephen appears to be able to provide greater continuity of care, and in Riley v Riley (1986) the court expressed a preference for children living with a parent who could provide continuity of care in one place as opposed to the parent who was constantly on the move. On the basis of the facts in relation to this issue, the scales appear to swing towards Stephen.

The age, sex, background and any other characteristics of the children are considered, together with the risk of harm to the child. There is no suggestion that Ryan is likely to harm the children, but more detail would be required to find out why Abigail dislikes him. If, for example, he was a harsh disciplinarian who frightened her on occasion, the court may regard it as not being in her best interests to live with him on a permanent basis. In contrast, if Jacob were diabetic and was used to Fiona rather than Stephen administering injections, this might swing the scales in her favour as regards the children remaining with her. Any possibility of Fiona and Ryan relocating would be regarded as potentially disadvantageous to the children's education.

Lastly, the capabilities of the parents and any other person of meeting the child's needs must be considered. There is an obvious advantage if a parent can show that they have established a suitable relationship with a substitute parent, as the child's best interests are often best met in a two-adult household. In the present situation Fiona and Ryan's relationship is relatively new and there is a suggestion that he and Abigail have an awkward relationship. Stephen has no partner that we are told of, but he has been a very caring parent who has a good relationship with both of the children and he has full support from his mother in looking after them. Therefore, Stephen appears to have a good chance of obtaining a residence order.

On the facts provided in this scenario, having settled the residence issue the court would very likely order generous contact in favour of the non-resident parent, as the court takes the view that both parents should still play an important role in their child's life regardless of the outcome. There is an assumption that children benefit from contact with their siblings or parents: Re L (A Child) (Contact: Domestic Violence) [2000] 2 FLR 334, [2000] FCR 404. Only where it can be shown that there are compelling reasons involving a significant risk to the child will the court not order contact in a non-resident parent's favour.

To reach a decision in the present case the judge would need more information about the following:

- the relationships between the children and Ryan;
- Fiona's work patterns;
- the couple's future plans in view of their demanding careers;
- the children's happiness/stability in their new surroundings, including their schools;
- whether the children were missing their former home.

To conclude, Stephen would appear on the facts to be in a strong position for obtaining a residence order in his favour, unless Fiona could provide more evidence to show that the children are happy and settled in their new home and that she is capable of providing them with stability and continuity of care.

In the family courts there are certain presumptions suggested by case law, as highlighted, which the courts will usually follow. However, they will not definitely affect the judge in reaching a conclusion about what is in the child's best interests in a particular case as each case is considered individually, recognizing that no two sets of circumstances are identical. Presumptions are likely to change over time if the dominant view in society changes. The law is informed by current thinking and responds to the publication of expert research from a whole range of professionals. This informs judges and ultimately influences the decisions they make. In this way the law evolves to reflect the dominant discourses in society at a given moment in time.

Human rights and family law

The Human Rights Act (1998) has had a significant effect on the way in which family cases are decided. For example, courts have had to recognize, under article 8, a right to respect for family and private life. This has had especial influence in relation to the issue of contact following separation. Consequently, the court will seek to promote contact between children and their parents and between siblings wherever possible. Thus on divorce, both parents have a right to contact with a child unless there is strong evidence to support the contrary view. However, this can be problematic in reality as the residential parent is the one who ensures that the child is available for contact sessions, and under the Human Rights Act (1998) it could be argued that in some circumstances the making of a contact order interferes with the residential parent's right to respect for a private and family life, a clear violation of article 8.

Conclusion

The main legislation in England and Wales governing the decisions made to settle disputes which involve children and their families, whether between parents or between families and the state, are the Children Act (1989) and the Family Law Act (1996). Although apparently straightforward at first reading, their application demands judges to make extremely complex judgments through careful consideration of a multiplicity of factors, whilst skilfully balancing the interests of all the parties involved. Herring (2001) argues that the law struggles to balance the interests of parents, both genetic and social, between protecting children and recognizing that they have rights and between protecting children and allowing parents freedom to raise their children in the way they consider is best for them. He argues that the way in which the law strikes the balance has changed over time and will continue to change in the future. How judges settle such disputes appears to a great extent to depend on the prevailing values, attitudes, beliefs and understanding at the time the decision is made. The law is shaped or moulded by current thinking and consequently evolves over time, taking its lead from and ultimately reflecting the dominant views of society at the time it was created.

References

Barton, C. and Douglas, G. (1995) *Law and Parenthood*. London: Butterworths.
Bowlby, J. (1951) *Maternal Care and Mental Health*. Geneva: World Health Organization.

Goldstein, J., Solnit, A., Goldstein, S. and Freud, A. (1996) *The Best Interest of the Child*. New York: Free Press.

Herring, J. (2001) *Family Law* (2nd edn). London: Pearson Longman.

Llewellyn, K. N. (1941) *The Cheyenne Way: Conflict and Case Law in Primitive Jurisprudence*. Norman: University of Oklahoma Press.

9 Child protection

John Powell

Introduction

This chapter will consider the ways that historical and social constructions influence how 'child protection' and its associated practices may be envisaged. It will attempt to connect to the concerns of students as they come into contact with this often emotive area of study and begin to translate it into more thoughtful ways of understanding the dilemmas often faced by a range of early childhood practitioners. The chapter will discuss 'child protection' as a complex set of insights and concepts that views children as having fundamental human rights, which may be overlooked by parents and professional carers alike. Whilst responsibilities for children usually reside primarily with parents, their care may become a cause for concern and come to the attention of external professional practitioners such as social workers, teachers and medical practitioners, who may initiate a process of intervention. There is an attempt throughout the chapter to problematize the language of 'child protection' that may, through continual use, otherwise become taken for granted.

A social constructionist approach

The term 'social construction' needs to be clarified since it will be referred to throughout this chapter and throughout the book. The tutors are keen to support students in their pursuit of developing a range of insights into different topics and subject areas so that definitive meanings, if presented, may be seen to be fragile and worthy of challenging:

> [We must] appreciate the power of redescribing, the power of language to make new and different things possible and important – an appreciation which becomes possible only when one's aim becomes

an expanding repertoire of alternative descriptions rather than The
One Right Description.

(Rorty, cited in Gergen, 1999: 62)

Rorty's view coincides with this book's concerns to question rather than
accept apparently absolute positions as necessarily thorough and complete
ones. Indeed, because child abuse practices very often take place in private,
and children are often unable, unwilling or afraid to articulate their concerns,
our students begin to appreciate that early years practitioners need both an
inquiring, open minded approach and an understanding that a decision may
need to be made based on what appear as tentative insights. There are occasions, however, which nonetheless require practitioners to proceed with
authority and act in the 'best interest of a child'. Dilemmas can already be
detected about how to understand child abuse and develop effective child
protection measures leading to decisions that will be in the best interests of a
child.

The terms 'child abuse', 'child protection' and 'best interests of the child'
are part of an existing child protection discourse to be found in documents
offering advice, such as the brochure *What To Do If You're Worried a Child Is
Being Abused* (DoH, 2003). However, the above terms are often rather inscrut-
able if exact meanings are being sought. In many contexts the job of making
meanings from the language that is used to describe aspects of child abuse and
protection is carried out when practitioners, or students for that matter, are
facing and discussing specific concerns that relate to particular children.

Browne (2002: 50) suggests ways that 'child abuse' as a set of definitions
can be linked to Browne *et al.*'s book *Early Prediction and Prevention of Child
Abuse*, which identified three '. . . major forms of child maltreatment: physical,
sexual and psychological or emotional abuse. Each type of maltreatment is
characterised into "active" and "passive" forms' (1988: 23).

A range of definitions of child abuse is specifically described in current
government advice (see DoH, 2003: 3). However, the assessment of situations
as abusive or not may also rely on a practitioner's cultural practices, which
include personal as well as professional values and attitudes in decision making.
There is an important point being made here, since this may mean that each
practitioner approaches a specific concern with different sets of beliefs and
attitudes, making it likely that there will always be a range of differing perceptions as to what counts as abuse or ill-treatment (see Laming, 2003).

Holland (2004) discusses the advantages and disadvantages of a social
constructionist approach to assessment, arguing that it has the advantage of
potentially showing that there are several 'truths' present in any situation, so
that the emphasis on practitioners discovering the 'truth' becomes a fool's
errand. Equally, the need to find an appropriate way forward becomes less a
result of one practitioner acting from their position as 'expert' and more the

consequence of consultation between other appropriate practitioners. In this approach the views of each of the participants is carefully considered, including those of the parents/carers and the child. Holland also points out that:

> ... maintaining an awareness that much of our knowledge is cultur-ally constructed also brings about the potential for anti-oppressive practice by critically examining our own social constructions and attempting to form an understanding of others.
>
> (Holland, 2004: 3)

On the other hand, depending solely on social construction could mean that a range of social issues would tend not to be treated as part of the 'real world', but more one constructed from personal imagination and fantasy. In this situation child protection may be considered as unrepresentative of a wider set of societal problems, with real and often devastating outcomes for children and their carers.

The language presented by most child protection guidelines and manuals suggests a definitive way of understanding and grasping its complexities. This regulatory approach to child protection is often necessary for direct work with children, especially where they are considered to be at risk of being harmed and urgent action is necessary. However, the tutors through the discussion of social construction offer an opportunity for students to participate through questioning in disturbing and expanding ways of appreciating the complex manifestations that abuse takes and how this may impact on children.

Historical constructions

A brief and rather selective history is used here to introduce students to the sug-gestion that a number of influential stories have become integrated into a com-mon set of social constructions concerning the protection of young children.

A case of key historical significance in the development of insights into the construction of abuse and protection is that of Mary Ellen Wilson, an American child in the late nineteenth century who was 'rescued' from con-tinuous ill-treatment. This was achieved, according to myth, by citing animal welfare legislation because childcare legislation did not at that time exist. However, the American Humane Society offers an alternative account of the case based on reconstructed aspects of the legal proceedings, which apparently did not call on animal welfare legislation and indeed show that redress through the courts was already part of the legal system of the time:

> At that time, some jurisdictions in the United States had laws that prohibited excessive physical discipline of children. New York, in fact,

had a law that permitted the state to remove children who were neglected by their caregivers.

(http://www.americanhumane.org/site/maryellenwilson: 2)

In this account there is apparently evidence that a haphazard system for protecting some children was present. However, there was still an apparent lack of
childcare legislation with broader national considerations, and intervention
was perhaps more arbitrary than it appears to be in contemporary western
societies. In the case of Mary Ellen, she appears to be constructed as both
'vulnerable' and as 'property' that belonged to the family, a construction recognized as still relevant in contemporary society (see Reder *et al.*, 1993). These
'constructions' are extremely important for students as they help them to
recognize issues of power that may operate between adults and children in
abusive or damaging relationships.

In the American Humane Society article, a number of factors are identified as having a significant impact on Mary Ellen and the care she received.
These include macro socio-economic factors such as poverty and deprivation,
which led to her being 'looked after' because her mother, a single parent, was
unable to care for her. The connection to animal welfare appears to be rather
loose, coming about through the actions of a concerned neighbour who con-
tacted Henry Bergh, a leader of the animal humane movement in the United
States and founder of the American Society for the Prevention of Cruelty
to Animals, requesting him to intervene on Mary Ellen's behalf (Holland,
2004: 3).

Although she was only ten when the case was heard in the court, Mary
Ellen gave a statement, which was recorded in the media at the time:

> On April 10, 1874, Mary Ellen testified:
> . . . My father and mother are both dead. I don't know how old
> I am. I have no recollection of a time when I did not live with
> the Connolly's. . . . Mamma has been in the habit of whipping and
> beating me almost every day. She used to whip me with a twisted
> whip—a raw hide. The whip always left a black and blue mark on my
> body. I have now the black and blue marks on my head, which were
> made by mamma, and also a cut on the left side of my forehead,
> which was made by a pair of scissors. She struck me with the scissors
> and cut me; I have no recollection of ever having been kissed by any
> one—have never been kissed by mamma. I have never been taken on
> my mamma's lap and caressed or petted. I never dared to speak to
> anybody, because if I did I would get whipped. . . . I do not know for
> what I was whipped—mamma never said anything to me when she
> whipped me. I do not want to go back to live with mamma, because

> she beats me so. I have no recollection ever being on the street in my
> life . . .
>
> (http://www.americanhumane.org/site: 3)

The statement referred to above offers an insight to students of the ways that
Mary Ellen was able to describe her life. In class, we are able to relate that to
other children's stories such as Victoria Climbiè, a child from recent times who
was also abused but who did not survive the ordeal and indeed was not able to
make such a coherent statement as Mary Ellen. These are significant differences to reflect on when there seems much more official attention and concern about children's well-being in modern times and yet, despite this, children
are still being identified as victims of abuse.

Students explore the cases in question, discovering that in 1874 when this
came to the attention of the public there were no statutory agencies dedicated
to working solely with children in either the UK or the USA. However, the
importance of neighbours willing to act led to the court being able to act on
the child's behalf, giving Mary Ellen the opportunity to voice her concerns
publicly. This aspect of the case is worth noting, as the voice of the child,
which is nowadays considered to be essential, might nevertheless be overlooked at a number of different stages, including the point where a court
might be involved.

Students discuss how the case of Mary Ellen (who was never the subject of
any inquiry) speaks to current concerns arising from later inquiries into the
deaths of children such as Maria Colwell (see DHSS, 1974) and Victoria
Climbiè (see Laming, 2003). Students discuss in class how Maria Colwell made
it clear that she wished to remain in the care of her aunt and uncle but these
wishes were not considered to be in her 'best interests'. This view was influenced by professional practitioners, privileging the belief that most children's
emotional and social needs were generally better met if they were living with
their natural parents. Consequently, Maria was returned to live with her birth
mother where she later died at the hands of William Keppel, who was living
with Maria's mother. Victoria Climbiè's first language was French, which acted
as a barrier to her communicating her concerns whenever she came into
contact with practitioners. The construction of the child here, therefore,
is as a human being whose basic human right to have their views heard
was not recognized by either family or care agencies and who was therefore
placed in a situation that proved to be fatal. For students, discussions lead to
concerns that personal, institutional and cultural views can be cast in stone
and lead to unthinking prejudice. This set of thoughts highlights for students
the need to apply coherent assessment strategies to gain a wider range of
views, including wherever possible those of the child, to develop a way
forward.

Our students learn that following the Mary Ellen case childcare legislation was introduced and the New York Society for the Prevention for Cruelty to Children was formed. These concerns were picked up in the UK and the NSPCC was formed shortly after, with the Prevention of Cruelty to and Protection of Children Act becoming law in 1889 (see Reder *et al.*, 1993), initiating a trend that has been noticeable ever since. This trend sees child protection concerns shipped from the USA to the UK on a fairly frequent basis, and through this the USA can and often is identified as an influential partner regarding child protection matters. Further, as Reder *et al.* point out, there is a relationship between inquiry findings, legislation and professional practice:

> The 1974 inquiry report into Maria Colwell's death was soon followed by the 1975 Children Act. The Jasmine Beckford inquiry in 1985 and the Kimberley Carlile inquiry in 1987 preceded the Cleveland Inquiry (1988) . . . The 1989 Children Act followed hard on the heels of these three inquiries.
>
> (Reder *et al.* 1993: 18)

To the above can now be added the Laming Inquiry in 2003, which followed the death of Victoria Climbiè in February 2000 and which subsequently led to the green paper *Every Child Matters* in 2003 and the Children Bill (2004) (now enacted). Students are therefore able to make a clear link between the influential part that inquiries have played in informing and helping to construct legislation and professional practices that are reviewed each time concerns are given a high profile through the process of public scrutiny.

The developing construction of children and childhood in child protection contexts

So far, the discussion has highlighted how students begin to appreciate that child abuse is complex and constructed at different times by historical, social and cultural influences. In addition to this, students consider historical and contemporary ways in which practice operates and whether there is a growing tendency to view all children as vulnerable and at risk from being abused. This set of questions is considered by both tutors and students in an attempt to develop their understanding of the ways that children are depicted in contemporary society and the difficulties that exist when strong emotions for children's safety are aroused. The initial reaction from students is that there should be more ways of checking that children are safe and unlikely to be put at risk. However, Kitzinger points out that overlooking the child's ability to deal with situations for themselves may create greater vulnerability:

... the logical extension of the image of the innately passive child and the refusal to recognize children's resistance strategies is to rely totally on adult protection to prevent, or interrupt abuse ...

(Kitzinger, cited in Prout and Prout, 1997: 174)

Students are invited to discuss the above concerns and to consider the consequences for children perceived as 'innocents' in a world where childhood is characterized by anxieties about the risks that wait to ensnare them. In this scenario children are at risk all the time and therefore a requirement of diligent childcare is for parents and carers to maintain a high state of surveillance so that the child's safety can be assured. This surveillance is often directed outwards towards strangers in the community. However, as Richardson and Bacon (2001: 9) argue, '... a society where the main focus on abuse is the stranger leaves children vulnerable', thus locating the home as the most likely place where abuse is likely to happen.

However, as students begin to appreciate, assuming that the majority of abuse will take place in the home does not always prepare one for identifying who will actually be the perpetrator of any abuse. Gibbons *et al.* (1995: 27) found in their research that 'the child's injury was inflicted by female caregivers in 40% of cases; and by the male caregivers in 43%'. This is a rather surprising finding for some of the students since it appears to defy the usual stereotype of the adult male perpetrator, suggesting that females are almost as likely to ill-treat children as males.

Students are clearly able to appreciate that there are dilemmas for child protection strategies. For example, one of the key purposes of child protection is to make the world a safer place for children, yet this begs the question, 'At what cost?' Students recognize that some situations containing risk are often useful learning situations for children, but the concept of risk has become increasingly associated with unconstructive outcomes such as hazard, trouble and injury (Parton *et al.*, 1997; Douglas, 1986, 1992). Students are therefore prompted to ask whether children's lives really need to be placed under such a glare of continuous surveillance from anxious parents and carers. In addition, the gaze of professional practitioners is focused on a range of community contexts but particularly on the home as part of a process of scrutiny that may lead to intervention in an attempt to put a stop to potential child abuse. Even if this apparently sterile vision of childhood persists it begs a number of questions for students, such as who will police the care givers, whose gaze scans the world of the child for possible risk contexts, and who is to decide what constitutes risky situations? In addition to this, there are questions around the impact such a regime might have on children who are unable to have time when they are not the source of anxiety for their parents and carers.

During their studies the students are invited to discuss the power dynamics present in child protection contexts. This concern, with the child viewed at the centre of a discourse of risk, is a useful area for them to consider. They are introduced to a small selection of Foucault's writings concerning 'panopticism' through terms that have been raised throughout their studies such as surveillance and discourse. The discussion with students relating to panopticism starts by considering Bentham's prison tower, which is significant because of its powerful imagery:

> . . . one can observe from the tower, standing out precisely against the light, the small captive shadows in the cells of the periphery . . . The panoptic mechanism arranges spatial unities that make it possible to see constantly and to recognize immediately . . .
>
> (Foucault, 1975: 200)

This quote leads students into a discussion concerning being able to 'see' in the ways described by Foucault and how this seems to uncover a sense of disciplinary power present within the gaze of the watcher. In other words, applying this to child protection, whilst the child clearly starts off as the focus of concern their nature remains determined by the adult (which may be reasonable for the very young). In symbolic terms children are the 'captive shadow' being watched by concerned adults seeking to 'recognize immediately' anything that may be constructed as risky. Students appreciate that this can become restrictive as the child grows older and becomes more interested in exploring their environment as a part of the process of growing and developing. Also, surveillance could be argued to transmit a set of values between the watchers and those who are being watched that set out the norm, which in the case of child protection appears to be primarily about safety and avoiding risk.

Students discuss how this may have the unintended consequences of training children to behave in ways that are not clearly related to safety and risk avoidance but may be more to do with the adults retaining their privileged position in a hierarchy. As one student pointed out recently:

> *There is also the possibility that potential perpetrators of abuse are able to develop imaginative ways to remain undetected by learning what the limitations of the professional gaze may be and taking advantage.*

Students can appreciate that practitioner surveillance may produce more questions than answers, leading to feelings of impotence as assessment processes become more demanding and tortuous whilst at the same time less illuminative. A recent social work visitor pointed out that ironically this excess of regulation in terms of coordination of services and assessment procedures may lead to less effective child protection services for children, resulting in more rather than fewer vulnerable children.

Students perhaps reluctantly tend to conclude that it appears more than likely that the world can never be assumed to be safe. One student adding that:

> . . . the very people who are trusted to have the best interests of children at the forefront of their thinking should be treated cautiously since they may be potential child abusers.

Another student argued that:

> This in effect means that a strong sense of cynicism can develop in children, parents and practitioners as they begin to absorb the belief that no one is as they appear to be.

Students are able to make connections to the apparent difference between the times of Mary Ellen and more modern times, in that there are many more practitioners now (in addition to parents and carers) involved in scanning the world for risk, placing all children more at the centre of adult concerns than ever before with real power to intervene or not (see Laming, 2003). Students comment that the support available for Mary Ellen was clearly lamentable, but this is also mirrored in many cases in more recent times. Students, through their discussions, perceive that contemporary society through its overpowering sense of concern and anxiety felt for children may lead them to becoming more nervous and feel less safe and vulnerable despite all that is in place to protect them. As one student pointed out:

> Children and practitioners often seem unsure what to do – everything seems far more complex these days than in the days of Mary Ellen. It doesn't surprise me that practitioners are often portrayed in the media as uncertain and indecisive. They have so many considerations to take into account that it can result in uncertainty about what is a priority and lead to little action being taken with a possible life-threatening outcome for the child.

The child's views

Throughout discussions students show a keen interest to address those issues that particularly relate to children and they are aware that there have been a number of significant moments in history that have offered reference points for developing a set of informed opinions. The study of child protection inquiries (see DoH, 1991; Reder *et al.*, 1993) suggests that there have been a number of practice concerns that have not been satisfactorily managed and perhaps may never be. Students discuss how in 1974 the inquiry into the death of Maria Colwell raised questions about the weight that might be given to the child's views (her wishes were not taken into account). Subsequent legislation included the requirement for the child's views to be sought. This is an important aspect of child protection work and points out that part of the powers and duties of a children's guardian, who may have an important role in representing the child, as set out in Rule 4.11 of the Family Proceedings Rules (1991) is to advise the court:

> . . . whether the child is of sufficient understanding for any purpose including the child's refusal to submit to a medical or psychiatric examination or other assessment that the court has power to require, direct or order. In addition the guardian should advise the court of the wishes of the child in respect of any matter relevant to the proceedings, including his or her attendance at court.
>
> (Powell, 2001: 81)

As students begin to understand, the general rule tends to be that the older the child the more weight is given to their views. The duty to take the child's views into account arises from the Gillick v West Norfolk and Wisbech Area Health Authority case in 1986:

> . . . where the House of Lords recognized that a child under the age of sixteen could give valid consent to medical treatment without parental consent or knowledge provided she or he was of sufficient age and understanding.
>
> (Powell, 2001: 18)

It seems to students in discussing this that in effect these rights also contain what may be constructed as a test that must be considered by practitioners, with the child needing to satisfy whether their age and level of understanding are adequate to give their consent. This suggests that there are likely to be variations amongst guardians and other practitioners about the children they have contact with and their ability to convincingly meet such a test. To many students this appears to reveal a further manifestation of the adult world's way of constructing children as needy, vulnerable and inarticulate.

Students often reflect at this juncture on the case of Mary Ellen, who was invited to give her account of the treatment that she received at the hands of Mary Connolly. The questions that may be raised by students relate to whether this was an arbitrary decision by the court and they contemplate how they might have acted if she had denied that she had been ill-treated.

Students are interested to discover that the cases that have been referred to throughout their studies all appear to have concerns that relate to inadequate communication. This, as students point out, has meant on occasions that children have been left unsupported because of deficiencies in the ability of different agencies to share concerns. In addition, students are aware of the failure to take the child's views into consideration in the case of Maria Colwell, where the emphasis was placed on Maria living with her birth family (even though she was clearly happy to be brought up as a looked after child and said so) (see Reder *et al.*, 1993).

The discussion throughout this chapter has emphasized the complex nature of child abuse and the dilemmas present at virtually every point, particularly when child protection strategies are being developed. For students it is important to be alert in order to recognize that there are moments for all practitioners when intervention is necessary, perhaps even vital, and that some children sometimes show signs that are clearer to identify than at other times. Throughout their studies, students develop more confidence in their ability to question orthodox arguments and, whilst not leading them to 'truth', an enquiring attitude is often an asset to developing understanding and insight.

References

Browne, K. (2002) 'Child abuse: defining, understanding and intervening', in K. Wilson and A. James (eds) *The Child Protection Handbook* (2nd edn). Edinburgh, London and New York: Bailliere Tindall.

Browne, K., Davies, C. and Stratton, P. (1988) *Early Prediction and Prevention of Child Abuse*. Chichester and New York: John Wiley and Sons.

Children Bill [2004]. London: The Stationery Office Ltd.

Culpitt, I. (1999) *Social Policy and Risk*. London: Sage.

Department of Health (1991) *Child Abuse: a Study of Inquiry Reports 1980–1989*. London: HMSO.

Department of Health (2003) *What To Do If You're Worried a Child Is Being Abused*. London: Department of Health.

Department of Health and Social Security (1974) *Report of the Committee of Inquiry into the Care and Supervision Provided in Relation to Maria Colwell*. London: HMSO.

Douglas, M. (1986) *Risk Acceptability According to the Social Sciences*. London: Routledge and Kegan Paul.

Douglas, M. (1992) *Risk and Blame: Essays in Cultural Theory*. London: Routledge.

Foucault, M. (1975) *Discipline and Punish: the Birth of the Prison*. Penguin: London.

Gergen, K. J. (1999) *An Invitation to Social Construction*. London: Sage.

Gibbons, J., Gallagher, B., Bell, C. and Gordon, D. (1995) *Development After Physical Abuse in Early Childhood: Studies in Child Protection*. London: HMSO.

Holland, S. (2004) *Child and Family Assessment in Social Work Practice*. London: Sage.

Kitzinger, J. (1997) 'Who are you kidding?', in A. Prout and A. Prout (eds) *Constructing and Reconstructing Childhood*. London: Falmer.

Lord Laming (2003) *The Victoria Climbie Inquiry*. London: HMSO.

Parton, N., Thorpe, D. and Wattam, C. (1997) *Child Protection: Risk and the Moral Order*. Basingstoke: Macmillan.

Powell, R. (2001) *Child Law. A Guide for Courts and Practitioners*. Winchester: Waterside Press.

Prout, A. and Prout, A. (1997) *Constructing and Reconstructing Childhood* (2nd edn). London and Washington: Falmer Press.

Reder, P., Duncan, S. and Gray, M. (1993) *Beyond Blame; Child Abuse Tragedies Revisited*. London: Routledge.

Richardson, S. and Bacon, H. (2001) *Creative Responses to Child Sexual Abuse: Challenges and Dilemmas*. London and Philadelphia: Jessica Kingsley Publishers.

The Real Story of Mary Ellen Wilson: http://www.americanhumane.org/site (2004).

10 Integration, inclusion and diversity

Rosemary Boys

Introduction

Society has always had issues with the ways in which children who are perceived to be educationally and physically different should be educated. Even in the twenty-first century there is still a lack of consensus between professionals, parents and lobby groups. The continuing evolution of society's recognition of the right of all children to participate fully in society and be included in mainstream education has affected legislation, educational requirements and practice. Despite this, however, much of the prejudice and marginalization of children with special educational needs (SEN) continues. In some instances this is based on lack of awareness, whilst in others it is the consequence of underfunding and inadequate resources.

For those involved with the recognition and implementation of the rights of children with SEN, their inclusion into mainstream education is identified as a precursor for their effective inclusion in mainstream society. As yet the provision of 'wrap around care', which would ensure that all children with SEN have prompt access to adequate and appropriate multiprofessional support, is in its infancy. For this reason the focus of this chapter is on the development and role of inclusive schooling. Within the educational context the term 'inclusion' is one that embraces a wide range of diverse needs. Mittler states that:

> Inclusion implies a radical reform of a school in terms of curriculum, assessment, pedagogy and grouping of pupils. It is based on a value system that welcomes and celebrates diversity arising from gender, nationality, race language of origin, social background, level of educational achievement or disability.
>
> (Mittler, 2001: 10)

Within this chapter we will be addressing inclusion with reference to Mittler's final categories – educational achievement and disability – recognizing that the concept and practices of inclusive education can provide a secure and effective social and learning context for all children. We will explore the ways in which student engagement with some of the difficult ideas embedded within the topic of children with SEN is encouraged and the struggles we initiate in order to provoke further contemplation.

The chapter begins by examining the influence of international human rights legislation on our national recognition of the rights of children with SEN. Contemporary understandings of the term SEN will then be discussed. Specifically, the definition introduced with the Education Act (1996), which is the definition presently used in all schools and settings, will be evaluated. The historical development of our present provision will then be discussed. This begins with a brief examination of initial legislation that affected children with SEN, introduced at the end of the nineteenth century, before proceeding to examine the progression towards current legislation, practices and changes in society's attitudes towards children with SEN. The chapter concludes by considering current advancements towards inclusion and reviewing some of the issues that still need to be addressed.

International influences and the rights of the child with SEN

In November 1989 the UN Convention on the Rights of the Child (UNCRC) affirmed the right of all children to equal education without discrimination within the mainstream education system. The ratification of this Convention has led to the introduction of legislation that should have a profound impact on the educational rights of children with SEN in England and Wales. The legislation seeks to recognize their rights by reforming educational practice from the integration of *some* of the children with SEN into mainstream education, to the provision of an educational system that enables *all* children with SEN to be taught through mainstream, inclusive education.

In the early stages of their studies, students have explored some of the intricacies around children's rights in relation to children with SEN. They have begun to contemplate the complexities embedded within legislation. 'The Rights of the Child' has afforded them opportunities to consider how the UNCRC can be interpreted in a range of contexts. At this point, this chapter draws from, builds on and broadens these initial contemplations in a way which enables what we hope to be a thoughtful, considered and informed approach to SEN legislation.

The international recognition of the rights of all children was further advanced in June 1994 by the Salamanca Statement of the UNCRC World Conference on Special Needs Education: Access and Quality. The government's adoption of the Salamanca Statement in 1997 led to the green paper *Excellence for all Children*, which sought to confirm its commitment to the principles of the Statement. However, the statement that '. . . we shall promote the inclusion of children with SEN within mainstream schooling wherever possible' (DfEE, 1997) indicates that there is recognition that it is not considered desirable or appropriate for all children with SEN to be included.

The journey of mainstream schools from the integration of some children towards the inclusion of all has been long and difficult. The changes required have enormous implications not only for our schools and educational system, but also for the ways in which they are challenging society's perceptions of SEN and those who have them. Many in our society maintain a view of SEN and disability that is located within a 'medical' model. Here, it is the affected person who is seen as a 'problem', rather than the social and physical barriers that hinder their access and inclusion into society. To upholders of this model it is therefore acceptable that children with SEN are educated in segregated communities because mainstream schools are considered to be unable to cater for their needs. The medical model of 'integration' and the associated acceptability of segregation have become juxtaposed with a notion of 'inclusion'. The premise of inclusion is based on a 'social' model of disability in which segregation is unacceptable and the problems are perceived to lie with schools and their absence of facilities and support. Within the social model of disability all children are valued as individuals and their strengths as well as their needs are recognized. This model welcomes diversity and perceives education to be a social and interactive process that encourages the eventual establishment of an inclusive society.

At present, however, such diversity is not always valued. Some children are still socially stigmatized and demonized, particularly those with social, emotional and behavioural complexities. For many professionals positively involved in the inclusion process, it is felt that effective social integration and positive acceptance are basic to effective inclusion. For effective change to take place, consideration must be given to society's perception of children with SEN, as well as recognition of their human rights and their educational needs.

To avoid students digesting legislative, rhetorical and ideological shifts as a straightforward and uncomplicated progression towards a more wholesome and in effect 'better' society, tutors create hesitancies and conceptual spaces for them to intervene, pose questions, problematize and engage more critically with ideas. We try to stimulate students' engagement with issues around these shifts in a range of ways, which includes drawing from their experiences across their studies. An example here would be their growing awareness of multiprofessional perspectives and the role such multiprofessional collaboration might have upon inclusive practices. Change within the SEN landscape has broader implications for educational decision makers. These include such practical issues as adequate and appropriate staffing of mainstream schools, the training of teachers and support staff, and the access to practitioners from other agencies supporting children with SEN into mainstream schools. The design of school buildings and furniture still needs to be considered, as well as the access and availability of specific resources.

The complex issues around multiprofessional working that recognize the different approaches, languages, ideologies and models that disciplines bring to each case conference or particular experience of any one child has become increasingly important if training with, and access to, a range of practitioners is to work in an enabling way. We return students to the multiplicity of meanings captured within the term 'multiprofessional' and focus here upon the term as the development of a creative interface of services in the interests of the young child with SEN. Discussions within the classroom have included evolving partnerships between parents/carers, teachers, social workers, educational psychologists, speech and language therapists, physiotherapists and paediatricians. It was recognized that although we need to continue to work towards developing a common framework and language with which to talk about and understand the child's and professional's experiences, the very different expertise and particular skills of each professional has the potential to be an enriching contribution to the totality of partnership work. Over time it was deemed possible for professionals to become more sensitized to each other's 'languages' and professional identities, that initially may seem disparate, and as connections and relationships emerge, productive support and enabling systems for each child may be facilitated. As a result of the time invested in talking about young children and SEN, the symbiotic learning that could potentially take place could serve not only to enhance multiprofessional understandings about children, their rights and needs, but also to enrich professionally entrenched visions, opening up different ways to 'read' events and behaviours, ways to understand and be with children. It is perceived that the byproduct of this mutual learning could have a more diverse influence upon the way different professionals approach many aspects of their work. All of these changes are costly and time consuming but essential if all children are to be educated together successfully.

Defining the term 'special educational needs'

So what exactly do we mean by special educational needs (SEN)? Defining the term is difficult and depends upon one's perceptions and experiences. Professionals who work with children with SEN usually give definitions with evidence of a strong commitment to children's rights and needs. They perceive children as individuals and would support Wilson's assertion that 'it is critically important to recognize that a child with a disability is first a young child who is more like his or her typically developing peers than different' (1999:

10). Consider the definition used in the SEN Code of Practice (2001). This document provides the mandatory framework for 'effective school-based support' for children with SEN in England and Wales:

> A child has a special educational need if he or she has a learning difficulty, which calls for special educational provision to be made for him or her.
>   A child has a learning difficulty if he or she:
>
> (a) has a significantly greater difficulty learning than the majority of children of the same age
> (b) has a disability which either prevents or hinders the child from making use of education facilities of a kind provided for children of the same age in schools within the area of the local education authority
> (c) is under five and falls within the definition at (a) or (b) above or would do if special educational provision was not made for the child. (p. 6)
>
> Children must not be regarded as having a learning difficulty solely because the language or form of language of their home is different from the language in which they will be taught.
>   Special educational provision means:
>
> (a) for children of two or over, educational provision which is additional to, or otherwise different from, the educational provision made generally for children of their age in schools maintained by the LEA (Local Education Authority), other than special schools, in the area
> (b) for children under two, educational provision of any kind.
>
> (Section 312: Education Act 1996)

As well as sensory and physical disabilities this definition is based upon academic, social and behavioural non-achievement, and comparison with capable peers. The Code of Practice recognizes some elements of causation and also includes the following definitions from the Children Act (1989) and the Disability Discrimination Act (1995):

> A child is disabled if he is blind, deaf or dumb or suffers from a mental disorder of any kind or is substantially and permanently handicapped by illness, injury or congenital deformity or such other disability as may be prescribed.
>
> (Section 17 (11), Children Act 1989)

A person has a disability for the purposes of the Act if he has a physical
or mental impairment, which has a substantial and long-term adverse
effect on his ability to carry out normal day- to day activities.

(Section 1 (1), Disability Discrimination Act 1995)

Many professionals believe that the categories of children considered to have
SEN are too narrow and should be more inclusive. The definition from the
Education Act 1996 used in the Code of Practice does not recognize special
educational needs (SEN) that arise as a consequence of a child's background,
from them having English as a second language or being gifted and talented
(Clark and Callow, 2002). Each of these can have implications for learning,
even though the situation might be transitory.

The historical changes in perception and practice

When examining with students the ways in which perceptions and practice
have changed towards the education of children with SEN, it is important that
the legal and historical contexts influencing their education are considered.
We explore whether changes demanded by legislation result in the gradual
change in society's perceptions of children with SEN, or conversely, that it is
through changes in society's perceptions for the recognition and acceptance
of, and provision made for, diversity and differentiation that changes in the
legislation have been made. Monk argues that the law relating to children
provides a code of behaviour for society, but that it should be viewed as 'a
continually shifting cultural and social text' (2004: 161). This is supported by
Alcott (2002), who recognizes that as attitudes change, so does legislation. As
the legislation most relevant to the educational needs of children with SEN is
examined, students are asked to consider who promoted the legislation and
how children with SEN benefited from it. It also needs to be acknowledged
that whilst some legislation has obviously been based upon good intentions,
without the funding to implement change there can rarely be a positive
impact on practice.

Within this chapter we feel it is important to explore the historical background of SEN as this is what the students would themselves experience in
order to support and stimulate a re-examination of current legislation, contemporary practices and their own values and beliefs in relation to children
with SEN.

Recognition of the need to consider children with SEN first arose at the
end of the nineteenth century with the introduction of compulsory education.
As Britain gained ascendancy in manufacturing and industry, the utilitarian
need for a literate and numerate workforce was acknowledged. The Education
Act of 1870 introduced the first compulsory school attendance laws. Although

the principle of education for all was the ideal, the lack of teachers and places for all children led to the segregation of those considered idiots, imbeciles, backward and feeble minded. Some children were placed in special schools or classes, a situation that persisted well into the twentieth century.

The British Mental Deficiency Act (1913) exacerbated the stigmatization of children with SEN by giving descriptive definitions to the labels used to categorize them. Those termed to be idiots were considered so defective that they '. . . could not guard themselves against common physical danger' (1913: 12–14). Imbeciles were '. . . defective to the degree that they could not manage their own affairs' (1913: 12–14). Those considered to be feeble minded (or morons) were those '. . . who needed supervision for their own protection, and the protection of others' (1913: 12–14), whilst those who were termed as backwards were '. . . unable to learn as quickly as their peers' (1913: 12–14) and were thought to disrupt the learning of 'normal' children. Many children were permanently institutionalized, often in what were termed mental asylums.

This time also saw the rise of the Eugenics movement. This powerful group, which included many leading psychologists, was perceived to have provided a theoretical rationale for the fixed endowment of intelligence. In his publication, *The Fight for Our National Intelligence* (1937), Catterell argued that mentally defective mothers would give birth to defective children, which would lead to the degeneracy of the British race. Consequently, those considered to be mentally defective were segregated and incarcerated in single-sex institutions where their lives were controlled and their sexuality denied them. There were no clear or specific criteria for the selection. Tilstone argues that '. . . (t)his segregation of mentally defective adults and their children as a possible danger to society largely contributed to the stigma often attached to special schools today' (1991: 5).

With the development of the branch of psychology called defectology and its use of psychometric testing in the early twentieth century, the former descriptive labels were given a scientific legitimacy. The classification of the degree of what was termed retardation in early IQ tests was based on non-standardized performance tests. These were therefore little more scientific than the descriptive terms used following the 1913 Act. According to Terman (1917) in the original scale, the following IQ descriptions were formulated:

- Dull (personality classified as deficient)   IQ 80–100
- Backwards (sometimes classified as deficient)   IQ 70–80
- Morons (feeble minded)   IQ 50–70
- Imbecile   IQ 20–50
- Idiot   IQ–20

Whilst the use of such labels seems primitive and medieval, these terms continued to be used professionally by psychologists throughout the 1960s and

1970s. In his textbook for the training of psychologists, Lundin states that '. . . although some objections have been levied against a classification system based in part on a psychometric criterion, it has been in use for many years and the test of time has shown its usefulness' (1965: 179).

It should be remembered that children with physical disabilities were also segregated at this time and that accommodating schools were usually residential and often termed as schools for 'crippled' or 'spastic' children. These terms, like those for children with intellectual and learning needs, are still part of our lexicon, though they are rarely used other than as disparaging terms. Children with physical disabilities were virtually invisible, and for most their segregation was not only from mainstream schools, but also from mainstream society.

However, during the 1960s and 1970s innovative changes in the education of children with SEN were beginning. This was a time when perceptions about children, childhood and teaching practice were being seriously questioned and challenged. Both enlightened educators and the parents of children with SEN were beginning to seek recognition of educational rights for all children, favouring the integration of all children into mainstream education. The long-held concept of some children being ineducable was contested, and innovative teachers such as Stevens were able to give evidence from their own practice 'that even children with severe learning difficulties were educable with stimulating teaching, and well trained, committed teachers' (1971). Two-year training courses were begun through the Training Council for Teachers of the Mentally Handicapped in 1964. These courses recognized the value of holistic education for children with SEN and placed emphasis on their social, emotional and intellectual development. The first innovative moves towards multidisciplinary practice also began at this time, and students are encouraged to continue to build upon their developing awareness of multiprofessional work in order to contextualize this shift.

It is argued that the real changes in what are now considered appropriate policy and practice in relation to children with SEN began with the publication of the Warnock Committee Report in 1978 (Hegarty and Alur, 2002; Jones, 2004) and the subsequent Education Act (1981), which was supposed to support the Warnock recommendations. For the first time the concept of integration was being discussed openly and a means of implementation was being considered. The Warnock Report suggested three forms of integration – locational, social and functional. Locational integration included special units or classes in a mainstream school, or a special school on the same site as a mainstream school. Social integration would occur alongside locational inclusion, where social interchange could take place between children with SEN and those in the mainstream school. Functional inclusion would involve children with SEN joining their mainstream peers in mainstream classes on a full- or part-time basis. The Warnock Committee had argued that:

> . . . all schools should have the responsibility to identify and meet pupils' needs, and that all children with Special Educational Needs should be educated alongside their peers as long as their needs could be met and it is practicable to do so.
>
> (DES, 1978: 16)

It estimated that 20 per cent of children might have special educational needs (SEN) at some time during their schooling, including children not previously considered to have SEN.

Both the Warnock Report and the 1981 Act recognized the need to remove the negative categorization of children with SEN. They therefore dispensed with the psychometric labels and gave official recognition to the more flexible concept of special educational needs (SEN). Whilst many of those working with children with SEN saw this as an opportunity to move away from stigmatizing labels, this change also had its critics. Many psychologists maintained that the definition was vague and imprecise (Adams, 1986), whilst sociologists Lewis and Vulliamy (1980) argued that the definition was both methodologically and theoretically misguided as it neglected the relevance and importance of social factors in the creation of learning difficulties.

For the first time the role of parents as partners in the education of children with SEN was recognized. The Warnock Report states that 'the successful education of children with special needs is dependent on the full involvement of their parents . . . Unless parents are seen as equal partners in the education process the purpose of our report will be frustrated' (1978: 9.1). This aspect of the 1981 Act gave parents the right to share in the decisions made concerning their children for the first time.

Whilst the recommendations made by the 1981 Education Act upheld the principle of ending segregation, it should be pointed out that this Act went through parliament with no financial memorandum attached. Consequently, there was no allocation of additional funding to local education authorities. The absence of funding raised concerns that government support for the education of children with SEN was rhetoric rather than positive commitment. The practical consequence of this lack of funding was that vulnerable children with SEN were placed in mainstream schools with low staffing ratios and without specialist teachers or an appropriate curriculum, buildings or equipment. The unplanned, under-resourced integration of children with SEN into already large classes was frequently met with hostility by overburdened teachers who felt they lacked the training, resources and support to educate all children, and by parents who were aware that the quality of education their children were receiving was inadequate and inappropriate. The consequences for most of the children with SEN themselves included placement in a totally inappropriate learning environment in which many were subjected to social isolation and bullying.

The newly introduced assessment process that was supposed to provide all children in mainstream education with assessment, and access to the support and help they required, was available only to the most needy of children. These were the two to four per cent of children who received a Statement of Special Educational Needs. The choice for many parents of children with SEN was segregation in a special school, if these had not been closed, or inclusion in an inappropriate learning environment that frequently resented their presence. Consequently during this period, parents began to organize themselves into groups. Some groups were for mutual support, whilst others became lobby groups that questioned and challenged their children's lack of educational and social rights.

Is the 'same' provision the appropriate provision?

The students are asked to contemplate whether the notion of 'same' encapsulates or addresses equality of opportunity; the right of the child to appropriate educational experiences and differentiated support; and whether or not an individual's needs can be effectively met within a context of 'sameness'. As tutors, we offer the students a number of ideas to explore in the light of this question. Within the present educational context most educators recognize that all children have the right to be included, some even arguing that all special schools should be closed (CSIE, 2002). However, there still needs to be consideration of the desires and requirements of children with SEN and their parents/carers. As well as children's rights, the effective education of all children must be considered (Lindsay, 2003), as must the provision of adequate care and support (Low, 2001). This is confirmed in article 3 of the UN Convention on the Rights of the Child, which states that '... the best interests of the child shall be a primary consideration' (1989: 17) in decisions that are made to include individual children with SEN. For many children and their parents/carers, the security and specialist teaching available in a special school might be considered a more appropriate option than a mainstream school.

Both of the Education Acts (1988 and 1993) that gave schools the National Curriculum state that all children have the right to a 'broad, balanced, relevant and differentiated curriculum'. Whilst few would argue with such aspirations the same problems that blighted the Education Acts of 1870 and 1981 still exist – the problems of implementation, the appropriateness of the learning context and social awareness. The National Curriculum (1999) identifies three principles for inclusion with reference to planning and teaching. These are:

- setting suitable learning challenges;
- responding to pupils' diverse learning needs;

- overcoming potential barriers to learning and assessment for individuals and groups of pupils.

Whilst some children with SEN are able to access the same programmes of study as their classmates, some may need to be taught from earlier key stages that are more appropriate to their abilities. For pupils whose attainment falls significantly below that of their peers, resources are available for teachers that provide guidance on planning. This requires planning a much greater degree of differentiation for lessons, and setting suitable learning challenges can be difficult for teachers with little or no training in special education.

For many schools the impact of included children with learning disabilities on test results can cause concern. League tables of schools' academic performance have encouraged comparisons between schools. As many parents still assume that high academic results are the best indicator of a successful school, the inclusion of children with SEN is often resisted.

To respond to children's diverse needs teachers must recognize and address all children's social and emotional requirements. This includes assuring that all children within a class are aware of each other's needs, strengths and experiences. Whilst schools outlaw the use of the many derogatory labels formerly used to identify children with SEN, many are still used within the current vernacular. Other new but equally insulting words are also evident as a result of the diagnosis of newly recognized disorders (for example, adders – children with Attention Deficit Disorder; scopes – children with cerebral palsy). These indicate that despite current legislation, attitudes towards children with SEN can still be negative and cruel. We therefore ponder with students whether, despite legislative and ideological shifts, the underpinning attitudes and subsequent emerging practices suggest a hierarchical imposition that may lack multiprofessional awareness, practical and philosophical commitment from those being required to implement the changes.

With the inception of the Children Bill (2004), schools are now expected to have access and basic facilities for pupils who have physical and sensory disabilities, many of whom do not have learning disabilities. For children with physical and sensory disabilities the provision of appropriate equipment and resources can support their successful inclusion. This Bill also recognizes the need for children to have access to other professional attention and promotes the concept of schools that accommodate these professionals, such as speech and language therapists, educational psychologists and social workers.

For many schools and for students alike, the most difficult children to include are those with social, emotional and behavioural disorders, who are perceived to have the capacity to disrupt classes and prevent other children learning and thriving. Some children displaying challenging behaviour are often identified as being 'naughty' when they actually have disorders such as autism. It is therefore important that early assessment is available to all children who give cause for concern. Such identification is increasingly evident through the increased provision of what is regarded as 'good quality' early childhood education, and community and family based initiatives as the Sure Start programme. There is a wealth of slippery and ambiguous ideas to unpack with students here and tutors use these interesting starting points to debate notions around the power of terminology and labelling; the complexities inherent within assessment and identification; and the amorphous monster that is 'good quality early childhood education'. Could we ever rest assured that, with what is deemed 'accurate' early assessment and appropriate support and resources, most children can be successfully included into mainstream schools? This provision is expensive, it requires coordination, an increase in those providing multiprofessional support, an increase in teacher education in SEN and community awareness. In addition, it pre-supposes an understanding that those professionals undertaking a commitment to inclusion have a grounded belief that all children have a right and entitlement to effective, rather than tokenistic or blasé inclusive practices.

There also needs to be consideration for those children with SEN for whom inclusion might be considered inappropriate and how we, as professionals, arrive at that decision. This includes those who do not want to be included in a mainstream school, those requiring a high level of individual personal and physical care, and those whose inclusion would be to the detriment of their peers. As stated previously, the DfEE has recognized that inclusion into mainstream schools should not be considered desirable or appropriate for all children with SEN. It could be argued that such a statement gives balance and maintains an element of choice in the issue of inclusion. It could also be argued that such a statement acts as a get-out clause for the DfEE. Personal stances towards this can only be made in the light of evidence, experience and ongoing debate.

References

Adams, F. (1986) *Special Education*. Essex: Longman.

Alcott, M. (2002) *An Introduction to Children with SEN*. London: Hodder and Stoughton.

Catterell, R. B. (1937) *The Fight for Our National Intelligence*. London: Houghton.

Centre for Studies on Inclusive Education (2002) *The Right to Belong to the Mainstream*. Bristol: CSIE.

Children Act (1989) (c.41) London: The Stationery Office Ltd.

Children Bill [HL] (2004) London: The Stationery Office Ltd.

Clark, C. and Callow, R. (2002) *Educating the Gifted and Talented*. London: A NACE/Fulton Publication.

Dale, P. (2003) The implementation of the 1913 Mental Deficiency Act, *Social History of Medicine*, 16(3): 403–418.

Department of Education and Science (1978) *Special educational needs: Report of the committee of enquiry into the education of handicapped children and young people* (The Warnock Report). London: HMSO.

DfEE (1997) *Excellence for all Children*. London: DfEE.

DfES (2001) *Special Educational Needs: Code of Practice*. London: DfES.

Disability Discrimination Act (1995) (c.50) London: The Stationery Office Ltd.

Education Act (1981) London: HMSO.

Education Reform Act (1988) London: HMSO.

Education Act (1993) London: HMSO.

Education Act (1996) London: HMSO.

Hegarty, S. and Alur, M. (2002) *Education and Children with Special Needs: From Segregation to Inclusion*. London: Sage Publications.

Jones, A. J. (2004) *Supporting Inclusion in the Early Years*. Maidenhead: Open University Press.

Lewis, I. and Vulliamy, G. (1980) Warnock or Warlock? The sorcery of definitions: the limitation on the report on special education, *Educational Review*, 32: 3–10.

Lindsay, G. (2003) Inclusive education: a critical perspective, *British Journal of Special Education*, 30: 3–12.

Low, C. (2001) *Have disability rights gone too far?* City Insights Lecture, 3rd April 2001. London: City University.

Lundin, R. W. (1965) *The Principles of Psychopathology*. Columbus, Ohio: Charles E. Merrill Books Inc.

Mittler, P. (2001) *Working Towards Inclusive Education*. London: David Fulton Publishers.

Monk, D. (2004) 'Childhood and the law: in whose best interests?', in M. L. Kehily (ed.) *An Introduction to Childhood Studies*. Maidenhead: Open University Press.

Stevens, M. (1971) *The Educational Needs of Severely Subnormal Children*. London: Edward Arnold.

Terman, L. M. (1917) *The Measurement of Intelligence*. New York: Houghton Mifflin Company.

Tilstone, C. (1991) *Teaching Pupils with Severe Learning Difficulties: Practical Approaches*. London: David Fulton Publishers.

United Nations (1989) *The United Nations Convention on the Rights of the Child*. Geneva: United Nations.

Wilson, R. A. (1999) *Special Education in the Early Years*. London: Routledge.

Wilson, R. (1995) 'South and north: special educational provision in New Zealand, Britain and the United States', in P. Potts, F. Armstrong and M. Masterton (eds) *National and International Contexts*. London: Routledge.

11 Health in childhood

Caroline Bradbury-Jones and Jane Bates

Introduction

In this chapter we seek to provide an insight into the issues that we explore with students to facilitate their understanding of health in childhood. We examine the concept of health with particular reference to children's perceptions, and the determinants of health are explored in relation to two significant health issues for children in contemporary society: poverty and obesity. We share our experience of teaching undergraduate students, and their narratives are utilized in an attempt to capture the essence of our classroom discussions.

Our primary concern is for students to focus on children's 'health' rather than on childhood 'disease' or 'illness', and in so doing we aim to dispel the perpetual dominance of the negative model of health. Despite the attempts of those concerned with health promotion to promote a holistic view of health, the notion of health as the 'absence of disease' and measurement of health in terms of 'not being ill' still reflect the most dominant views of health held in western society. In attempting to define health, students will often frame their response in language that supports the 'absence of disease' paradigm. For example, they tend to attribute their own 'healthiness' to not having a cold or the flu and will rarely comment on their mental or social well-being.

On the face of it, health should be a rather simple concept to explore; after all, we all experience it, either for better or for worse. In other words, at any point in our lives, most of us are able to express the state of our own health in terms of whether we are healthy or unhealthy. Some prefer to conceptualize this as being 'more or less' healthy (Iphofen, 2003). There is an underlying complexity in attempting to define health, however, and once we start to examine the concept we discover that it is rather nebulous and ambiguous. The word 'health' actually derives from the old English word *haelo* meaning 'whole' or 'healthy' and in its earliest definitions simply meant the absence of disease. In 1948 the World Health Organization (WHO) published what has become the most widely accepted definition, describing health as a 'state of complete physical, mental, and social well-being and not merely the absence of disease' (WHO, 1948). This definition is sometimes criticized as being too idealistic, on the basis that a complete state of health is unachievable, and has therefore been modified to encompass the notion of health as a resource for living rather than an end in itself. In some definitions there is also an acknowledgement of the environment as a determinant of health (WHO, 1984).

Our perspective of the healthy child acknowledges the WHO's perspective but can also be extended to encompass the philosophy of health that underpins *Birth to Three Matters* (DfES and Sure Start, 2002). Here a healthy child is defined in terms of their emotional well-being, their growth and development, their safety and their ability to be involved in making healthy choices. We suggest that adopting this approach to conceptualizing children's health enables a move away from the reductionist, developmental stages focus that has been popular among child health promoters for too long.

With respect to 'making healthy choices', it is the voice of the child that particularly concerns us because children, especially very young children, are often unable to express their views or make choices about their health and thus are reliant on others to do this for them. A questioning of the extent to which children are actually engaged in decision making in relation to their health is fundamental to our classroom discussions. We feel, as Hooton (2000) suggests, that it is only through developing an understanding of how children view their own health that we can find ways to empower them to take more responsibility for it.

One of the notions that we aim to dispel in our exploration of children's views about health is one that has dominated research in the past – that is, that the child is an incompetent person or an immature adult (Pridmore and Bendelow, 1995). Foley *et al.* (2001) argue that a transition towards recognizing children as 'knowers' is significant. This transition involves an acknowledgement that children are not merely passive recipients of knowledge in relation to their health and bodies, but are also able to generate knowledge in relation to their own health. The significance lies in the fact that if not recognized, children become mere objects rather than active participants in relation to their health. It seems reasonable to accept, on the one hand, that children are relatively dependent on adults for some things, but there is a need, on the other hand, to resist the argument that dependency equals passivity (Alanen, 1994, cited in Foley, 2001). It is important for students to appreciate that children even as young as six do actually hold quite well-defined views about health and illness (Hooton, 2000). It is equally important for them to recognize that to achieve a child-centred, empowering approach to health issues, children's ideas and beliefs must be respected and acted upon.

Children's views about health appear to develop in ways that mirror Piaget's model of concept development (Eiser, 1991) and are mediated not only by age but also by personal experiences and culture. To encourage an appreciation of the significance of the above, children's drawings and writings are utilized as a resource within the classroom. Students are encouraged to explore the difference that a variable such as age can make to children's perceptions. For example, drawings by a group of six and seven year olds (Hooton, 2000) are used to demonstrate how young children will invariably perceive a healthy person as young, sporty and active and an unhealthy person as elderly, male and in need of a walking stick. Drawings by young children of unhealthy people are often accompanied by representations of pools of sick, which may relate to the children's most vivid recollection of their own illness.

Research with older children reveals that they have an increased knowledge of many determinants of health, including nutrition, exercise and smoking (Hooton, 2000). Older children are also able to recognize the contribution that they themselves make, either positively or negatively, to their own physical health and will often link their health status to diet and exercise. The majority of children will usually describe their health as 'good' or 'fairly good' (Brannen and Storey, 1996) and may find it easier to recognize ill-heath in others rather than in themselves.

Lay beliefs also appear significant in constructing children's perceptions of health. Through the normal process of socialization, children begin to learn the 'causes and cures' of illnesses from those around them. Most students are able to draw on recollections of the lay perceptions that they 'learnt' in childhood. Their narratives seem to reflect the significance of how embedded such notions as not to go out with wet hair, or having to wear a vest, lest they 'catch a cold' can become (Richman, 2003). A consequence of such lay views within childhood is that young children may perceive illness as a punishment for doing something wrong and see cures like 'rubbing your knee better' or putting ointment on a cut as almost magical. As children get older, however, they start to see illness as being a result of contagion and by the age of 11 are conversant with germ theory and the medical model of health.

Whilst searching for our ultimate definition of health we have to be mindful that health is a state of being that is subject to wide, individual, social and cultural interpretation and results from the interplay between individual perceptions and social influences. It is essential therefore that within our discourse we do not neglect to place the wider determinants of health as the central tenet. Our classroom discussions in relation to children's health are based therefore not only around perceptions of health, but importantly on an exploration of the intricate relationships between meanings of health, experiences, values and social circumstances. These would include: individualized lifestyle factors; social and community influences; living and working conditions; and general socio-economic, cultural and environmental conditions (cf. Dahlgren and Whitehead, 1991). Such a useful model allows us, on the one hand, to explore the multiplicity of determinants on children's health by treating them almost as discrete entities. On the other hand, it permits us to emphasize that these determinants are in fact inextricably linked, allowing us to espouse a holistic paradigm.

The scope for exploring the determinants of children's health is so extensive that for the purpose of this chapter we have chosen to demonstrate how the model can be applied to just one significant health issue: obesity. However, we feel that there is no health issue in childhood, even one as important as obesity, that can be divorced from the issue of poverty and the resultant inequalities in health. It is for this reason that for each determinant that we discuss within this chapter, consideration will be given to the enduring problem of inequality in children's health.

Obesity has increased, even among children (Wanless, 2003), and globally has reached almost epidemic proportions. The extent of obesity worldwide is such that the WHO has coined the phrase 'globesity' to highlight the problem (WHO, 2003). Similarly, the House of Commons Health Committee (2004) has highlighted the fact that we have a generation growing up in an 'obesogenic' environment, with one in five boys and one in four girls either overweight or obese. It must surely be an issue of national concern that these figures represent a sharp increase from those in 2002, where one in 20 boys (5.5 per cent) and about one in 15 girls (7.2 per cent) were obese (House of Commons Health Committee, 2004). The consequences of this are far reaching in that it is possibly the first time that the life expectancy of an entire generation will be reduced and some children will die before their parents due to obesity in childhood (House of Commons Health Committee, 2004).

In exploring the issue of childhood obesity with students, an appropriate starting point in relationship to the aforementioned model is to consider the fixed determinants of age, sex and constitutional factors. Although clinical obesity – that is, obesity associated with disease – is still comparatively rare, obesity due to other factors has more than trebled in the last two decades (House of Commons Health Committee, 2004). The most significant predisposition for children appears to relate to the health status of their parents. Children have an 80 per cent risk of becoming obese if both parents are overweight and a 40 per cent risk if one parent is overweight. The risk reduces considerably to only 20 per cent if neither parent is obese (Cheung and Richmond, 1995).

Students are surprised by the implications of a mother's physique on the long-term health of her children. For example, children of women who are overweight have an increased risk of coronary heart disease as adults (Acheson, 1998). The inequality in health lies in the fact that women from lower social classes are more likely to be obese than women in higher social classes, and therefore their children are likely to suffer the consequences as adults (Acheson, 1998).

Although the search for 'fat' genes continues, the idea that genetic factors such as metabolic defects are a major contributing factor in obesity has largely been abandoned. Instead, attention has been focused on lifestyle as a major determinant. The importance of establishing healthy eating patterns and developing a healthy lifestyle early in life is widely recognized (Department of Health, 2003). However, despite the recognition of the importance of a healthy diet in the prevention of adult coronary heart disease and strokes, children's diets are generally far from healthy. Typically, their diets remain high in fat, a known risk factor, and are also high in sugar (James and James, 2004).

Obesity develops as a consequence of an imbalance between the amount of energy consumed and the amount expended. In terms of lifestyle, therefore, obesity can be seen to result from either 'gluttony or sloth' (Jebb and Prentice, 1995). Students enjoy engaging in debate in response to the provocative question of whether children are either greedy or lazy. Many students will express the view that children are simply greedy and that they indulge in a diet that is high in 'crisps and sweets'. Data from the Sodexho School Meals Survey (2002) does appear to support this view, with 45 per cent of children identifying that they eat too many sweets and chocolates.

The counter argument, of course, is that children are not greedy, but lazy. Students will cite examples of the typical 'couch potato', sitting in front of the television or computer. Again, research seems to indicate that these views may be valid in that children themselves attribute playing on their computer or watching television as reasons for not getting enough exercise (Sodexho, 2002). Levels of walking and cycling have fallen dramatically in recent years (House of Commons Health Committee, 2004). One could argue that the gluttony and sloth debate may be somewhat academic when contextualized in a framework within which the ability for children to articulate their choice is questionable. In other words, there is almost a sense of injustice in criticizing children for their behaviour or lifestyle 'choices' in relation to diet and exercise, when in reality these 'choices' may be restricted. In relation to the sloth debate, parental concerns with respect to child safety needs to be considered because road traffic accidents remain the biggest single cause of accidental death amongst children and young people. Each year in England nearly 180 children die and almost 4800 are injured as pedestrians or cyclists. Many children are killed when playing or walking close to their home (Department of Health, 1999). The physical danger of traffic, coupled with the perceived 'stranger danger', so cruelly illustrated by the deaths of Jessica Chapman and Holly Wells, are sufficient to persuade any caring parent to keep their children 'safe at home'.

Whilst lifestyle factors are important with respect to childhood obesity, the influence of the family cannot be overemphasized. Home is where the behaviour patterns that shape a child's norms in relation to food and eating are formed. We therefore encourage students to consider the implications of society and the family as a determinant of health. Children's eating habits are a fascination for students. For example, when presented with data that suggests that 35 per cent of children have tea on their knee while watching TV and 7 per cent at a table on their own (Sodexho, 2002), we ask students to consider the implications of this for socialization. We encourage them to explore the consequences of eating in isolation and the lack of opportunity to learn about food that is associated with this increasing social phenomenon.

A 'spin-off' from the sloth debate with students is an exploration of what children are actually exposed to when they are watching television. Students reflect the pervasiveness of advertising as they readily give accounts of advertisements for food and drink aimed at children. Recent research has revealed that food advertisements are screened more frequently during children's programmes than those of adults and that 95–99 per cent of the adverts promote food that is high in fat, sugar and/or salt. There is a paucity of advertisements for fresh fruit or vegetables aimed at either children or adults (House of Commons Health Committee, 2004). The House of Commons Health Committee expresses concern about the nature of such advertising and has called for a voluntary withdrawal of advertisements for unhealthy foods. Their concern is readily reflected in our discussions with students, who see quite clearly the power of the media in relation to the active promotion of unhealthy foods and the susceptibility of children to the media's persuasiveness.

The milieu of school in relation to nutrition is one that we consider important, not least because of the changes in policy over the past few decades. During the early 1970s some 70 per cent of children were staying at school for a midday meal (Daniel and Ivatts, 1998). Within the same decade policy changes implemented by the Conservative administration removed the requirement for local education authorities to provide free school milk to children aged over seven years. In the 1980s, as part of the 1980 Education Act, local authorities were no longer required to provide a school meal service to all children (except for the provision to children entitled to free school meals).

According to Daniel and Ivatts (1998), there is considerable evidence that the nutritional quality of meals eaten in school has deteriorated. There have been some positive policy changes implemented by the current government that include, for example, the (re)introduction of nutritional standards for school meals. Initiatives such as the Fruit in Schools Scheme (where every four to six year-old child is given a free piece of fruit every day) have also been introduced. One of the problems with attempting to improve nutrition in schools is that what children eat at midday is generally not regarded as the responsibility of either the education authority or the school (Mayall, 2001).

In relation to health services, our biggest concern is one that is recognized by others, in that they are all too often designed with adults in mind (Department of Health, 2003). Some argue that '. . . current health policies aimed *at* children are not very effective health policies *for* children' (James and James,

2004: 165). Policies seem more concerned with the notion of investment and a construction of children as the next generation of adults rather than '. . . what this might mean for the current health status of children as actors and agents in their own right' (James and James, 2004: 165). We encourage students to consider children's agency – that is, their *own* behaviour and decision making in relation to health – as one that may be slow to manifest in contemporary policy, but as James and James (2004) highlight, it is a factor that has long been recognized by the manufacturers of sweets and 'junk food'.

Attempts to explain health inequalities began with the work of Sir Douglas Black in the 1980s (Black *et al.*, 1980). Social inequality in terms of income, education and housing has a proven effect on health (Department of Health, 2002) and is one of the most significant global public health concerns. There is a plethora of research linking poor health to 'disadvantaged' social background, and this research suggests that it is the relativity that is significant in influencing health rather than the absolute difference in income. It is the gap in income between rich and poor that has the greatest effect and in the countries where this gap is the greatest, the poorer the health of the population (Wilkinson, 1996, cited in Iphofen, 2003). While the overall health of the population (in the UK) has improved over the past century, as measured by life expectancy and infant mortality and morbidity, the difference in health status between the richest and the poorest within society has increased. In other words, the health chances of a person who is poor are not favourable in comparison to a richer counterpart. This phenomenon has been variously described as the 'health divide' (Whitehead, 1987); 'inequality in health' (Acheson, 1998); and the 'health gap' (Department of Health, 1999).

Contemporary wisdom holds socio-economic factors as the most significant contributory factor in determining health and thus several policies have been aimed at addressing inequalities from this perspective. The current UK government commissioned an independent inquiry into inequalities in health (Acheson, 1998) and the political rhetoric seems to reflect a commitment to reducing the enduring nature of the problem. Initiatives to improve childhood nutrition in the form of those already discussed are examples of the implementation of such policy.

There appears to be a dichotomy in the student narratives in relation to the discourse of health inequalities in childhood. In relation to our discussion concerning obesity, some students are keen to attribute health inequalities to behaviours such as laziness and ignorance. They support this view by arguing that cheap food is readily available (at least in the UK) and that there is no excuse for an unhealthy diet. These students tend to suggest that poor people, including children, must therefore choose to eat an unhealthy diet. However, this notion is often vehemently opposed by other students who criticize this view as being both naive and victim blaming. These students prefer to frame their argument in terms of the socio-economic factors associated with inequalities in health. In other words, they are able to perceive of the effects of social deprivation in terms of poor housing and low income as significant factors in adversely affecting health.

We can only attempt both here and in the classroom to highlight the importance of social inequality as a determinant of children's health. In this chapter we have had to take a rather 'broad brush' approach to the vast area of health in childhood and we trust that this has not resulted in a diluted account. We are acutely aware of the risk of trivialization and superficiality associated with an attempt to address such a complex area within one chapter. It is for this reason that we have focused on childhood obesity as one health issue rather than being tempted to expand our discussion more widely. However, the framework we have used can be equally applied to explore the factors associated with any child health issue such as safety, dental health, mental health and play. We have also tried to ensure that the importance of recognizing children as their own agents in terms of making decisions about their health forms the cornerstone of any attempts to promote their health.

The first few years have been marked by exciting policy implementation, which should have significant implications for children in the UK. The Children Bill (2004) received Royal Assent in November 2004 and has become the Children Act (2004). The Act forms the legal backbone for the national strategy aimed at improving the lives of children and should ensure more integrated services and enhanced multidisciplinary working. It also means that England can at last have a Children's Commissioner who will be responsible for services provided for children and will be charged with ensuring that children have a 'voice'. The responsibility will include arrangements to safeguard and promote the well-being of all children, but particularly the most vulnerable who may otherwise be unable to make their views known.

In addition, 2004 saw the long awaited publication of the National Service Framework for Children, Young People and Maternity Services (2004). This ten-year plan sets standards to improve health, social and educational services for all children and again places children firmly at the centre. A concern for the well-being of the most vulnerable children is evident, as is a commitment to reducing inequalities. It is too early to determine the outcome of such policies and to speculate whether they will amount to any more than mere rhetoric, or whether rather more optimistically they will prove to have a measurable effect on improving the health and well-being of children.

References

Acheson, D. (1998) *Independent Inquiry into Inequalities in Health Report.* London: The Stationery Office.

Black, D., Morris, J., Smith, C. and Townsend, P. (1980) *Inequalities in Health: Report of a Working Party*. London: Department of Health and Social Security.

Brannen, J. and Storey, P. (1996) *Child Health in Social Context*. London: Health Education Authority.

Cheung, L. and Richmond, J. (1995) *Child Health, Nutrition, and Physical Activity*. Leeds; Champaign, Ill.: Human Kinetics.

Dahlgren, G. and Whitehead, M. (1991) *Policies and Strategies to Promote Social Equity in Health*. Stockholm: Institute of Futures Studies.

Daniel, D. and Ivatts, J. (1998) *Children and Social Policy*. Hampshire: Palgrave.

DfES and Sure Start (2002) *Birth to Three Matters: A Framework to Support Children in their Earliest Years*. London: DfES.

Department of Health (1999) *Saving Lives: Our Healthier Nation*. London: Department of Health.

Department of Health (2002) *Tackling Health Inequalities: Summary of the 2002 Cross-Cutting Review*. London: Department of Health.

Department of Health (2003) *Getting the Right Start: National Service Framework for Children. Emerging Findings*. London: Department of Health.

Department of Health, Department for Education and Skills (2004) *Core Document, National Service Framework for Children, Young People and Maternity Services* www.dh.gov.uk.

Eiser, C. (1991) It's OK having asthma – young children's beliefs about illness, *Professional Nurse*, March: 342–345.

Foley, P., Roche, J. and Tucker, S. (2001) *Children in Society*. Buckingham: The Open University Press.

Hooton, S. (2000) 'Promoting child and family health through empowerment', in J. Kerr (ed.) *Community Health Promotion: Challenges for Practice*. London: Baillière Tindall.

House of Commons Health Committee (2004) *Obesity: Third Report of Session 2003–04*. London: The Stationery Office.

Iphofen, R. (2003) 'Social and individual factors influencing public health', in J. Costello and M. Haggart (eds) *Public Health and Society*. Hampshire: Palgrave Macmillan.

James, A. and James, A. (2004) *Constructing Childhood*. Hampshire: Palgrave Macmillan.

Jebb, S. and Prentice, A. (1995) Obesity in Britain: gluttony or sloth? *British Medical Journal*, 311: 437–439.

Mayall, B. (2001) 'Children's health at school', in P. Foley, J. Roche and S. Tucker (eds) *Children in Society*. Buckingham: The Open University Press.

Pridmore, P. and Bendelow, G. (1995) Images of health: exploring beliefs of children using the 'draw-and-write technique', *Health Education Journal*, 54: 473–488.

Richman, J. (2003) 'Holding public health up for inspection', in J. Costello and M. Haggart (eds) *Public Health and Society*. Hampshire: Palgrave Macmillan.

Sodexho (2002) *The Sodexho School Meals and Lifestyle Survey*. Sodexho.

Wanless, D. (2003) *Securing Good Health for the Whole Population: Population Health Trend*. London: HMSO.

Whitehead, M. (1987) *The Health Divide: Inequalities in Health in the 1980s*. London: Health Education Council.

World Health Organization (1948) *Preamble to the Constitution of the World Health Organization as adopted by the International Health Conference*, New York, 19–22 June 1946; signed on 22 July 1946 by the representatives of 61 States (Official Records of the World Health Organization, no. 2:100) and entered into force on 7 April 1948.

World Health Organization (1984) *Report of the Working Group on Concepts and Principles of Health Promotion*. Copenhagen.

World Health Organization (2003) Controlling the global obesity epidemic. www.who.int/nut/obs.htm WHO

PART 3
Children's Childhoods

12 Exploring representations of children and childhood in history and film: silencing a voice that is already blue in the face from shouting

Rachel Holmes and Ian Barron

Introduction

This and the following chapter reflects upon the course's integrating mechanism for the ways that students are encouraged to study the different ways in which children have been and are understood. Conceptually, it is an aspect of the students' experience that they find challenging. In order to enable an appreciation of the historical, cultural and intellectual backdrop to this chapter, the discussion is extended over two chapters. This first chapter seeks to situate and disturb representations of children and childhood in history and film within the students' broader experience; to explore the historical and ideological framework from which this chapter has emerged; to consider how students tend to view children and childhood; and to begin to look at the ways in which, at the early stages of their studies, students' beliefs begin to be destabilized. The chapter also provides an introduction to the central theme, that of 'othering'.

Chapter 13 develops in considerably more depth this central theme by opening up questions around who is 'other' and who is 'non-other', as propagated and provoked through visual narratives. Taken together, the chapters examine the ways in which exploring representations of children and childhood within different media create an evolving context for engaging with discourses that both reflect and of themselves construct the child. It explores ways to deconstruct narratives and other symbolic representations of the child and seeks to facilitate the reframing of deeply embedded concepts and understandings. The chapters were conceived as symbiotic and in conceptual harmony with all other chapters. They were created to manifest a conceptual 'space' for discussing and challenging traditional, western 'regimes of truth' (Foucault, 1977) constructed throughout history and sustained in some contemporary arenas.

The invention of childhood

It could be asked, however, why there is the need for such study. After all, it could be claimed that we all know about children. Certainly, students generally begin their studies believing this to be the case. They 'know', for example, that children are innocent, vulnerable, can misbehave and need to be helped to behave appropriately in the adult world. They 'know' that their growth and development takes a particular course and some of them believe that the work of writers such as Sheridan (1997) has told them what this is. They 'know' that children are carefree, do not get ill and do not die or, if they do, it is not to be expected. They think they know all of this. The concern of Explorations is to enable students to explore the assumptions, ideologies and discourses on which these ideas are based.

Widespread interest in childhood as a distinct phase of human life is generally considered to be a relatively new phenomenon. As Aries (1962) notes, in medieval societies children were seen essentially as small adults and were expected to behave and dress in the same sorts of ways. Life was little different from that experienced by adults and death just as commonplace as in the adult population. As Hendrick (1997) comments, it was only with slow improvement in the health of children and with some decline in infant mortality in the late eighteenth century that the way that children were perceived began to change and to take on more of the characteristics of how children are commonly understood today. It was in this period that the bipolar nature of how children are often understood today first appeared. At one extreme was the childhood paradigm expounded by Rousseau in *Emile*, where childhood was seen as a special phase of human life to be nurtured through experience of the natural world in order to feed children's natural goodness so that they would grow into well-balanced adults. Romanticism, as we have noted in Part 1 of this book, was to develop these notions further, with Wordsworth promoting childhood as a period not only of goodness but also of special qualities that gave children the capacity to 'see into the life of things' (*Tintern Abbey*). At the other extreme was the concern of John Wesley to 'break the child'. In the nineteenth century, this latter view of children was developed by the Evangelical movement, whose view of human nature was premised upon the notion of Original Sin and saw all children as born sinful and needing to be rescued from evil.

Whilst childhood meant different things at these two extremes, what is important to note is that childhood had come to be seen, in both cases, as a distinct phase of human life. Historically, children have had a significant role within the economy as workers, but the greater economic prosperity of the middle and upper classes meant that childhood took on a different complexion, with a greater emphasis on education (particularly for boys). For the working classes, however, children remained an important source of income well after the Industrial Revolution.

The prosperity generated for the upper and middle classes by the Industrial Revolution did lead them to pay much greater attention to the needs of the working class poor. As Hendrick (1997) notes, from their different polarities, the Romantic and Evangelical movements both sought to construct childhood for the working classes as a period that should be concerned not with work but with education and preparation for adult life. Whilst the Romantics were concerned to protect the special status of childhood and prevent children from being brutalized by work, the Evangelicals were more concerned with children's moral development and also disturbed by the unrest within the working classes during the nineteenth century. They feared the possible political consequences for the middle and upper classes if working class children were not removed from the turmoil. Out of these concerns came renewed interest in the possible dangers of juvenile delinquency and a belief that education was the answer to the problem if society was to be provided with young adults ready for the world of work and with appropriate moral principles. Hultqvist and Dahlberg argue that this led to a contradictory set of beliefs about childhood:

> On the one hand, childhood was a natural process; on the other, it was to be realized through the practices of educators and others who sought to save the child's soul from the same uncertainties that made childhood possible as a historical project.
>
> (Hultqvist and Dahlberg, 2001: 4)

With children visible in identifiable classrooms, so further changes occurred in how children and childhood were viewed. Children now came to be studied for the first time. A particular impetus to the interest in studying children was the near defeat of the British army in the Boer War. The poor health and physique of young men was seen as partly responsible and this led to the development of medical screening processes and the child study movement. As noted by James (1999) and as reported in Part 1 of this book, for much of the twentieth century (and beyond) developmental psychology came to dominate how children were understood.

The past ten years, however, have seen a questioning of the supposed lessons of developmental psychology (see, for example, Burman, 1994, 1999; Morss, 1996; James, 1999), a growth in the influence of sociology in the study of children and childhood, and growing recognition that how we view children is in large part a social and cultural construct. There is now greater recognition of the role that social institutions play in how children are perceived. In the recent past, the impact of advertising and the media has been, in part, to construct children as consumers. From time to time, however, the bipolar view of childhood reasserts itself and concerns are expressed about the loss of the special status of childhood and/or about the descent into immorality that is seen to be besetting childhood.

This account of how notions of what is meant by childhood in Britain have changed over time is intended to give some context to the sorts of beliefs that are commonly held by students and by society in general. What it demonstrates is that the beliefs that are held do not have the status of 'truths' as might at first appear. They are constructs that result from particular periods in time and which reflect economic and political circumstances and particular philosophical and religious beliefs. They are also notions that reflect class, culture, race and gender. As Hultqvist and Dahlberg comment:

> There is no natural or evolutionary child, only the historically produced discourses and power relations that constitute the child as an object and subject of knowledge, practice and political intervention.
> (Hultqvist and Dahlberg, 2001: 2)

How is it then that certain beliefs have come to influence the way that we understand children and childhood? How we understand childhood could be seen, in part, to be based on what might be termed 'taken-for-granted knowledge' or 'commonsense assumptions'. It could be argued therefore that certain beliefs about children are held because they are quite evidently sensible. An example might be the notion that babies experience a period of dependency. Even such seemingly straightforward assumptions, however, are anything but. They tend to reflect belief systems that seek to mark adults and children out as fundamentally different and opposite. As Jenks notes:

> . . . childhood is spoken about as: a 'becoming'; as a tabla rasa; as laying down the foundations; as shaping the individual; taking on; growing up; preparation; inadequacy; inexperience; immaturity, and so on. By contrast (The) adult world is not only assumed to be complete, recognizable and in statis, but also, and perhaps most significantly, desirable.
> (Jenks, 1996: 9)

Whilst infant dependency has some basis in reality, all too often it is not sufficiently nuanced – babies are not equally dependent in every sense. Seeing babies as dependent also sets up a binary relation in which adults are seen as independent, when again this is not true in any straightforward sense. A relation is created in which children are seen as deficient without regard to what is particular and distinctive about being a child in any positive sense.

Thus children are marked out as 'other' because they are seen to lack the qualities that are valued by adult (male, white, heterosexual, middle class) society. The solution, of course, as Jenks explains is for adult society to 'extend a welcome to the child and to invite him to cast off the qualities that ensure his differences' (1996: 9). Where children do not conform to these expectations (for reasons over which they may or may not have control), they are marked out not only as deficient but also as deviant and as an affront to how 'decent' and 'normal' children ought to behave. This again points to the bipolar manner in which we perceive of childhood: a period of innocence but also a period of possible immorality.

How is it then that particular ways of viewing children come to hold currency? The work of Foucault (1977) helps us to understand how certain views or constructions in relation to childhood come to dominate individual and public perception. He explains that societies bring together a range of voices, ideas and beliefs into overall discourses that offer ways of explaining the world. As noted in Part 1, discourses are therefore conceived of as a set of belief systems underpinned by relations of power. The power or influence may emerge from a particular professional group, such as teachers or social workers, but it will be significant only where those groups are afforded power by political or economic factors. Foucault also notes that societies have several discourses to make sense of the world and that discourses change over time. In Foucault's view, the apparatus of the state acts to ensure that we comply with dominant discourses, which enact how the world is to be understood. Those who do not fit with what is seen as important and central or who do not comply with the gaze of the dominant group are 'othered'.

From a white, middle class, western, heterosexual, non-disabled male perspective, those who are 'othered' are those who do not have those characteristics. This will include women, children, the working classes and other races and cultures. As Hultqvist and Dahlberg note:

> The contradictions of childhood thought . . . led to the construction of the normal child with a normal way of reasoning and emotional and aesthetic experience, but they also produced their opposites: otherness and the fears and anxieties that surrounded the figures of the non-normal child, the racially 'inferior' child, the proletariat boy and girl – characters that would, should these threats not be counteracted, disrupt the sanitary logic of the child's nature.
>
> (Hultqvist and Dahlberg, 2001: 6)

Thus a female, black, non-Christian, working class, gay and disabled child will be particularly 'othered'. It can also be seen that 'othering' occurs when dominant institutions become afraid of what they have constructed, which leads to moments of discontinuity. The reinvention of children as miniature adults who dress in small versions of adult clothes, as discussed earlier, also led to a moral panic about the loss of the special status of childhood when thongs and bras were marketed to children under the age of ten. The result was to 'other', to condemn, those who sold the underwear as well as those who bought or wanted to wear it, conveniently forgetting the role that all had played in creating the demand in the first place. Part of the media frenzy surrounding the murder of the toddler Jamie Bulger by two ten year olds in the early 1990s reflected a concern about the sort of children that society and the media had created. The answer was to 'other' the boys as 'freaks of nature'.

Disturbing the silence: reading visual narratives

The idea within this chapter of reflecting upon visual representation as a way of engaging students in discussions about representation of children and their families arose from our belief that visual forms have powerful ways of commenting on the historical, cultural and political milieu from which they are borne and, similarly, powerful ways of actually constructing, mediating and publicly circulating notions that propagate ideals (Mills and Mills, 2000). In recognizing that visual imagery does not represent 'reality' but a particular translation or version of it, we were interested in how the process of visual representation gives ideas public expression and has potential to become ideological in its collusion with dominant ideas of 'other'. We also considered how for any audience, images could become the vehicle for different reflexive readings, differentiated understandings, and the site of struggle and disturbance.

Debates had surfaced around ways in which visual imagery in the 1980s had begun to reflect an increasing cultural 'depthlessness' and how 'style and surface' had become priorities (Jameson, cited in Sim, 2001: 100). However, Hill and Every, in relation to film, recognize that 'in the wake of this change, postmodern film criticism has celebrated the intensity of the surface and the multivocal readings against the grain that it allows' (cited in Sim, 2001: 101). The idea of 'multivocal readings against the grain' presented a number of issues for us, which we believed could be mirrored in classroom discussions with students. In order to advocate the multivocal possibilities of reading imagery, it had to be established, first, that there was a 'grain' to read against and, second, what 'the grain' actually constituted. We pondered whether modernist constructions of the viewing audience categorized them as seeking a point of enlightenment, revelation, insight or an affirmation of widely held values. We also reflected upon 'the grain' that pervaded the imagery that positioned the audience within the realms of dominant discourses, such as the advocacy for and virtues of heterosexuality and middle class values manifested within a white, patriarchal, capitalist society.

It seems that the narrative within moving imagery interpreted within a modernist framework was not intended to be contested but rather affirmed in its relationship with the powerful aforementioned values. What postmodernism has potentially brought to this is that, although it may still be underpinned by these values, the 'multivocal readings against the grain' suggest that the audience engaging with these values is able to appreciate and critique the struggles embedded within them. The challenge herein seems to lie within an individual's propensity to reflect upon how and why his or her response to the imagery is governed (Wolfreys, 1998); how and why he/she reads the imagery in particular ways; and how he/she is able to re-read the narrative in ways that allow for indeterminate moments pervading the visual text. By using imagery of childhood and family life within sessions, we would be able to explore with students what was being assumed of the imagery as message-giver and the audience as consumer/critic, which could allow a disturbance of 'the grain' and support the facilitation of 'multivocal readings'. By discussing a carefully selected film, we anticipated engaging with the ways different students reflexively read 'othering' narratives, ways they perceive and make different interpretations of the dominant voices and ways to facilitate a discussion around how they conceptualize the construction of these voices.

Cinematic silence: representations of 'other' within film

At Stage 1 of the course, we selected the film *East is East* (Khan-Din, 1999) as a vehicle to focus upon 'othering', representations of Asian and Muslim culture, and notions of gender and identity within a dual-heritage family. We intended to use the film as an opportunity for students to become aware of and unpack the positions they take when presented with images of 'otherness'; how they relate to difference; and how this might afford them greater awareness of their own points of self-reference. Derrida (1972) argues that there is always a relation of power between the poles of binary opposition. The significance of this idea within *East is East* is that this film could be seen to portray binaries in terms of non-other (including, for example, white, non-Muslim) and other (Muslim, non-white). Derrida's point is that the relation of power inherent within these binaries creates an interesting notion for contemplation. Hill and Every suggest:

> . . . the scenarios found in many postmodern films express a number of repetitions, particularly around the issues of . . . ethnicity, that make the notion of free-floating signification problematic.
> (Hill and Every, cited in Sim, 2001: 101)

We understand multivocal readings to pertain to free-floating significance and considered in what ways their repetition is problematic. An interesting interjection here is that the film's director Khan-Din is himself of dual heritage and the film itself is a partial autobiographical account of his childhood in

Salford. As a 'free-floating' audience we pondered how Khan-Din's own values, expressed through the film, made reference to dominant values by representing the struggles that lie within them. We considered, furthermore, the ways in which the audience might be seduced into engaging with these. A site of tension arises when we consider that the representation of ethnicity or race within post-modern film is such a popular theme (*My Beautiful Laundrette*, Kureishi, 1985; *East is East*, Khan-Din, 1999; *The Bhudda of Suburbia*, Kurieshi, 1999; *Bend it Like Beckham*, Chadha, 2002; *My Son the Fanatic*, Prasad, 1997; *Bhaji on the Beach*, Chadha, 1993; *Monsoon Wedding*, Nair, 2002).

Derrida suggests that 'Identity is never known until perceived in a particular form' (cited in Wolfreys, 1998: 61), and our concern arises out of whether this recurring theme merely replays a 'particular form', albeit in different guises and therefore depends heavily on the 'free-floating' capacity of the reader to make significant conceptual shifts. Furthermore, what is the consequence if these shifts do not emerge? Is there a danger that the identity of 'other' remains embalmed within a staid set of white, western values, without the audience having to find new ways to inhabit the narrative?

On first viewing, we read the film as a comical portrayal of a deeply complex set of circumstances, where the director drew from personal life experiences and placed them into a context that might interest audiences by entertaining, whilst also communicating subversive messages. Within the context of 1970s Salford, where ethnocentricity seems to saturate the terraced backstreets, the children of a father who is constructed as entrenched in Pakistani culture, trying to maintain a voice alongside his white, female partner, are each radically different in their approach to cultural and religious allegiances. The constructed awkwardness of the children's relationship with their father is positioned as a dual-identity struggle, where the dutiful expectations of their father are positioned in stark contrast to their mother's acknowledgement of her children's struggles. We found the interesting interplay between race and gender in terms of dominant voices, post-colonial and feminist notions of 'othering' to create a focal point. The father is constructed as exerting his patriarchal prowess by 'subordinating' his wife, yet simultaneously being rendered disempowered by his minoritized racial status, homogenized by his wife and her colluding neighbour into a marginalized sense of 'they'. The daughter is portrayed as having characteristics that could be read as assertive and rebellious, while some of her brothers seem considerably more timid, and the father seems to find the fluidity of these gender roles difficult to negotiate.

The film utilizes humour and at times we found this difficult. There were moments when particular characters were portrayed as 'larger than life' Asian stereotypes, intended to be representative of 'other' in a way that could be seen to humiliate, disempower and, in a subversive way, perpetuate feelings of superiority or reassurance for the white or non-Muslim section of the audience.

DuGay *et al.* suggest that 'culture depends on giving things meaning by assigning them to different positions within a classificatory system' (1997: 132), but the film unearthed some of the dilemmas facing those who seemed to defy this classificatory system, who fell between categories and therefore outside the mindsets of those who rely upon categorization to make meaning. This film seemed to play on this inter-category identity as both a struggle and source of entertainment, and our own struggles making meaning from this seemed interesting for discussion within the classroom.

Watching and discussing extracts from the film *East is East* became the focus of one session and the students were encouraged to document representations of children and race. Considering the positions taken when presented with images of 'otherness', it was interesting that traces of the child as a 'blank slate' and the strong perception of children's vulnerability were found in students' responses, whilst also an element of the cultural dilemmas borne from the notion of free will emerged. Comments ranged from:

> That kind of identity crisis is natural when parents are from different cultures.

> It's a message about how you can't expect teenagers who have been born in Britain, with parents born somewhere else, to lead an old-fashioned lifestyle in British society.

to:

> It's showing that life's always going to be hard for some children because they've got parents who are only concerned about their own culture instead of looking at where they're living and being more reasonable.

In order to explore more fully how the students position themselves and how they relate to the notion of difference, we intend to spend some time focusing on the students' uses of particular terms here. Those of interest to us were: 'identity crisis'; 'natural'; 'old-fashioned lifestyle'; 'British society'; 'only concerned'; and 'looking at where you're living'.

The idea of the powerless victim who was presented by the student as being 'naturally' confronted with an 'identity crisis' was understood to be embedded within the notion of the child as a 'blank slate'. Within this film, the parents conjure their own complexities, as they are constructed as a fractured couple, represented as culturally, racially and religiously dichotomous. For the student, the child read as a passive recipient of such a divisive experience seems to have been constructed and understood as in crisis. This crisis seems to become a mirror of the struggle between mother and father, Muslim and non-Muslim, Asian and white identities, and the child positioned as 'natural' victim, as if somehow the realities for the child within this duality create a definitive truth.

The phrase 'old-fashioned lifestyle' suggests a comparative judgement having been made by interpreting the cinematic imagery and swirling narratives around the representation of 'other' within the film. This comment was made by a white, non-Muslim student and as such becomes interestingly enmeshed within Said's 'othering' dialogue: '. . . western power, especially the power to enter or examine other countries at will, enables the production of a range of knowledges about other cultures . . .' (1993: 205).

The inclusion of Said's idea here signifies our own contemplations of how what we interpreted as his reference to particular beliefs about 'other' could translate into university classroom encounters; the ways in which the debris of such translations become deeply entangled with our own and students' readings and framing of ideas; and consideration of what is needed in order to create a disturbance of this translation process. The 'knowledges' Said refers to could suggest a power-based claim not only to know 'other', but to deem 'other' to be 'inferior' or 'old fashioned', characterized by the dominant discourses around 'us and them' polarities and the inherent inequalities manifested within the process of 'knowing'.

In order to manoeuvre this chapter into a conceptual space where the experience of discussing the film could afford a greater awareness of the students' positions, borne from their self-referencing, we intend this chapter to illuminate any assumed 'knowledges' as artefacts of, and being sustained by, the social processes that surround each individual. Young (1995) locates the possibility of 'knowing other' to be a process of shifting positions by heightening awareness and developing critical analysis of discourses embedded within imagery. In order to begin this process, the student must become more open to the ideas located within social constructivism by challenging the single-mindedness and constraining consequence of any one personal truth transcending, consuming and dominating 'other'.

As tutors in the process of listening and responding to stories told by students in a way that disturbs or unsettles 'taken-for-granted knowledge', we consider the opportunity to tune into nuances of 'othering' discourses to be a prerequisite to nurturing the students' own self-exploration by engaging them in discourse analysis. Expressions such as '. . . identity crisis is natural when parents are from different cultures', '. . . old-fashioned lifestyle in British society' and '. . . parents who are only concerned about their own culture' could indicate stagnated beliefs which the students interpreted as being reaffirmed by the extract from *East is East*.

In an attempt to offer a further catalyst for discussion, a quotation by Godfrey was used, reflecting upon representations of British Asians in contemporary British cinema. He suggests that '*East is East* seeks to reassure white audiences of the practical adequacies of western culture and society' (2004: 5).

His expression focuses upon the white viewing audience, almost posing them the question, 'What does it take to be white?' By suggesting the need for reassurance, he seems to be claiming white cultural practices are forcefully maintained in a power-based relationship with Asian cultural practices in ways such as the production of films laden with white-affirming narratives. Could it be argued that some of the students were 'reassured' of their own adequate culture by positioning 'other' as inadequate ('old-fashioned lifestyle' and 'parents who are only concerned about their own culture')? Could the notion of 'other' be rendered as such in order to maintain the status and authority of 'non-other' (here the white or non-Muslim audience) and to maintain the mythical 'adequacy' of western culture and society? Does this film seek to portray 'other' in a position of inadequacy and subordination, storied from the position taken by the pseudo-knowledges of western manifestations of power?

We revisit the question, 'What does it take to be white?' Could being white necessitate the maintenance of stereotypical representations and the undermining of difference, positioned against what could be described as the romanticism of white lifestyles, where the white ideals of individualism, freedom to have a 'secular outlook' and gender equality face the construction of the harsh stereotypes of Asian collectivism, possession, religious commitment and gender role differentiation? Framed within untenable binary opposition, could some of the students be eager to engage with stereotypical constructions of 'other' in order to gratify their own understandings and 'knowledges' of both self and other ('life's always going to be hard for some children')? Could they be interpreting the representations of difference within the film as deficit models within contemporary society because these models serve to secure their own cultural inheritance ('only concerned about their own culture instead of looking at where they're living and being more reasonable')? Interestingly, an Asian student expressed a view that was followed by a haunting silence in the room:

> Perhaps the filmmaker and some of the audience don't want to challenge these stereotypes. Maybe it would be too threatening . . . because of the way they are comfortable seeing Asian culture.

This returns us to Said's notion that the more 'knowable' (that is, the more stereotyped) the object becomes, the more 'other' it remains (1993). Our challenge to all students was to consider how individual and free *any* life can actually be. In predicting the complexity of responses to that challenge, we left them to consider Naib's subversive reflection on *East is East*: 'the film silences a voice that is already blue in the face from shouting . . .' (2002: 63).

We challenged them to consider whose face is blue from shouting, from shouting what and shouting to whom? Why does this voice remain silenced amidst a film that could be perceived to give voice? In what ways has this voice already been unheard? Where do the students position themselves amongst all this silenced shouting and how might this position inform and satisfy or challenge their beliefs and practices? Are they the voice being silenced or are they the silencer? If they are the silencer, why might they find listening such a challenge?

Destabilizing the process of silencing

Rather than write a conclusion to this chapter, we intend to recognize the many ideas that remain swirling in what Zizek suggests is an '. . . ideological space . . . made of non-bound, non-tied elements . . . whose very identity is open . . .' (1989: 87) and intend to reflect upon some of the journeys that we hope have at least served to destabilize. In a series of interesting tutor/student discussions, we have become more aware of the essentialist tendencies of our own assumptions, challenged by our own positions and disturbed in the comfort of our own ideas. The unpacking of constructions of children and childhood will be continued in the following chapter, where we begin to try to reframe ideologies. A claim to any kind of victory narrative would undermine everything we continue to do, and in our struggles to find new ways to facilitate and support the development of students' and our own ideas, we reflect upon our encounters with caution and a penchant for 'free-floating significance'.

References

Aries, P. (1962) *Centuries of Childhood*. Harmondsworth: Penguin.
Burman, E. (1994) *Deconstructing Developmental Psychology*. London: Routledge.
Burman, E. (1999) 'Morality and the goals of development', in M. Woodhead, D. Faulkner and K. Littleton (eds) *Making Sense of Social Development*. London: Routledge.
Derrida, J. (1972) *Positions*. Chicago: University of Chicago Press.
Du Gay, P., Hall, S., Janes, L., MacKay, H. and Negus, K. (1997) *Doing Cultural Studies: the story of the Sony Walkman*. London: Sage/Open University Press.
Foucault, M. (1977) *Discipline and Punish*. London: Allen Lane.
Godfrey, W. (2004) *Them and Us and 9/11: Representations of British Asians in Contemporary British Cinema*. Paper given at symposium ('Issues Of Representation In Film') presented by Postgraduate Studies in Visual Representation, School of Art and Design, Bradford College (see http://www.bradfordfilmfestival.org.uk/ 2004).
Hendrick, H. (1997) 'Constructions and reconstructions of British childhood', in A. James and A. Prout (eds) *Constructing and Reconstructing Childhood* (2nd edn). Brighton: Falmer.

Hultqvist, K. and Dahlberg, G. (2001) 'Governing the child in the New Millenium – introduction', in K. Hultqvist and G. Dahlberg (eds) *Governing the Child in the New Millenium*. London: RoutledgeFalmer.

James, A. (1999) 'Researching Children's Social Competence', in M. Woodhead, D. Faulkner and K. Littleton (eds) *Making Sense of Social Development*. London: Routledge.

James, A. and Prout, A. (1997) *Constructing and Reconstructing Childhood* (2nd edn). Brighton: Falmer.

Jenks, C. (1996) *Childhood*. Routledge: London.

Mills, J. and Mills, R. (2000) *Childhood Studies: A Reader in Perspectives of Childhood*. London: Routledge.

Morss, J. (1996) *Growing Critical: Alternatives to Developmental Psychology*. London: Routledge.

Naib, H. (2002) *The New Seriousness*. Bradford: Funkaarh Muvment.

Said, E. (1993) *Culture and Imperialism*. London: Chatto and Windus.

Sheridan, M. (1997) *From Birth to Five Years: Children's Developmental Progress*. London: Routledge.

Sim, S. (2001) *Postmoderism*. London: Routledge.

Sinister Wisdom Collective (1990) 'Editorial', *Sinister Wisdom*, 42(4): 1–6.

Wolfreys, J. (1998) *Deconstructing Derrida*. London: Macmillan Press.

Young, R. (1995) *Colonial Desire: Hybridity in Theory, Culture and Race*. London: Routledge.

Zizek, S. (1989) *The Sublime Object of Ideology*. London: Verso.

13 Exploring representations of children and childhood in photography and documentary: visualizing the silence

Rachel Holmes

Introduction

As noted in Chapter 12, the central theme of 'othering' will now be developed in considerably more depth by opening up questions around who is 'other' and who is 'non-other', as propagated and provoked through visual stories. We intend to present an aspect of how we work with students to deconstruct aspects of early childhood, where 'othering' is considered within photographs. We will revisit this later in the chapter as we consider how early childhood could be reframed within the exploration of ways 'other' can be re-engaged with through documentary. In the latter stages of the students' studies, the concern is to move beyond the specific use of the term 'other' that was introduced in Chapter 12 in order to consider broader and interdisciplinary notions of 'othering', which have proliferated over centuries (including, for example, Lacan, 1968; De Beauvoir, 1973; Said, 1993; Arendt, 1986; Williams and Chrisman, 1994). In recognizing how different uses of this term have shifted paradigmatically, along with the interpretations that frame its particular meaning within different theoretical contexts, we intend to explore how these differentiated interpretations can all impact upon the child. Within this chapter we are not intending to subsume all uses of the terms 'other' or 'othering' to a single meaning, as we fully acknowledge that any sense of meaning belongs only to a slippery moment. It is proposed that the complexities inherent within this theme will be mindfully explored, being sensitive to the transient moments that afford different meanings to students, embedded within and expressed through language, discourse and narrative.

From a psychoanalytical perspective, Lacan (1968) framed 'othering' as part of the 'de-centering process' of the developing young infant. The notion of 'other' within this context was used to accommodate the 'mirror phase' of growth, where the infant imagines self reflected in the 'mirror' of the other's look, the omnipotent infant wishing to idealize their subject. 'Othering' for Lacan was about the opening of the child's relation with symbolic systems outside themselves and the beginnings of symbolic representation (Hall *et al.*, 1992). Within 1970s feminist literature, De Beauvoir identified woman as 'other', with the male positioned centre stage. She suggested that the male position is conceived of as gender neutral, he is the subject – she is the 'other'. Within post-colonial discourse, Said (1993) suggests that the white western world empowers a eurocentricity, aimed at 'othering' and primitivizing the non-white western world. The focus on western representations of its 'others' rests on a theory of dominant western imperial power and agency, pointing to a very familiar, widespread and stable form of 'othering' whereby the people being othered are homogenized into a collective 'they'. Said suggested that this 'othering' process is used to create, define and solidify the 'west'.

Searching for significant threads that transcend these interpretations of 'othering', we consider in more depth themes that first emerged in Chapter 12. We ponder, first, how 'non-other' seems to remain invisible, almost without scrutiny, without becoming an object of study. Second, we consider how 'other' seems to encapsulate the notion of the silenced voice, homogenized through a complex and systemic process of colonizing power and knowledge, thereby seeming to subjugate notions of difference. We arrive at these perspectives having reflected on the position of 'other' within these dichotomous discourses and find it to be rendered as such in order to maintain the status and authority of the 'non-other'. Two further points are added to these contemplations: De Beauvoir claimed that 'other' is posed as such by the 'One' in defining himself as the 'One' (1973); she also suggests that 'other' has been 'known' in the shadows of an ill-informed sense of 'pseudo-knowing', which is built on by Said's suggestion that the more 'knowable' (that is, the more stereotyped) the object becomes, the more 'other' it remains (1978).

Photographing silences: representations of 'other' within photographs (de-constructing early childhood)

Building on the use of film at Stage 1, this chapter contemplates photography that uses children and notions of childhood as its subject, which we believed could open up challenging readings of the still image as a political statement. Living in a world of photographic images, we considered an interesting opportunity would be to engage with such images as fragments contributing to the processes of 'othering' within early childhood. Uses of the photograph within, for example, art, photojournalism and advertising render it a familiar fixture, potentially having visual impact on a daily basis and able to physically and subliminally infiltrate a range of viewing contexts. It is considered to have the potential to penetrate the awareness of the consuming public, with a message that can be manipulated, deconstructed or framed in whichever way is deemed necessary. The focus within this chapter lies in the photograph utilized as a tool of advertisement, being complex in the ways its impact and meaning could be deconstructed. At stage 2 of the course, the advertising campaigns of Barnardo's, 'Stolen Childhood' (2002) and 'There are No Silver Spoons for Children Born into Poverty' (2003), were selected for their provocative imagery and in order to consider how organizations concerned with children's welfare subliminally construct or reconstruct children and aspects of childhood in certain ways.

Before moving onto its use in the classroom, some thoughts about our choice of photography as a reflexive tool of engagement seem useful. After 30 years of emergent post-structuralist thought (Derrida, 1972; Foucault, 1977), both the constructor and viewer of images could be perceived as having become insatiable deconstructionists. It could also be argued that the narratives brought to each photograph within this process of deconstruction emanate autobiographical tendencies, which could emerge as dominant transgressions informing interpretations of any subject visually represented. This notion of an autobiographical narrative is perceived here as the motives, understandings and perspectives of the photographer and viewer. Linfield (2001) suggests the photograph is a 'fictive construct' and proliferates 'discourses of power' that reveal only its own prejudices, that it expresses privilege. Furthermore, Pink suggests any 'ethnographicness of photography is determined by discourse and content, for example as a site of cultural production, social interaction and individual experience' (2001: 50).

Our responses to these thoughts relate to the idea that the photograph as a political tool could energize cultural and emotional relationships emerging from a reflexive engagement, with the image as symbolic representation. We accept that any symbol represents something else by convention or by association, but also in its representation it is socially and culturally defined, varying across different groups of people and time. The context and subject of each photograph therefore might determine the ways in which the image is 'read' and emerge as meaningful to the image-maker, as well as to the viewer. With this in mind we brought photography into the classroom.

The students were introduced to the uncompromising images used within the aforementioned Barnardo's advertising campaigns. The photographs have been digitally manipulated to juxtapose the body of a child, sometimes with the face of an adult, positioned alongside a suggested behaviour that the viewer might associate with sexual or substance abuse. The images do not claim to be in any sense 'real' or 'truthful', but present the viewer with an overt and deliberate reconstruction.

We accept that a photograph's ability to convey any kind of 'truth' has become controversial and limited, expressed in the mid-1980s by the critic

Grundberg (1985), who used the phrase 'crisis of the real' to describe the state of post-modern photography. He proposed that the photograph metaphorically has become a stained document, whereupon each image has the potential to become endlessly constructed, deconstructed, manipulated and 'rephotographed' – anything other than actually document self, other or the world. Our intentions were to use photographs to explore how thinking can sweep between reality and metaphor, where events and depictions have the potential to become embellished or constrained, depending upon the context in which they are 'translated'. The manipulation employed by Barnardo's seems to be used purposefully to raise awareness, to challenge assumptions and beliefs.

A Stage 2 student, Ruth Jacobson, reflected upon a number of images from the campaigns in detail and we intend to draw on some of her writing in order to engage with her response to the use of photography in the construction of 'other'. We will deconstruct aspects of her writing to explore the contemplations and deliberations we feel she may have gone through. Rather than Ruth taking an empathetic stance, which arguably could be the campaigns' primary intention – 'a potential victim, someone who is visibly at risk, which Hoffman believes "moves us to help the 'sufferer' " . . .' (cited in Goleman, 1996: 105) – her writing offered an account of what she perceived to be the campaigns' covert inference:

> Given the current emphasis on 'ideology of the child-centred society' (James and Prout, 1997: 1) we chose to examine discourses of childhood through the controversial Barnardo's advertising campaigns. These campaigns reflect childhoods that are not often seen or heard and therefore contest the view that groups (such as children) in western societies have 'obtained the right to be heard' (James and Prout, 1997: 85).
>
> (Jacobson, 2004)

Through a hint of western complacency, she seems to be subverting the assumption that the rhetoric of a 'child-centred society' has empowered the child to a position of 'non-other', whereby the child's previously silenced voice has now found listeners. The very birth of these campaigns for Ruth seems to have brought questions to a western society that in its complacency perhaps assumes relative self-assurance that 'the childhoods that are not often seen or heard' are an exception to otherwise well-adjusted community relations. This takes us back to the notion of the silenced voice from Chapter 12 that is '. . . already blue in the face from shouting' (Naib, 2002: 63) and the process of 'othering' that conveniently forgets the role that all have played in creating the conditions that spawn such hidden and silenced experiences. Within our focus on 'other', Ruth seems to have questioned the subtle power differentials embedded within the widely held belief that children have 'obtained the right to be heard'.

Linfield's (2001) suggestion that the photograph is itself a 'fictive construct' and proliferates 'discourses of power' brings an interesting interception
into the dynamic. Although it is made clear that the campaign has constructed
the photographs in the most literal sense, Ruth hints at their more covert
constructions, in that they can be read as visual narratives espousing abuses of
power and positions of powerlessness. Her choice of the term '*controversial*'
acknowledges the public furore that surrounded their release (with a record
472 complaints), but also suggests that their implicit connotations might be
constructed by the viewer as untenable within a society that advocates rights
for the child. The identification of such issues emerged from her justification
for the focus of her writing, which seem to situate her within the realm of
reflexive contemplation as her writing continues to ask difficult questions of
the images, of herself as a viewer, of the organization and of the consuming
public. She continues:

> ... On the issue of child prostitution ... these childhoods contradict popu-
> lar assumptions of childhood and its 'supposed embodiment of innocence'
> (Mills and Mills, 2000: 148), how child sexual abuse challenges 'trad-
> itional beliefs about childhood' (James and Prout, 1997: 1) and how prosti-
> tution can still only be possible in specific cultural conditions (Cusick,
> 2002: 230).
>
> (Jacobson, 2004)

Here, Ruth seems to recognize conceptually the intention of the image-makers
to challenge 'regimes of truth', by placing the physicality of the child (constructed through symbolic associations of powerlessness, fragility and vulnerability) in binary opposition to the world of adult powerfulness, manifested to
the point of exploitation. In her writing she proposes that the cultural positioning of these images challenges the viewer to consider any assumptions
they have about which groups are affected by prostitution.

Our engagement with her writing considers Giroux's notion of the dangers of the 'aestheticisation of politics', suggesting some images are so sen-
sationalized as 'horror' that the viewer can only respond to them on this
level, without being able to respond critically to them nor digest the social
politics surrounding them (1994: 18). Ruth's analysis prompts us to reconsider
the way in which Giroux places the viewer in a particular position that seems
to deny the potential for 'free-floating significance'. She seems to have
engaged with the images on a level beyond that of any surface interpretation
and we are drawn into understanding her engagement as an expression of
interpretative reflexivity (Lynch, 2000: 32), whereby she has attempted to
identify non-obvious narratives within more habitual ways of thinking. Our
tentative suggestion is borne out of her subsequent writing, in which she
interprets the use of shock tactics (perceived as a tool of engagement) as

advancing the organization's efforts to subvert the practices 'of western culture':

> . . . based on exclusion and the discourse of 'otherness' where groups such as children are placed as 'outsiders' . . . (Barrett, 1997: 1).

> (Jacobson, 2004)

We understood the narratives that she located within one of the images to be those she perceives as circulating amongst some of the viewing public in relation to adult drug abusers, positioned as 'other', disconnected from and maybe disowned by a moral highground-taking public. With reference to other images, Ruth goes on to suggest this shock tactic technique distracts from the implicit reinforcement of more subliminal stereotypical messages. She cites Barnes *et al.* (2003: 133):

> There is a place for shock tactics where the purpose is to inform debate and public opinion, but we are concerned and uneasy about the way in which the complex issue of child poverty is linked specifically to drug abuse and alcoholism . . .

> (Jacobson, 2004)

In relation to what we understand as her reflexive interpretation, Giroux argues that individuals produce rather than receive meanings (1994: 19), and we believe the student has gone on to 'produce' an interpretation of this idea in her writing:

> . . . Through their controversial campaigns, Barnardo's may have contributed to dispelling certain popular assumptions about childhood but may have also built on stereotypes of what it means to be poor . . .

> (Jacobson, 2004)

In her conclusion, Ruth presents a cautionary note:

> . . . it is important to explore the issue of childhood as a socially constructed discourse and how the 'concept of childhood has become problematic' (James and Prout, 1997: 1) largely because there is not one childhood but many.

> (Jacobson, 2004)

She recognizes the impact that these campaigns could potentially have in their construction and publicizing of an 'alternative childhood' that sits in binary opposition to the 'embodiment of innocence' (Mills and Mills, 2000: 148). However, she also intimates that in their visual singularity they do only offer one perspective or snapshot of a much more complex and wider picture. Photographs surely show the viewer something, but just as surely they are complex, intricate, demanding and need to be viewed as representative of multiple 'truths'. Their substitution of a single moment for the fluidity of connected events – connections through which we discover meaning – render photographs as objects, which as Sontag (1977) intimates cannot themselves explain anything but are inexhaustible invitations to deduction, speculation and fantasy.

Ruth's writing has afforded us fascinating points of reflection into the ways she deconstructed the visual imagery used in these advertising campaigns. As a concluding adjunct, we feel it is important to summarize issues relating to her interpretation of photography as a political statement. She seems to recognize that the viewer cannot 'know' an experience from a photograph any more than a reader can 'know' by isolating one phrase from a paragraph. We believe that she is alerted to the temptation to substitute the part for the whole, to confuse speculation with context, to mistake the emotional impact that photographs provide for an actual 'knowledge' of the complex web of events, human choices and social conditions. In the same way that Lyotard draws caution to writing that '. . . pretends to be complete . . .' (1988: 127), the photograph in its simplicity can claim to represent the completeness of a moment, allowing for an otherwise transient moment to be contemplated, revisited and reconsidered. However, rather than assume the logic of the present could be 'revealed' through the eye of a rational photographer and read as if embracing some form of definitive 'truth' by the viewer, Ruth acknowledges that the photographs offer an isolated fragment of something larger and as a fragment, is perceived as laden with competing personal and professional narratives.

It seems that a photograph's ability to convey 'truth' is becoming ever more open to speculation, and the potential for the 'multivocal readings' of film suggested at Stage 1 could also be placed onto the photograph at Stage 2. Furthermore, the viewing film audience who face the post-modern challenge of bringing 'free-floating significance' to the narrative can find a similar challenge awaiting them in the newspaper, magazine or art gallery.

The silences go on: 'othering' within documentary (early childhood reframed)

Having begun to disturb constructions of 'other' in film at Stage 1 (as we saw in Chapter 12) and now in photography at Stage 2, students are invited to re-engage with the thematic representations of 'other' through visual narratives in Stage 3. Channel 4's documentary *The Last White Kids* (Shona Thompson, 2003) concerns a white family living in a predominantly Asian district. We chose to use this documentary as it presented an interesting view of a well-documented area of the UK, often constructed in the national press as a region where intercultural relations are fractured and where mutually hostile communities are in turmoil, at times engaging in 'race riots' (see national press, May/June 2001). A number of reports have emerged out of such media-related storying. As an example, *Community Cohesion: A Report of the Independent Review Team* could be perceived as making gestures in an attempt to redress complex issues of 'other' and 'othering' with traces of superficial rhetoric:

> We believe that there is an urgent need to promote community cohesion, based upon a greater knowledge of, contact between, and respect for, the various cultures that now make Great Britain such a rich and diverse nation.
>
> (Community Cohesion Unit, 2003: 16)

Such claims to politically correct sensitivities could be construed as merely academic discourse, transgressing the incandescent autobiographical narratives that energize complex intercultural relations, as Farrar suggests:

> The concept of 'riot' is the organising tool for the discourse that is generated not only in the media, tabloid, broad-sheet, radio and television, but also in most of the official reports that are sometimes produced after these events. It functions to block a proper debate about what is really at stake . . .
>
> (Farrar, 2002: 4)

He goes on to talk about the media images that construct 'mobs' as aggressive and threatening, which:

> . . . must be the dominant, hegemonic reading [Hall 1980] of these images and texts. Alongside the myth of their primitive barbarism, the preferred reading of these words and images is that these people are unpredictable, irrational, uncontainable . . . These Others violently challenge all that the 'Normals' hold dear.
>
> (Farrar, 2002: 5)

Furthering these epic constructions of 'other', a number of recent television documentaries, including, for example, *Trouble Up North* (2002) and *Edge of the City* (2004), seem to have reinforced these provocative discourses, with transmission of *Edge of the City* being delayed after the programme was found to be advertised on the British National Party website as a 'party political broadcast'. We considered this a bleak 'othering' landscape, with documentary-makers struggling to address issues that could perhaps offer the viewer a different perspective from which to reconsider the disparate experiences of the communities who find some sense of 'home' within this region. With these preoccupations in mind, we selected the documentary *Last White Kids* to use with students at Stage 3. In an attempt to find ways to reframe constructions, we intended to open up and explore the concept of fluid identities as evolving intricate processes that could be seen to inform and shape inter-racial communities, thereby challenging what could be perceived as homogeneous and static media-perpetuated processes of 'othering' manifested by the fractious construction of this northern city.

Reflecting on the documentary, Sarfraz Manzoor ponders: 'What's it like to be white – and a minority' (2003: 33). He documents how the Gallaghers are the only white family on their street and in their whiteness are portrayed as feeling minoritized as representatives of one-third of the population of this area. He notices a curious difference between the reactions of the girls and their brothers to this assumed 'minority' status. On one level, the girls are constructed as wanting to be Muslims: reading Islamic books; experimenting with wearing hijabs and jilbabs; regularly taking part in the prayers and teachings within the local mosque; and reciting extracts from the Qu'ran. They can read and speak extracts of Arabic. What struck us as fascinating was the sense of spirituality that Ashlene, one of the daughters, was portrayed as being in the process of finding within Islam. In stark contrast to this, her 11 year old brother Jake and cousin John discuss their constructions of the world, divided into two groups: one group who are Muslims and the other group in binary opposition who include people who are white, black or mixed race, but what unites them is that they are not Muslim. The two boys include themselves in this group and give the group the name 'porkies' because, unlike the Muslims, they eat pork. Manzoor seemed interested in the way the boys placed themselves in opposition to the Muslim families, perhaps making an important comment about their own developing sense of identity and 'belonging' within a changing sense of urban community where the cultural, religious and racial mix is increasingly blurred.

What we perceived to be the documentary's inflammatory title, *Last White Kids*, seems to play on a notion of extinction, perhaps suggesting 'struggles to survive' a larger, stronger force working to banish, consume or eradicate. Before watching the documentary we asked students how the impact of this title might affect the viewing audience, and with what ideas and assumptions might an audience enter into a reading of this documentary? A student responded:

> *It might make you feel Britain's in a state of being over-run or that because of all the Black and Asian immigrant families, the white people in Britain feel they're being taken over.*

We interpreted her initial use of the term 'Britain' to represent an unstated relationship between a construct of Britain and the 'whiteness' that Britain historically embodied. Perhaps Britain still has not accepted its multiracial identity that is so often glibly assumed. Nevertheless, the student seemed to identify a pre-conditioning of the white audience that perhaps renders engagement with the documentary an almost foregone conclusion, in that the viewer might read a narrative of reassurance whereby their initial interpretation of 'extinction' finds affirmation.

On viewing the documentary, although the focus is the 'last white kids', what also interested us was its construction of the silenced community amongst which this white family lives. The stark use of polarities between white and Asian seemed to position the intricacies of ethnicity, religion, race and culture as confused, dilemmic and almost unimportant against this backdrop of simplistic differentiation. The Gallagher children were portrayed as struggling with these inter-relational complexities, whereas their mother was constructed as needing to distinguish herself clearly from her neighbours. We interpreted her dissatisfaction at being described as white and instead asserting herself as 'English' as a construction of her need to create a broader sense of sameness and collectivity, recognizing that some of her own extended family were mixed race.

Within its post-modern genre, the documentary seems to leave a prevailing dichotomy between the presence and absence of different voices in a whirlpool of conjecture. Interestingly, Conomos suggests:

> A documentary aware of its own artifice is one that . . . understands the mutual dependence of realism and 'artificiality'. . . . it recognizes the necessity of composing life in living it or making it . . .
>
> (Conomos, cited in McIlroy, 1993: 4)

Within the documentary, we interpret the consistently slippery use of terms such as 'white', 'Asian', 'Muslim', 'mixed race', 'English', 'Pakistani' and 'Bangladeshi' to facilitate the 'mutual dependence of realism and artificiality'. That is, the documentary's representation of the children's struggles with their emerging sense of identity set against their mother's certainty in defining herself seems to construct stories around the presence of particular personal journeys, where the viewer can find prevailing strategies of absence to reach their own relative truths. The mechanism of absenting the voice of the community surrounding the Gallagher family (despite being invisibly portrayed as overwhelmingly influential over the female white children) seemed to be a vehicle used to suspend the restlessness of this dichotomized absence, being subverted through the frame of the defining presence. As Dyer suggests: '. . . white people have had so very much more control over the definition of themselves and indeed of others than have those others . . .' (2002: xiii).

With reference to the strikingly silent voice of the wider community, filtered through the white mother's reflections, a student suggested:

> *I could see how their mum might see her daughter's involvement with the Mosque as 'brainwashing', particularly with her name being changed from Ashlene to Ayeshah . . . You know like part of her family's identity is being taken away.*

We considered whether this student, in her attempts to destabilize her own initial reading of the imagery, might be trying to explore alternative cultural narratives that, despite the deliberate polysemous aestheticization of experiences within the documentary, are still constrained by conventional and established cultural patterns of representation and interpretation. In other words, in the process of being destabilized, could the student only fall as far as the safety net of white consciousness would allow her? Another student commented:

> *It's easy though to just say she's being brainwashed. I thought Ashlene really got something from going to the Mosque . . . it's as if she needed to be there because when she wasn't able to go, she seemed lost . . .*

An immediate response to this came from another student:

> *Yes, and I think that although her mum said she thought her daughter was being brainwashed, later she arranged for her to go back to the Mosque which I think was a really brave thing to do.*

Here, we witnessed what we perceived as the unfolding thoughts of students' fascinating conceptual journeys. The discussion had been positioned by a student expressing her empathy for Ashlene's mother, but with indications that she was beginning to disturb what she might have otherwise left unexplored. A second student then responded by suggesting the misleading scapegoating process of assigning blame (brainwashing) could be a comfort zone for unquestioned beliefs, serving to shield Ashlene's mother from much more complex dilemmas in relation to her own cultural position. The third intervention almost demonstrates this, when the student refers to Ashlene's mother as being 'brave' for stepping outside of what could be read as her cultural constraints.

Extending this notion of constraint, another student suggested the role that language plays in her reading of this documentary:

> *What's interesting to me is the idea that there doesn't seem to be any language to express what lies in the middle of binary constructs. The*

language to describe opposites is well established and maybe that's why we stay situated there rather than find new ways to talk about the messiness of real life.

We considered this idea within the light of Greene's assertion: 'When people cannot name alternatives, imagine a different state of things, share with others a project of change, they could remain anchored or submerged . . .' (1988: 9). This shift to a focus on language then flourished as students began to find ways of reconsidering the visual and autobiographical narratives represented within the documentary and began to explore what Conomos proposes: 'Documentary has come to suggest incompleteness and uncertainty, recollection and impression, images of personal worlds and their subjective construction' (cited in McIlroy, 1993: 6).

As they contemplated the language they were using to describe their responses to the documentary, the students also started to consider the language the Gallagher family were using in trying to express their sense of difference and sameness, lying within the context of the active presence of the documentary-maker, who asked particular questions, took up particular issues and focused on particular passing comments made by the family. A student pointed out how the Gallagher girls were keen to distinguish between their own Wahabi mosque and the nearby Sunni mosque, which she felt suggested an influence of the community they lived in, perhaps the emergence of multiple cultural narratives that lay within a particular religious ideology.

Against a post-colonial landscape of 'other', we asked whether the documentary-makers intended to construct the Gallagher family as 'other' in an inter-racial context where whiteness has historically been perceived as 'non-other'. Dyer suggests that '. . . whiteness as power is maintained by being unseen' (2002: 45), and perhaps the Gallagher family were now being constructed as 'seen' and as losing a sense of power (reference to notion of extinction) because of the documentary's portrayal of some of the children's cultural transgressions. Interestingly, Dyer goes on to say white people have the right 'to be various, literally to incorporate into themselves features of other peoples' (2002: 49), which offers a further issue for contemplation. The prolific increase in white people's acceptance, consumption of and relationship to black music and dance suggests that some are comfortable incorporating cultural differences into their own sense of self, but perhaps there are subtleties at work here. Are we detecting a nuanced hierarchy of 'otherness', which might relate back to the Gallagher boys' differentiated construction of Muslims and 'porkies'? Within the context of this documentary and in relation to the Gallagher girls, the characteristics of being Muslim focused upon embracing Islam as a way of life and experimenting with dress, perhaps two areas constructed within the documentary as constraining rather than emancipating. Within the 'white western world' where a sense of individual freedom is valued and 'normalized', is it conceivable that the 'othering' interpretations of Islam and associated dress codes have created a particular dilemma for the Gallagher mother and boys? Perhaps their preclusion of 'other' has found form in their understandings of Islam as a vehicle of constraint and absolutism, as the antithesis of personal freedom? Ironically, could the construction of Ashlene's spiritual journey embody her search for a sense of personal identity and freedom *through* Islam?

Perhaps within the documentary's attempt to make a political statement about the family's forced responses to their position, whereby the binaries of assimilation or ostracism became the only presented options, Henson's controversial thoughts might find some allegiance: 'We know that people can undergo a sudden change of thinking and loyalties under threat of . . . intense social pressure and isolation' (2002: 345).

In discussing Henson's seemingly essentialist position a student brought an interesting concept into the dynamic:

> *Do you think being 'othered' depends on where you are and who you're with? If, for example, I lived in a predominantly non-white country, perhaps being white would make me feel othered, whereas I don't here . . . not because of my whiteness anyway . . . it just seems that being 'othered' isn't a condition that's static.*

This student seems to be suggesting that in a context where her whiteness has historically been the 'norm', she feels she does not have to consider this as part of her identity: her skin colour and everything that this represents in Britain renders it invisible. Her inference to fluidity, destabilization and shifting notions of self in relation to 'other' is understood as this student's struggle to locate a position for herself amongst these linguistic and conceptual tendencies to find solace within binaries. Her reflexive engagement suggested to us that she was exploring some difficult ideas around power, politics and polarities, amidst media representations of a world where the 'messiness of real life' has become invisible. With reference to this idea, an Asian student reflected:

> *I have to say that even though I have the skin colour and religious beliefs to be othered within this country, I don't feel othered . . . maybe it's about my own self-confidence in my sense of identity . . .*

The process of 'othering' is positioned here as a white construction and this construction of 'other' has not been received or understood by this student as part of her sense of identity. With reference to her comment, we reflected upon the emergence of this notion of 'other', understanding it to have been borne from academic discourses, which could be perceived as being rooted in the 'masculinization of thought' (Boler, 1999: 10), thought that in itself remains defined by the dominant ideologies of 'non-other'. The discussion also has resonance with Barth's conception of ethnicity as:

> . . . the cumulative result of a number of separate choices and decisions made by people acting vis-a-vie one another . . . patterns are generated through processes of interaction and in their form reflect the constraints and incentives under which people act.
>
> (Barth, 1966: 2)

For Barth (2000), ethnic identity is not fixed but generated through interaction with others and is a performance in relation to a boundary. However, as he notes, that boundary is permeable and plastic rather than fixed:

> . . . we can assume no simple one-to-one relationship between ethnic units and cultural similarities and differences. The features that are taken into account are not the sum of 'objective' differences, but only those, which the actors themselves regard as significant . . . Some cultural features are used by actors as signals and emblems of differences, others are ignored . . .
>
> (Barth, 1969: 14)

This student's contribution led us to reflect more extensively upon these notions of non-static positions, shifting cultural and gendered identities, having opened up fascinating areas for ongoing deliberations in the classroom.

We consider that the journeys started over the duration of this chapter have presented us with the opportunity to destabilize further as well as beginning to facilitate the reframing of students' understandings of self in relation to 'other'. By doing so, students might be encouraged to continue to explore 'situated' or embodied knowledges, perhaps working towards what McCarthy and Crichlow suggest 'making visible what is rendered invisible when viewed as the normative state of existence . . .' (1993: 193).

The complexities of absence . . .

In the spirit of a free-floating consideration of how children and childhood have been constructed and our attempts to deconstruct and challenge apparent certainties, we move not to the victory of conclusion but to the complexities of absence. The invisibility of 'non-other' alongside the silenced 'other' have become threads emerging from all three forms of visual narrative in the present and previous chapter, which in different ways have perpetuated a recognition that: 'No one should ever "speak for" or assume another's voice . . . it becomes a form of colonization' (Sinister Wisdom Collective, 1990: 4). Instead of 'the silenced object' and 'the invisible subject' being perpetuated in binary relation to each other, the notion of absence has taken different forms and served different purposes at different times, which has left us with many ideas to contemplate. The language struggles lying within an emerging sense of complexity continue to present new challenges as students contemplate more intricate nuances of experiencing which might otherwise have been systematically compartmentalized to satisfy some kind of conceptual equilibrium. Zizek, discussing the notion of 'floating signifiers', suggests they become structured into:

> . . . a unified field which 'quilts' them, stops their sliding and fixes their meaning . . . overdetermined by their articulation in a chain with other elements – that is their 'literal' signification depends on their metaphorical surplus-signification . . . the 'quilting' performs the totalization by means of which this free-floating of ideological elements is halted . . . they become parts of the structured network of meaning.
>
> (Zizek, 1989: 87)

Recognizing the intricate and consuming visual world carefully constructed around each of us, our use of film (in Chapter 12) and of photography and documentary (in this chapter) attempted to disrupt aspects of this 'structured network of meaning'. By probing some of the 'metaphorical surplus-signification' circulating within this visuality, we strived to interrupt students' 'knowing' of children. We attached what we interpret as 'nodal points', such as 'children who are mixed race' (*East is East*), 'children who are abused' (Barnardo's campaigns) or 'last white children' (*Last White Kids*), to try to open up what could otherwise be perceived as a neatly configured conceptual quilt of 'knowing' about children and childhood. In this way, by discussing the many different assumptions we associate with particular terms and by looking at the cluster of descriptors used to express understandings of sameness and difference, we attempted to explore an understanding of what Zizek describes as 'primal baptism' (1989: 87). That is, the ways words have been transmitted, along with particular meanings, in a chain of tradition. Questions have to be asked, including whether we could ever disturb this chain, or whether all struggles would only ever be different struggles that find other forms of the same expression, and, of course, whether or not this actually matters.

What we feel students have begun to do, as interpreted through their diverse comments and writing, is to take some time to deliberate what they might otherwise have discarded as 'old hat'. We used very familiar forms of visual narrative that within different social contexts might have been consumed in ways that reassured or satisfied their own sense of self, as well as their sense of 'other'. Wilkinson and Kitzinger refer to how intimately this process is related to how 'we' use the 'other' to define ourselves, how 'we' understand ourselves in relation to what 'we' are not (1996: 8).

With this in mind, our emphasis on these visual narratives in the classroom context may have served to interrupt the students' initial disregard for them as powerful message-givers and themselves as reflexive negotiators, whereby they can begin to 'see' each in different ways, or at least to contemplate them in a different context. When they next 'see' a film, photograph or documentary, they may feel interested enough to read each differently and perhaps begin to ponder: 'If I find myself through you, but no longer control the you that grants me my self, then I am forced to deal with a self that is beyond my control . . .' (Sampson, 1993: 153).

References

Arendt, H. (1986) *The Origins of Totalitarianism*. London: Andre Deutsch.

Barnes, M., Middleton, S., Millar, J., Room, G. and Tsakloglou, P. (2003) *Poverty and Social Exclusion in Europe*. London: Edward Elgar.

Barth, F. (1966) *Models of Social Organisation*, Occasional Paper no. 23. London: Royal Anthropological Institute.

Barth, F. (1969) *Ethnic Groups and Boundaries: The Social Organisation of Culture Difference*. Oslo: Universitetsforlaget.

Barth, F. (2000) 'Boundaries and Connections', in A. P. Cohen (ed.) *Signifying Identities*. London: Routledge.

Boler, M. (1999) *Feeling Power*. New York: Routledge.

Community Cohesion Unit (2003) *Community Cohesion: A Report of the Independent Review Team*. London: Home Office.

De Beauvoir, S. (1973) *The Second Sex*. New York: Vintage.

Derrida, J. (1972) *Positions*. Chicago: University of Chicago Press.

Du Gay, P., Hall, S., Janes, L., MacKay, H. and Negus, K. (1997) *Doing Cultural Studies: the story of the Sony Walkman*. London: Sage/The Open University Press.

Dyer, R. (2002) *White*. London: Routledge.

Farrar, M. (2002) *'Riot as the dominant framing device': Parallel Lives and Polarisation*. BSA 'Race' and Ethnicity Study Group Seminar.

Foucault, M. (1977) *Discipline and Punish*. London: Allen Lane.

Giroux, Henry A. (1994) *Disturbing Pleasures – Learning Popular Culture*. London: Routledge.

Godfrey, W. (2004) *Them and Us and 9/11: Representations of British Asians in Contemporary British Cinema*. Paper given at symposium ('Issues Of Representation In Film') presented by Postgraduate Studies in Visual Representation, School of Art and Design, Bradford College (see http://www.bradfordfilmfestival.org.uk/ 2004).

Goleman, D. (1996) *Emotional Intelligence*. London: Bloomsbury Publishing.

Greene, M. (1988) *The Dialectic of Freedom*. New York: Teachers College Press.

Grundberg 1985, cited in Grundberg, A. (1999) *Crisis of the Real: Writings on Photography Since 1974 (Writers & Artists on Photography)*. London: Aperture.

Hall, S. (2002) *Representation: Cultural Representations and Signifying Practices*. London: Sage Publications.

Hall, S., Held, D. and McGrew, T. (1992) *Modernity and its Futures*. Oxford: Blackwell Publishers.

Hendrick, H. (1997) 'Constructions and Reconstructions of British Childhood', in A. James and A. Prout (eds) *Constructing and Reconstructing Childhood* (2nd edn). Brighton: Falmer.

Henson, H. K. (2002) Sex, Drugs and Cults, *The Human Nature Review*, 2: 343–355.

Jacobson, R. (2004) *The Deconstruction of Early Childhood*, BA (Hons) Early Childhood Studies essay. Manchester Metropolitan University.

James, A. and Prout, A. (1997) *Constructing and Reconstructing Childhood* (2nd edn). Brighton: Falmer.

Jenks, C. (1996) *Childhood*. London: Routledge.

Lacan, J. (1968) 'The mirror phase as formative of the function of the I', *Écrits*. London: Tavistock.

Linfield, S. (2001) *The Boston Review*. New York: New York University Press.

Lynch, M. (2000) 'Against Reflexivity as an Academic Virtue and Source of Privileged Knowledge', *Theory, Culture and Society*, 17(3): 26–54.

Lyotard, J. F. (1988) *Peregrinations. Law, Form, Event*. New York: Columbia University Press.

Manzoor, S. (2003) Isle of White, *The Guardian*, 30th October.

McCarthy, C. and Crichlow, W. (1993) *Race, Identity and Representation in Education*. New York: Routledge.

McIlroy, B. (1993) 'Observing and Walking the Thinnest of Lines: Phenomenology, Documentary Film and Errol Morris', *Semiotic Inquiry*, 13(1–2): 288.

Mills, J. and Mills, R. (2000) *Childhood Studies: A Reader in Perspectives of Childhood*. London: Routledge.

Naib, H. (2002) *The New Seriousness*. Bradford: Funkaarh Muvment.

Pink, S. (2001) *Doing Visual Ethnography*. London: Sage Publications.

Said, E. (1993) *Culture and Imperialism*. London: Chatto and Windus.

Sampson, E. (1993) *Celebrating the Other: A Dialogic Account of Human Nature*. London: Harvester Wheatsheaf.

Sim, S. (2001) *Postmodernism*. London: Routledge.

Sinister Wisdom Collective (1990) 'Editorial', *Sinister Wisdom*, 42(4): 1–6.

Sontag, S. (1977) *On Photography*. London: Doubleday.

Thompson, S. (2003) *Cutting Edge: The Last White Kids*, 30th October. Channel Four.

Wilkinson, S. and Kitzinger, C. (1996) *Representing the Other*. London: Sage Publications.

Williams, P. and Chrisman, L. (1994) *Colonial Discourse and Post-colonial Theory*. Essex: Prentice Hall.

Wolfreys, J. (1998) *Deconstructing Derrida*. London: Macmillan Press.
Young, R. (1995) *Colonial Desire: Hybridity in Theory, Culture and Race*. London: Routledge.
Zizek, S. (1989) *The Sublime Object of Ideology*. London: Verso.

14 International perspectives

Sue Aitken and John Powell

Introduction

> The report concludes that half of all children in the world today suffer
> from some form of extreme deprivation. Whether it is lack of water,
> lack of health care, lack of schooling, or lack of protection; whether it
> is displacement in war, exploitation due to economic desperation, or
> the losses caused by HIV/AIDS, more than 1 billion children are being
> robbed of childhood.
>
> (9th December 2004, Unicef press release)

The above remarks highlight a familiar and easily recognizable picture of a
world where children can be vulnerable, deprived and exploited. It also
assumes, in common with the views of many of our students, that 'childhood'
is a simple concept possessing both universality and commonality. However,
one of the central challenges for tutors and students when exploring international perspectives is to try to understand childhood as highly complex and
multilayered (see Stainton Rogers and Stainton Rogers, 1992; Qvortrup, 1994;
James *et al.*, 1998; James, 1999). For many students, however, the statement
above characteristically distances them from the world of disadvantaged
childhoods as somehow existing beyond their own understanding.

Images of such childhoods, whether represented in visual or written
form or generated by news media or charities, suggest that they are being
'marked out' by deprivation or personal disaster that may serve to categorize
children and childhood. Through this type of process they acquire the label
of 'the starving child', 'the war torn child' and/or 'the exploited' and
'abused child'. Thus, within the supposed universality of childhood, the
notion of child as 'other' is established. It is also likely that the representation of children as described above can become a metaphor for all children
from non-western and essentially non-white societies. Holland suggests that
the 'press reports of wars, famine and natural disasters and appeals for aid

become synonymous with pictures of black and non white children' (1992: 148).

The aim of this chapter is to highlight and reflect upon the challenge to tutors and students of simultaneously exploring the impact of 'separating' and 'othering' whilst developing a sense of connectedness to childhood worlds in a range of contexts, both locally and globally. To achieve this aim, the chapter will explore notions of childhood by examining perceptions of 'work' and 'play' as central themes to help students develop a more coherent and dynamic relationship with international perspectives. In so doing, students are offered an opportunity to re-examine readings of childhood experiences in a national and international context, seeking to draw parallels and divergence within the lives of children across the globe. As the Unicef report highlighted above makes clear, poverty is not exclusive to developing countries:

> In 11 of the 15 OECD countries for which comparable data is available, there have been notable increases of child poverty rates over the course of roughly the last decade. At the beginning of the Millennium only three countries – Finland, Norway and Sweden – enjoyed a rate of child poverty of less than 5 per cent.
>
> (Unicef, 2004: 34)

The background

Historically, our teaching of International Perspectives encompassed the idea of a comparative study for students in their final year. The logical argument was that students who had acquired and experienced a range of settings in this country were now equipped to make comparisons with other systems and ideologies within a global context. Almost immediately, however, students were faced with a number of difficulties in developing their understanding through resources such as the Internet. These difficulties centred on barriers presented in language and the authenticity of the information and data gathered. What emerged for the students was an understanding that fact and truth are highly contestable and constructed notions that are validated within the various contexts in which they were given. For example, when looking at government statistics concerning the numbers of children who are diagnosed as having HIV/AIDS or the numbers of children who *don't* receive a full-time education, there were concerns that such figures were selective so as to present a particular picture. Equally, organizations such as Unicef and Save the Children tend to highlight needs of children as a marketing tool to raise contributions. As students wrestled with official and governmental spin and obfuscation, they experienced frustration and impotence. As one student remarked: 'how can I know what is really going on? Unless I experience it, see it, analyse first hand all I can gain is a superficial and one-dimensional account of provision in any country.' This student had articulated and implicitly identified a powerful dilemma that surrounds the collection and validity of secondary data versus first-hand experiences. However, some of our students believe that this dilemma may be overcome and objectivity achieved merely by being there to experience actions being performed that later represent data. But as Gunnar Myrdal observed:

> The faith of the student is his [sic] conviction that truth is wholesome and that illusions are damaging, especially opportunistic ones. He seeks 'realism', a term which in one of its meanings denotes an 'objective' view of reality.
>
> (Myrdal, 1969: 3)

As a reflection of these difficulties, the focus of this chapter now begins to shift from a straightforward comparative research study of provision to a study of the construction of childhood experiences and its diverse meanings across the world. Thus students were given the opportunity not just to compare but also to question the very premise on which that comparison had taken place, using concepts such as 'work' and 'play' as the vehicle.

One step backwards

Understanding the social and cultural construction of working children in a cross-cultural context requires an elaboration of many of the themes already encountered in this book, including power of discourses and theories related to 'othering'. As an exercise, students are asked why the map (figure 14.1) of the world is oriented the way it is, with Europe and North America at the top and Britain in the middle? Given that the world is a sphere floating in the void of space, there is no 'right way up', there is no correct orientation. The students are asked, 'How does our view of the world change when we see it this way up?' The map opposite highlights the western-centric nature of our construction of the world.

Students' responses include, *'we can't find "us"'* and *'Europe is really small in comparison to Asia'*, or *'Europe and the USA don't seem to dominate the world in the same way.'* The students' perceptions are altered; no longer do they take for granted the 'position' of Europe and the USA at the centre of the world. In a real sense what is familiar or constant in their world has been distorted.

Further distortions are undertaken when students are introduced to the idea of a map of the world being a 'representation' – a representation that reflects the past as much as it represents the present. It is an iconography that mirrors the power, politics and economic positions of dominant/powerful

Figure 14.1 An Australian mapmakers view of the world. Reproduced with permission © Hema Maps Pty Ltd.

cultures, thus giving a representation a seeming reality. Such representations occupy a position that Baudrillard (1994), in his articulation of the 'simulacra', regards as a simulation rather than a fiction. A hyper reality where consensual imagery and representation create a world that we consciously recognize as 'real' but subconsciously know it cannot be. The map also serves to 'other', to divide and dissect the world into binaries of rich and poor, west and non-west, developed and non-developed, as articulated by Said (1985) and Paechter (1998).

In trying to reposition students, the aim is to get them to take a step back from the here and now and the commonsense approach in order to seek a global overview that informs their understanding of the various positions in which children may be placed in different parts of the world. As part of their study they examine the way 'orientalism' (Said, 1985) has 'warped' other perspectives in understanding children and childhood. For many students who are first or second generation migrants to this country, this provides an arena to relate their own narratives concerned with being a child and childhood, where for some it has been experienced as feeling simultaneously both an insider and an outsider.

The discourse that encompasses a community of west and the rest, north and south, also creates positional distortions where descriptors such as 'third world', 'undeveloped countries' and 'developing country' serve to emphasize hierarchies. As Hall states: '(the) West is a historical, not a geographic construct. By "western" we mean a society that is developed, industrialized, urbanized, capitalist, secular and modern' (1992: 277). The west, according to Hall's argument, therefore includes Japan in the east, Australia to the south, Europe in the centre and the USA and Canada to the west in our standard 'right way up' map. However, following publication of the Brandt Report (1980), when the world was identified as being split between the wealthy north and the poor south, the term north/south began to be used to describe the economic 'haves' and 'have-nots'. Yet using a 'normal map' implies that there is a top and a bottom, where a sense of a hierarchy is still maintained.

The shadow cast by nineteenth and early twentieth century European imperialism and colonialism serves to structure many cultures in terms of language, custom and 'tradition'. Every continent outside Europe has its dominant European language, be it English, Spanish, Dutch or French. Imperialism and colonialism could be described as the mother and father of globalization, where homogenization and ubiquity are spawned. So a 'good' childhood will resemble a western one, where education replaces work, where childhood continues until the 18th year and where children can play freely and unhindered. As McKechnie and Hobbs observe:

> Countries such as Britain are sometimes treated as if they represent a model for the treatment of children to which economically under-developed economies should aspire. This is based on the assumption that Britain long ago 'solved' its child labour problem.
>
> (McKechnie and Hobbs, 2001: 9)

Students also examine why the 'other' can be presented as beguiling and superior, often seen as providing the panacea for the cracks that appear in a domestic context. Models such as Reggio Emilia, Te Whariki and the Scandinavian Paedagogic system can be read as both exotic and cherished and as wholly transferable models of excellence. Whilst each may present innovative ideas and positions on the care and education of children, each must be read within its own context, needs and political climate. Johnson (1999) suggests that we should perhaps cast doubt on the universality and transferability of such models. Students are therefore encouraged to investigate the import/export dynamics of understanding childhood. Just as pre-school models in Scandinavia and Reggio Emilia are deemed to be worthy of importation as a means of enriching children's development in western societies, at the same time western philosophies and practices are exported to non-western countries as solutions for poverty, ill-health and exploitation.

Why should this be of interest to us? Entirely because the concept of 'us' gives a sense of unity, with a sense of shared understanding and commonalities, but more importantly it sets up the possibility that there is also a 'them', those who aren't like us. In brief, they are 'other' to us. It is perhaps therefore a little ironic that in developing an international perspective our gaze is directed inward rather than outward. Here the ambition is both to explore and to deconstruct what we understand by 'work' and 'play' within a western discourse. These thoughts are then used to examine these notions in an international sense.

Playing with 'work'

Work is often seen as the antithesis of play. But what is work? Fyfe (1989) makes the distinction between child *work* and child *labour*. He argues that children often want to work; it is a rite of passage that can provide independence and status. However, he also stresses that such work should be non-industrial and should not be harmful. Finally, it should occupy a minor proportion of the waking day. In a similar vein, the International Labour Organization defines child labour as 'paid and unpaid work or activities that are mentally, physically, socially or morally harmful to children' (ILO, 2002: 5). In other words, it is not work *per se* which is considered to be harmful but the type and conditions of work that children undertake. Additionally, agency is clearly an issue, where within Fyfe's definition children who work have the freedom to choose to work or not.

Having established some of the difficulties in trying to clarify 'work' in a singular way, the students are then asked to think about the work/labour dichotomy by considering a number of scenarios within a western context. For example, is it work or labour to help out on the family farm or in the family shop or business? Is it work or labour to look after younger siblings or act as a main carer on a regular basis? Such activities are often not seen in terms of work or indeed labour but rather a family commitment or duty (Qvortrup 1994; Song, 2001). Yet such children could be working with heavy machinery or with dangerous agricultural chemicals, or indeed working extended hours in a family shop or restaurant. But it is questionable whether such practices are seen as exploitative or harmful. In our view they become invisible. After all, there are few public campaigns arguing for the abolition of children working in family businesses here in the UK.

Meanwhile, there is a sense in which children's work in the west is viewed as a positive experience, as 'character building', 'developmental' and part of 'adult apprenticeship'. Indeed, students themselves describe many instances of work as a child, whether helping around the house or assisting on paper rounds, in positive terms where they can remember a sense of independence.

However, those students who have had to work in family businesses describe it as an 'obligation' where 'there was no choice'. Similarly, Song refers to British-born Chinese children and the tensions created around participation in family-run Chinese takeaway businesses: 'Despite the widely reported belief in helping out, many young people reported a constant tension between wanting to help out and feeling that they had to help out' (2001: 65). Moreover, she goes on to suggest that children may play a key role in the successful operation of the business, especially where translation and interpretation skills are necessary.

Thus what may initially appear as unsophisticated in terms of understanding the meanings of 'work/labour' can be shown to be complex. Within industrialized and western states, working children are rarely seen as exploited in the sense that non-western children are. This leads students on to make a link between children working and poverty. However, the irony is that working children in Great Britain are less likely to be found in deprived homes than in affluent middle class ones (Hobbs and McKechnie, 1997).

Despite this, the notion that children only work in the most extreme of circumstances is still persistent. In our view this is because of how 'the child' and 'childhood' are configured within (western) discourse. Here, childhood is separated from adulthood; children therefore are discouraged from overtly participating in activities that are viewed by adults as being for adults, such as paid work. Thus a link is made between the need for children to 'play' rather than 'work' for the greater good of their development and education.

Whilst no one would suggest that young children should not be protected from exploitation, in any form, it is with reference to child labour in the less developed countries of the world and its links to poverty that for many students provide the most interesting challenges. It is the nature of this work, poverty and its contextualized meanings that, as in the examination of the world map, provides them with a different method of understanding these terms. For a number of students the only awareness of physical geography they have is triggered by media reports that highlight human suffering. For many it is only a famine, a natural disaster or war that helps them to locate the poorest places in the world. These states are therefore already constructed as comparatively less developed, poor and vulnerable.

Thus students, when considering the way children are constructed – as workers – will tend to do so with this pre-formed reading in mind. Many have been aware of consumer boycotts and campaigns against child labour and some may even have taken part. It therefore often comes as a surprise when they are asked to consider what a cessation of work might mean for child workers. By using material such as the following, students have to once again take a step back in order to reconsider preconceived ideas. The subsequent extract is taken from 'The Working Children's Report' (1998), submitted to the UN Committee on the Rights of the Child and initiated by 'Concern for Working Children, India' whose aim is to empower children by creating opportunities for them to influence the process of decision making:

Working children cannot be abruptly pulled out from work. Before that, alternative arrangements have to be made because all children have a right to survival.

When children have their own thoughts, society comes in their way. For example, if a girl chooses to plough in the field, the society says 'What a shame, she is a girl and she wants to plough'. The government should break down such barriers. Then children will be able to act on the basis of their thoughts.

We are working children. Why does the government want to send us to beggars' colonies?

(Taken from 'The Concern for Working Children' India website)

Such remarks call into question the frequently held belief that working children do not want to work or that work is undertaken under duress and that it often results from the impact of economic structure not personal agency. As Liebel points out:

When, in May 1998 some working children from Nicaragua were visiting Germany one twelve-year-old girl took the wind out of the sails of a woman journalist. In answer to her question as to whether she would not give up working if her mother alone brought home enough money, the girl answered: 'Why should I? It makes me proud to earn something myself. I learn how to look after money. It gives me independence'.

(Liebel, 2004: 1)

Indeed, increasingly there is evidence of children taking responsibility for their own work experiences. For example, organizations such as Bhima Sanga in Bangalore and Bal Mazdoor Sangh (Child Workers' Union) in Delhi represent on an informal basis working children who have collected together to lobby local, national and international authorities to recognize them as workers with equal rights. Swift states:

What the movements have done is build on children's ability to help protect themselves against the physical and psychological traumas that poverty and social exclusion expose them to. They have gone further, enabling children in varying degrees to become protagonists for their rights and for social change rather than victims of poverty.

(Swift, 1999: 10)

Students are asked to consider alternative strategies that empower children, rather than solutions such as consumer boycotts that are externally imposed. Boycotts are often considered to be at best unhelpful and at worse harmful – in the same way that economic and political sanctions seem only to harm the vulnerable rather than the intended target (as with the sanction against Iraq before 2002). Students begin to question whether western ideology in relation to children working is in all instances in the best interest of the child, when it might necessitate the loss of a means of survival. The ILO in 2002 recognized that only a small minority – 5 per cent of child workers – were involved in the production of exported goods and that western boycotts, whilst well meaning, sometimes resulted in the closure of factories employing underage workers who were then forced to find alternative employment, often in worse conditions.

A general view held by some in the west is that the way to eradicate children working is to provide them with compulsory schooling. This model is derived from Victorian Britain, which in the mid- and late nineteenth centuries combined legislation prohibiting child working with legislation for compulsory education (Fyfe, 1989; Weiner, 1991; Green, 1998). However, as students begin to appreciate, the separation of children from work and replacing it with education does not necessarily release children to play.

Playing with play

As already articulated in Chapter 3, 'play' is neither neutral nor benign. Within the social, educational and political context it serves a range of purposes. The discourse concerning the positive nature of children and play is a powerful one. However, its juxtapositioning with 'work' in the context of international perspectives allows for a reading of the dominant western-centric position that articulates a relationship of 'play' to 'work' that in many instances is oppositional. Students come to perceive, through various routes, that the western reading of 'play' is as socially constructed as that of work. Although 'play' has often become a metaphor for what is perceived as good for children as much as 'work' has become a metaphor for what is bad, is our understanding of 'play' any more real or tangible as a childhood practice than our western reading of 'work'?

Just as children's work has become invisible in the west, so children and play and its supporting rhetoric has become very visible. That said, there is sufficient ambiguity around the notion of play that prevents complacency. Students themselves report mixed messages about it. Those, for example, who experience placements in Key Stage 1 classrooms describe how play can be treated as part of packages that are aimed at instilling either 'good behaviour' or 'productivity of work'. So beyond the foundation stage it is not unusual to hear expressions such as 'when you have finished your work you can go and play' or 'you will have to stay in at break time to finish your work'. Moreover, those students who have experience in more affluent areas indicate a practice where children appear to be weaned away from play so that they might experience a more substantial diet, including undertaking 'paper and pencil' tasks aimed presumably at 'getting them ready' for formal schooling.

Meanwhile, outside of early years institutions confused messages circulate around play, some of which are pejorative. Think here of the child who is admonished for 'playing around' or the young one who is described as 'playing up'. It is by juggling with these mixed messages and meanings that coalesce around play that students can move beyond an overly simplistic, commonsense notion that positions play as the positive other to work. Moreover, by opening up 'play' (and 'work'), opportunities are created to rethink fixed notions.

Additionally, further ruptures are made by considering those countries where there is slippage between the work–play binary. For example, Liebel (2004) refers to the work of Ortiz Rescaniere (1994) and Rengifo Vasquez (2001), who when researching in the Andes identified an inseparability between play, work and life. Meiser (1995) too could discern no apparent separation of work and play or leisure and work in the Tongan people or children of the South Pacific. Liebel (2004) further cites Kummels' (1993) observation that Raramuri children in Chihuahua, Mexico, when aged about six are given jobs with responsibility such as looking after cattle. However, the children play games and have fun while caring for the animals. Similarly, Klute (1996), Nunes (1999) and Melaku (2000, cited in Liebel, 2004) have noted that in Brazil, central Africa and Ethiopia play and the responsibility for looking after animals go hand in hand. Casting our eyes back further to the seminal work of Margaret Mead (1928), she pointed out that Samoan children from the age of four or five performed definite tasks and duties within the community commensurate with their strength and intelligence. However, the time spent as such was more related to their lives than the six hours each day spent by American children in schools learning skills that seemingly had little to do with their lives. Mead in fact referred to schooling as an 'inexplicable nuisance with some compensations' (1928: 133).

Conclusion

Making sense of notions such as 'work' and 'play' within an international context is part of a process where students can develop 'agency'. Our concept of agency draws on Davies' work. Here an individual is one:

> . . . who **actively** makes sense of, rather than passively receives, the meanings available within discourses used by the groups of which

they are a member (and thus as one who can refuse discourses, or positions within discourses, who can stand outside of any particular discursive/interactive practices, who can take these practices up as their own, or not as they choose).

(Davies, 1996: 360, author's emphasis)

The ambition of this chapter has been to illuminate what 'actively' making sense can look like, where tutor and students re-examine notions including 'work' and 'play'. In attempting to reposition their engagement with these often emotive subjects, students are challenged to deconstruct the western-centric narrative and to recognize the many stories that exist in a myriad of locations.

References

Baudrillard, J. (1994) *Simulacra and Simulation*. Ann Arbor: University of Michigan Press.

Brandt, W. (1980) *North-South: a programme for survival. The Report of the Independent Commission on International Development Issues*. London: Pan Books.

Davies, B. (1996) Agency as a form of discursive practice: a classroom scene observed, *British Journal of Sociology of Education*, 17(1): 341–361.

Fyfe, A. (1989) *Child Labour*. Cambridge: Polity Press.

Green, D. (1998) *Hidden Lives: Voices of Children in Latin America and the Caribbean*. London: Cassell.

Hall, S. (1992) 'The West and the Rest: Discourse and Power', in Hall and Gibben (eds) *Formation of Modernity*. Oxford: Polity Press.

Hobbs, S. and McKechnie, J. (1997) *Child Employment in Great Britain: a Social and Psychological Analysis*. Edinburgh: The Stationery Office.

Holland, P. (1992) 'Cry babies and damaged children', in P. Holland (ed.) *What is a child: Popular Images of Childhood*. London: Virago.

International Labour Organization (2002) *A Future without Child Labour*. Geneva: ILO.

James, A. (1999) 'Researching children's social competence: methods and models', in M. Woodhead, D. Faulkner and K. Littleton (eds) *Making Sense of Social Development*. London: Routledge.

James, A., Jenks, C. and Prout, A. (1998) *Theorizing Childhood*. Cambridge: Polity Press.

Johnson, R. (1999) Colonialism and Cargo Cults in Early Childhood Education: does Reggio Emilia really exist? In Contemporary Issues in Early Childhood Vol 1 No 1 1999.

Klute, G. (1996) in M. Liebel (2004) *A Will of Their Own*. London: Zed Books.

Kummels, I. (1993) in M. Liebel (2004) *A Will of Their Own*. London: Zed Books.

Liebel, M. (2004) *A Will of Their Own*. London: Zed Books.

McKechnie, J. and Hobbs, S. (2001) 'Work and Education', in D. Mizen (ed.) *Hidden Hands: International Perspectives on Children's Work and Labour*. London: Routledge.

Mead, M. (1928) *Coming of Age in Samoa*. New York: Mentor Books.

Meiser, U. (1995) in M. Liebel (2004) *A Will of Their Own*. London: Zed Books.

Melaku, D. (2000) in M. Liebel (2004) *A Will of Their Own*. London: Zed Books.

Myrdal, G. (1969) *Objectivity in Social Research*. New York: Pantheon Books.

Nunes, A. (1999) in M. Liebel (2004) *A Will of Their Own*. London: Zed Books.

Ortiz Rescaniere (1994) in M. Liebel *A Will of Their Own*. London: Zed Books.

Paechter, C. (1998) *Educating the Other*. London: Falmer Press.

Qvortrup, J. (1994) 'Childhood Matters: An Introduction', in J. Qvortrup (ed.) *Childhood Matters*. Aldershot: Avebury.

Rengifo, V. (2001) in M. Liebel (2004) *A Will of Their Own*. London: Zed Books.

Said, E. W. (1985) *Orientalism: Western Concepts of the Orient*. London: Routledge.

Song, M. (2001) 'Chinese children's work roles in migrant adaptation', in P. Mizen (ed.) *Hidden Hands: International Perspectives on Children's Work and Labour*. London: Routledge Falmer.

Stainton Rogers, R. and Stainton Rogers, W. (1992) *Stories of Childhood: Shifting Agendas of Child Concern*. London: Harvester Wheatsheaf.

Swift, A, (1999) *Working Children Get Organised*. London: International Save the Children.

Unicef (2004) Speech delivered by Carol Bellamy, Executive Director, Unicef to launch *The State of the Worlds Children 2005*.

Unicef (2004) *The State of the World's Children 2005*. New York: Unicef.

Weiner, M. (1991) *The Child and the State in India: Child Labour and Education Policy in Comparative Perspectives*. Delhi: Open University Press.

The Concerned for Working Children (CWC), India: http://www.workingchild.org/.

Unicef Press Office: http://www.unicef.org/media/index.html.

15 Understanding development in early childhood

Ian Barron

Introduction

The essential starting point for 'understanding development' is the premise that an understanding of child development will be important to students' work with children. What has become evident in teaching this over a number of years, however, is that encouraging students to engage *critically* with the study of children's development is not as easy as it might at first appear. The first part of this chapter is concerned with the ways in which children's development has traditionally been conceptualized, understood and taught. The second part considers some of the problems that are seen to exist with the traditional model. The final section outlines the beginnings of a different way of thinking about children's development.

Studying children's development

As noted elsewhere in Part 3 (see Chapters 12 and 13), before the late nineteenth century there were very few attempts to study children's development in any systematic way. This is not to say that there had been no interest in children's development. In the seventeenth century John Locke had conceptualized children as being born as 'blank slates'. The contrasting position (as we see in Chapters 12 and 13) was that of the eighteenth century French philosopher Jean-Jacques Rousseau (1993), who believed that children are born with natural goodness and curiosity and those should be nurtured by providing pleasurable experiences of the natural world. However, it was only with the Child Study Movement, which began in the nineteenth century, that for the first time close systematic attention was paid to children's growth and development. Subsequently, as James (1999) notes, for much of the twentieth century (and beyond) developmental psychology dominated how children have been understood.

This chapter begins then with an attempt to establish what students know already about child development, or at least think they know. It seeks to engage students in thinking about the capabilities of children of different ages and challenges them to consider the basis for their knowledge. Students consider how far these capabilities apply to all children. Examples are explored in relation to individual difference and also in relation to how children's capabilities can be seen to be understood in similar ways across different cultures. Students are asked to think about the extent to which adults share or have different capabilities from those of children. They are then encouraged to identify what they believe to be the needs of children of different ages and to examine how far the needs of children reflect notions about children's capabilities. Where notions of need do not appear to reflect capabilities, students reflect upon how they have formed the ideas that they have. They consider how far children's needs are universal and how far they mirror the particular culture and point in time. They also reflect upon how far children's needs are similar to or different from those of adults.

What emerges is a sense that all aspects of children's development are interrelated and interconnected with adults, other children and the world in which they live. In attempting to address the notion of holism, Bronfenbrenner's (1979) ecological model of development is examined. We consider the implications of his contention that children's development is the result of the interactions between the child and significant others at the micro level of the family; the meso and exo levels of the communities and institutions of which the child forms part or which impact indirectly on the child's life; and, finally, the macro level representing the cultural, political, religious, moral and economic imperatives that govern life at the level of any given society.

Traditional accounts of development

What students realize from their reading, however, is that this way of understanding children is not especially widespread in the textbooks, where there is much more of a focus on theories that concern themselves with particular aspects of development and with whether development can be explained in terms of nature or experience. In essence, we enable students to engage with the ideas that have emerged from different theorists as they have engaged with the 'nature–nurture' debate. We encourage students to move to a more sophisticated conceptual understanding than an initial response from them that tends to be, 'It's a bit of this and a bit of that.' The concern is to enable students to explore the ways in which there are parallels, continuities and discontinuities in accounts of children's development.

A brief account is given of the polarities of the 'nature' versus 'nurture' debate. Students examine how some theorists (e.g. Gesell, 1928) have tried to explain changes in how children think and behave in terms of arguing that they are born with predetermined patterns of development and behaviour, which are determined by their genes. In this account, children are seen as being 'pre-wired' to develop in certain ways. Consideration is given to how many of these nature-based ways of explaining development reflect the seemingly 'natural' way in which children develop physically. By contrast, attention is then paid to the nurture model of development, which argues that it is the environment that explains the changes that occur in how children think, behave and develop. Students are encouraged to engage with the work of behaviourists such as Skinner (1957) and their claims that development is driven by the environment and achieved through operant conditioning and positive and negative reinforcement of behaviours. Bandura's (1977) work on social learning theory is then explored as a way of encouraging students to consider other factors that may be seen to determine how children develop and behave. Most students have an intuitive sense of the way in which children watch and imitate and also learn behaviours that they value, in the hope of obtaining the benefits of them for themselves. Students with their own children particularly engage with Bandura's move away from the strict behaviourist view that inner mental processes are irrelevant. They see much that makes sense to them in his later position, which maintains that children observe the consequences of a particular behaviour before deciding whether to pay attention to it.

What emerges from the discussion on the polarities of nature and nurture is a sense from students that both have a part to play. In order to explore this interplay, Freud's (1917) account of psychosexual development is examined. Here the pattern of development is seen as a naturally unfolding series of latent stages, whilst at the same time there is a belief that children's experiences with their parents can affect the path that development takes. Freud sees the child initially as self-seeking and concerned to gratify primitive impulses at all costs. Freud's view is that society cannot function according to this pleasure principle and therefore it is the task of parents to help the child to learn about outer reality and to learn the means of delaying and inhibiting impulse gratification. The source of all selfish impulses is the 'id' and later this is controlled by the 'ego', which restrains these desires. The 'superego' develops from parental controls but becomes internalized as a means of self-regulation. Childhood is considered to consist of a conflict between these three forces.

This same belief in interplay between internal mechanisms and external experience is further explored in relation to Piaget's (1975) contention that development occurs through the active interaction of the child with the environment. Piaget maintains that the development of knowledge and understanding occurs through a maturational unfolding of latent abilities. As the individual interacts with the environment, they seek to make sense of it in particular, predetermined ways. Mental representations of these experiences are then formed, referred to as schemas (more properly *schemata*). New experiences are categorized, either fitting into existing structures/schemas, in which case 'assimilation' occurs, or, if they do not fit, then cognitive conflict or disequilibrium occurs and schemas have to be adapted or new ones formed, and then 'accommodation' occurs in the process that he referred to as 'equilibration'.

Children are seen as having qualitatively different ways of making sense of experience at different times in their lives. These differences find expression in the Sensori-Motor Period (from birth to approximately 18 months), the Preoperational Period (before 6/7 years) and Operational Period (from 7 to approximately 11 years) of the Concrete Operational Stage, and the Formal Operational Period (from the age of approximately 11 onwards). In Piaget's account, the whole of development is to be conceptualized as a journey towards logical and abstract thought.

This emphasis on logical and scientific thought is challenged as attention is paid to the ways in which it can lead to children being judged as less competent than they are. Whilst Piaget characterizes the young child's thinking as essentially egocentric, Donaldson (1978) has been influential in refuting this view. Piaget's studies of the cognitive development of young children were based around a model of research that had its roots in scientific investigation. Donaldson points to the results of subsequent investigations by colleagues to suggest that Piaget's investigations did not necessarily reveal what he claimed they did. Donaldson's colleagues discovered that where the experiments were adapted to make 'human sense', the children performed quite differently from how they had in Piaget's own experiments. For Donaldson, this points to two significant issues. One is that the laboratory may not yield results which are typical of how children behave in other situations. The other is that the researcher and the researched may not share the same frame of reference and may not understand a situation in the same way. Paraphrasing Donaldson, what her colleagues discovered was that in strange situations, with strange adults, children behaved strangely.

Moving beyond the individual

What all of this points to is the importance of culture and context in children's development. In order to explore their significance, attention shifts initially to the work of Erikson (1963) and Vygotsky (1978). Erikson's account was, at least in part, a response to criticisms of Freud that pointed to the way in which Freud's theory appeared to emphasize only internal (and sexual) drives and imperatives. Erikson drew attention to the ways in which culture, context and society affect how children develop. The theory is again stage-based and focuses on crises that shape our identities. The movement, in childhood, is from identity as being developed essentially in interaction with the caregiver in the earliest months, to the influence of the family in pre-school years and onwards to the significance of interactions outside the home in the school years.

Whilst Vygotsky's theory of development has a stage basis to it, it has been very significant in drawing attention to the importance of culture and social interaction with others in shaping development. Vygotsky (1978) maintains that psychological development is not driven entirely by some form of internal force. The process by which children learn is characterized as a very social one: knowledge and understanding develop in social and cultural interaction between the child and significant adults. As Vygotsky notes: 'human learning presupposes a specific social nature and a process by which children grow into the intellectual life of those around them' (1978: 88). Thought is seen as having its origins in action and it becomes a way of controlling and organizing those actions. Language, however, plays a central role in learning (Vygotsky, 1962). The origins of language are seen as being functional: a means of communicating basic needs and desires, such as those for food, drink or comfort. The nature of language changes, however, and it becomes, with considerable adult guidance, a way of planning and carrying out action. Children are considered to learn with and through language, as well as with their hands and eyes. Language is used by the adult as a means of constructing, directing and teaching. The child does not learn in isolation: knowledge is acquired and development occurs in the interface where the learner meets more knowledgeable others. Vygotsky conceptualizes learning as occurring where children move just beyond their present stage of understanding and reach out to understandings just beyond their present capabilities. He referred to this as the 'zone of proximal development' (ZPD), which he explained as:

> . . . the distance between the actual development level as determined by independent problem solving and the level of potential development as determined through problem solving under adult guidance or in collaboration with more capable peers.
>
> (Vygotsky, 1978: 86)

Particular attention is paid to the significance of theorists such as Wood *et al.* (1976) in identifying the types of support that adults provide to support or *scaffold* children's learning in the journey through the ZPD.

The focus is then concerned with ensuring that students do become a little more sophisticated in their understanding than the seeming outcome of these critical engagements with the theoretical positions that all too often have led them to conclude that, 'Well none of them are right and none of them are wrong: development is the result of a little bit of this and a little bit of that.' The results of considering whether there really are significant differences between adults and children can also lead students to conclude that there are not. This is not particularly helpful since it tends to lead them to doubt whether children do have any particular characteristics to which they should be paying attention – an issue where students wish to work with children!

Consideration is therefore given to more recent approaches that seek to identify the influence of both nature and nurture. These have pointed out, on the one hand, that the nature theory fails to take sufficient account of the role of adults, culture and environment in children's development, whilst also pointing out that the nurture argument fails to take sufficient account of the ways in which children appear to have certain preferences and dispositions right from birth. Thought is also given to the ways in which children are different from adults and how this might be explained. Evidence is examined that suggests very strongly that babies are born with certain sensory preferences (e.g. for human faces) and with certain social predispositions, which make them sensitive to the action and expressions of other people (Murray and Andrews, 2000). Students are thus encouraged to engage with current theories that recognize the ways in which children appear to be born with certain predispositions, but that the nature of the child's experiences affects how those predispositions are played out in reality, possibly causing changes to the underlying brain biochemistry (Gopnik *et al.*, 1999; Shonkoff and Phillips, 2000).

As we noted earlier, the main focus of Understanding Development is to develop in students an ability to apply theory to their work with children. In many ways this is a difficult undertaking, given that some students have no prior knowledge of child development, whilst others have some existing basic knowledge from previous studies and some have basic knowledge and a great deal of practical experience of work with children. It is no easy task for students with no prior knowledge to develop sufficient knowledge to engage critically, whilst other students find it difficult to accept that their existing knowledge is relatively superficial and may need to be rethought. One final year student recently commented that she had only just recovered from the collapse that she experienced, almost two years previously, of what she had believed to be certainties.

Reconceptualizing development

We attempt to engage with these challenges and to encourage students to think critically, holistically and cross-culturally about their understandings in relation to young children. It must be admitted that success in achieving these aims tends to be rather mixed. Some students do manage to think holistically about the ways in which all aspects of children's development and experience affect other aspects but many do not. Perhaps this is hardly surprising given the relatively traditional way in which Understanding Development deals separately with the different aspects of children's development. Despite much rhetoric about holism, child development textbooks fall into the same traps and do little to support students' understandings about what holistic accounts of development might actually mean. As one student notes:

> There are many different theories about the various aspects of child development and many of them contradict each other. Most theories focus on one or two aspects of development, which gives people the information and ability to understand that aspect of a child's development. However by separating the theories into different areas it makes it difficult to gather a holistic view of children's development. Children develop at different rates and in different areas depending on the child, their environment and other influences, so it would be difficult to produce holistic theories . . . but without it, it is difficult to get an overall view of the child.

The question now to be asked, however, is whether conceiving of development holistically is helpful. The answer depends on what we mean by holism in relation to development. If we mean that accounts of development need to take account of the universal principles that govern all aspects of children's development, in the manner of Piaget, then it is doubtful whether this conception of holism is helpful. If we mean an awareness of the ways in which different aspects of children's development interrelate and affect each other, then this may have some value, particularly if we move away from conceiving of development essentially as being located within the child. What is clear is that despite exhortations to think of children's development 'holistically', students still tend to see development as a series of unconnected incidents. Whilst there are ways in which it may be just that, as we shall see, there has been no conceptual attempt to explore the reasons. Nor has there been enough attention paid to enabling students to truly understand development as an essentially social, political and cultural phenomenon. In short, many of the old certainties have been removed without enabling students to move towards an alternative way of viewing children's development.

What is called for is a major reframing of understanding development, one that conceives of development as occurring within a framework of social practices and under the gaze of culture and institutions (Foucault, 1998). The basis for the reconceptualization is thus variously in the work of Bronfenbrenner (1979), Lave and Wenger (1991) and Foucault (1998), who see learning and development as occurring through participation in social settings, activities and events. Lave and Wenger's theory was developed from research with apprentices, which explored the ways in which apprentices initially engaged in legitimate peripheral participation, undertaking non-crucial tasks that would not put the whole undertaking at risk if not completed wholly successfully, through to full participation. This marks a shift away from stage-based models that have argued for universal patterns of development. The child is conceived as participating, initially peripherally, in different communities of practice, with different participants with different levels of skills, understanding and behaviours. These communities of practice are formed from those who have a legitimate role in relation to particular understandings and ways of being. Thus they also involve relationships of power and surveillance (Foucault, 1998). They are the context within which children develop and learn about who they are. Development is therefore seen as occurring in the interactions that form part of particular communities of practice. What is being argued is that children's development, in all its aspects, is a social process but that different communities of practice will lead to the development of particular skills and understandings. In this sense, learning and development are situated in the particular community of practice in which they occur and the development of ways of being in one context does not necessarily transfer to another. What is also being suggested is that learning and development are 'out there' – they are not merely located within the individual.

Internalization of learning and development follows in the trail of social and community experience. The process by which they become located in the individual is conceived as occurring through the notion of apprenticeship – children engage in the things in which they are competent but become capable of new undertakings and are gradually introduced to greater complexity. Children's independent competencies are those which they have internalized. They have a wider range of competencies, however, as part of a community of practice, but these skills, understandings and behaviours are not performed independently: they are performed as assisted social practices. In this sense, the move from peripheral to central legitimate participation has much in common with Vygotsky's notion of the zone of proximal development. Competent learners are learners who have been and are supported by encouraging and sensitive adults, who make very careful decisions about the things that children can do and can learn for themselves and the things with which they need some help. This is similar to the way that Bruner (1977) conceptualizes as 'scaffolding' or Lave and Wenger (1991) as legitimate participation in a community of practice, or Foucault (1998) might conceptualize as the exercise of surveillance and power.

Post-modern understandings about development

It is hoped that this reframed way of looking at notions of holism in relation to children's development addresses some of the problems identified at the beginning of the chapter. Part of what is being suggested is that the notion of looking at children holistically is much more complex than has hitherto been suggested. Whilst Bronfenbrenner's ecological model need not be wholly abandoned, one needs to look again at what it might mean in a post-modern era. The micro, exo, meso and macro systems need to be considered not only in terms of their connections to the child but also in terms of the disconnections, false starts and contrary effects. This then reconceptualizes the ecological model as a dynamic framework within which life and development are played out. Discontinuities are seen to be as important as continuities in a model of development in which children engage as participants in different communities of practice under the gaze of the power exerted by adults and institutions over how children develop. The move away from traditional models has tended to lead to students struggling to come to terms with how to conceive of development if all the old certainties have been removed. What has been offered here is the beginning of a scaffold on which to begin to build a reconceptualized model of how to understand children's development.

References

Bandura, A. (1977) *Social Learning Theory*. Englewood Cliffs, NJ: Prentice-Hall.

Bronfenbrenner, U. (1979) *The Ecology of Human Development: Experiments by Nature and Design*. Cambridge, Mass: Harvard University Press.

Bruner, J. S. (1977) *The Process of Instruction*. Cambridge, Mass: Harvard University Press.

Donaldson, M. (1978) *Children's Minds*. London: Fontana.

Erikson, E. H. (1963) *Children and Society* (2nd edn). New York: W.W. Norton.

Foucault, M. (1998) *The Will to Knowledge*. London: Penguin.

Freud, S. (1917) *A General Introduction to Psychoanalysis*. New York: Washington Square Press.

Gesell, A. (1928) *Infancy and Human Growth*. New York: Macmillan.

Gopnik, A., Meltzoff, A. and Kuhl, P. (1999) *How Babies Think: The Science of Childhood*. London: Weidenfeld and Nicolson.

James, A. (1999) 'Researching Children's Social Competence', in M. Woodhead, D. Faulkner and K. Littleton (eds) *Cultural Worlds of Early Childhood*. London: Routledge.

Lave, J. and Wenger, E. (1991) *Situated Learning: Legitimate Peripheral Participation*. Cambridge: Cambridge University Press.

Locke, J. (1964) *Some Thoughts Concerning Education*. London: Heinemann.

Murray, L. and Andrews, E. (2000) *The Social Baby*. London: Richmond Press.

Piaget, J. (1975) *The Child's Conception of the World*. Lanham, Maryland, USA: Littlefield Adams Quality Paperbacks.

Rousseau, J. -J. (1993) *Emile*. London: Everyman.

Shonkoff, J. and Phillips, D. (2000) *From Neurons to Neighborhoods: The Science of Early Childhood Development*. Washington: National Academy Press.

Shore, R. (1997) *Rethinking the Brain: New Insights into Early Development.* New York: Families and Work Institute.

Skinner, B. F. (1957) *Verbal Behaviour.* New York: Appleton-Century-Crofts.

Vygotsky, L. S. (1962) *Thought and Language.* Cambridge, Mass: MIT Press.

Vygotsky, L. S. (1978) *Mind in Society.* London: Harvard University Press.

Wood, D., Bruner, J. S. and Ross, G. (1976) The role of tutoring in problem solving, *Journal of Child Psychology and Psychiatry*, 17: 89–100.

16 Concluding remarks

Liz Jones, Ian Barron, John Powell and Rachel Holmes

The writing of this book has been a year-long enterprise. During that time rough drafts of chapters have been exchanged and many, many conversations have been spawned where there has been a constant toing and froing between the writing, our practice and theories. So, in writing this book, what have been our intentions? As is often the case, perhaps by highlighting what we did not intend we may come closer to articulating our overall ambitions. We knew, for example, that we wanted to avoid writing that was prescriptive in nature and yet we did want to contribute towards generating knowledge, including that concerned with children and childhood. We also knew that we wanted to articulate aspects of our practice, but without inferring complacency or satisfaction at having got it 'right'. We also wanted to avoid linear accounts of practice, where the reader is offered 'step by step' guidance into, for example, the development of a multiprofessional perspective. True, the students begin in year one and progress through to year three. But the tussles that occur within this time, where intellectual growth and practical wisdom deepens and intensifies, defy explanations that are rooted in modernist conceptions of linear progress. There is undoubtedly progression, but it is one that is characterized by erratic zigzagging rather than a smooth or even route.

Overall, we have come to see the process of writing this book as 'ground-clearing' (Trinh, 1989: 41) activity. Effectively, the writing has allowed us to dig away at practice and, in so doing, create openings where there have been possibilities for us to reconsider familiar and well-trodden territory. We have noted, for example, that many of our commonplace activities where, say, we describe and categorize young children and their families are both essential and yet deeply questionable. So, when writing, we have tried to avoid offering solutions. We have also become critical of and therefore wary of overarching or meta narratives that offer us generalized accounts of early childhood. However, it should be noted that being wary is not the same as outright rejection. Rather, it demands a relentless activity on the part of the practitioner where commonsense understandings are interrogated, questioned and reconsidered.

As has been noted, a traditional metaphor that has been used in order to summarize young children and their development has been 'the garden', where careful nurturing of the roots will favour strong growth. However, much of the preceding writing has been critical of development that is embedded in what could be described as a 'root tree' metaphor (Deleuze and Guattari, 1987). So, if we can no longer depend on the 'root tree' metaphor as a means for capturing the fragmentation of lived experiences, do we have any other metaphorical choices as we look to the future?

Patti Lather (1993) favours the 'rhizome'. We too find resonance in the rhizome as a metaphorical way of conceptualizing the terrain of early years for two reasons. First, it is still embedded in nature, so there is a sense of the continuing conversation that needs to be had with the past as we set about anticipating the future. Second, they 'function' in extraordinary ways and it is the activity of the rhizome, its movements as well as its physical manifestations that 'metaphorically' appeal to us:

> Rhizomes defy the regularity of linear growth. They do not have a central or main trunk. Nor do they emerge from a single root. Instead, with their underground stems and aerial roots, they upset all preconceptions that are brought to notions of growth.
>
> (Brown and Jones, 2001: 179)

So, as a metaphor, rhizomes work against the constraints of authority, regularity and common sense and open up thought to creative constructions. Moreover, they have a disregard for prescribed order and patterned ways of being. In place of 'the smooth unfolding of an orderly growth' (Lecercle, 1990: 132–3), there is an appreciation of haphazard and random growth. As a way of continuing to 'function rhizomatically' (Lather, 1993: 680), we end the book with some further pressing questions.

What do we understand childhood to be in the post-modern era?

As discussed earlier, traditional studies of young children have tended to focus on debates, which have long since become tired, about whether development should be understood to be driven by 'nature' or by 'nurture'. Concerns that 'nature' theories lead to determinist views of outcomes for children and that the 'nurture' argument leads to a feeling that children are born without any skills or abilities have tended to create a situation in which many accounts of young children's development seem to go little beyond arguing that both are somehow involved.

Much thought on young children has also tended to argue for a holistic approach, whilst continuing to work with the conventional separate aspects, such as intellectual, linguistic, social, emotional and physical. Penn (2005) draws attention to the notion of these categories as constructs, created by North American and European psychology. More generally, it could be argued, the legacy of western psychology has been to create views of young children as deficient and going through 'stages' on a journey towards adult competence. Little is said about the ways in which adults are not universally competent and much is made of what young children cannot do, despite evidence of the many skills and attributes that they demonstrate from very early in their lives. It is also the case that such accounts of young children and their development have given a privileged position to the development of logical thinking, which has been seen as the necessary precondition for social and emotional under-standing, which are then viewed from the same stance.

More recent approaches to studying young children have sought to address some of these issues but have raised others. Whilst more attention has come to be paid to social and contextual aspects, development has also tended to be viewed still as something that occurs within the child, though it is con-cerned with understandings about the world and other people in relation to and beyond the child. Some theorists have also sought to emphasize the com-petence that young children are seen to demonstrate from birth, or very soon after, and have argued that the first three years have lifelong consequences (see, for example, Shore, 1997). Others, such as Bruer (1999), have argued that development is much more plastic, right through to middle childhood, and argue against special significance being attached to this period as one critical to lifelong development. There have also been some recent attempts (see, for example, Morss, 1996) to argue that the notion of development itself is a myth, but care needs to be taken, perhaps, that sufficient attention is paid to the relative dependency that very young children do experience.

So what view of the young child are we left with at the end of this book and in the post-modern era? First, it must be acknowledged that young chil-dren can only ever be understood as the constructs and products of the society and culture in which they live. This is not to say that the child's role is passive and that they do not influence the society and culture in turn. However, even here, any claims for the active role of the child are the result of political and cultural permissions and construction. Certainly in the west, there are reasons to claim that the interplay of children's early dispositions, skills and under-standings with social and cultural experience leads to competence as children engage actively with others in making meanings. But these claims are the result of how young children are constructed in particular industrialized coun-tries, and the construct of young children and their development is a situational one.

The form that young children's lives take and the sense that they make of the world in which they find themselves are therefore to be understood as constructs that are negotiated in the moment in interaction with significant peers, adults and the culture of which they form part. These interactions are marked by discontinuity and interruption as children engage in different developmental performances and practices under the gaze of the power exerted by adults and institutions within a cultural and historical context. The young child is perceived as a social being whose experience of life and the world is filtered through gender and, later, through other aspects, such as ethnicity, sexuality and class. The development of the young child is therefore understood not only to be the result of cognitive processes but also of social and cultural practices played out amongst discourses of power. This conception has much in common with Bourdieu's position, when he argues that the individual is and becomes what the historical, social and cultural confines of the habitus permit:

> . . . the *habitus* makes possible the free production of all the thoughts, perceptions and actions inherent in the particular conditions of its production – and only those . . . the *habitus* is an infinite capacity for generating products – thoughts, perceptions, expressions and actions – whose limits are set by the historically and socially situated conditions of its production.
>
> (Bourdieu, 1990: 55)

Young children's development is therefore perhaps best thought of as both personal and structural, both internal and external, both continuous and discontinuous, and both open and bound.

How can services capture and support the fragmentation of lived experiences?

Earlier we identified a shift from the notion of development as embedded in a 'root tree' metaphor (Deleuze and Guattari, 1987) towards the concept of a rhizome – movement that works against the constraints of authority, regularity and common sense. We consider the concept of the rhizome to offer us more creative ways to explore social phenomena. With this in mind, we intend to contemplate how we can begin to reframe the services that function to support early childhood experiences. In a way that unleashes different ideological positions and interrogates historical debris that may bind provision and practices to a traditional and formulaic 'root tree', we hope to reconceptualize service-based initiatives and the ways they could begin to celebrate more diverse, haphazard and random development.

In keeping with the spirit of the metaphor of childhood as 'the garden', early childhood services may symbolize the apparatus of support and intervention known to most gardeners attempting to ensure the best growing conditions. This metaphor paints a picture of the 'child' as a delicate plant requiring careful tending by a host of intervening and watchful personnel – an army of gardeners. One reading of the nursery could be as a place for providing early nurturing and protection for the fragile plantlings or children from the severity of the wider environment. The increasing range of practitioners could be understood as skilled gardeners equipped with the necessary knowledge and understandings to attentively nurture uniformity of growth and provide appropriate intervention when any signs of 'hindered' or 'irregular' development are identified.

However, there is a sense that all has not been well in the childhood garden for some time and Beck argues that we have become involved in an elaborate fantasy that centres on the child:

> . . . the child is the source of the last *remaining, irrevocable, unexchangeable primary relationship*. Partners come and go. The child stays. Everything that is desired, but not realizable in the relationship, is directed towards the child.
>
> (Beck, 1992: 118, authors' own emphasis)

Embedding this idea within the services we provide for young children, it could be argued that, embroiled within such adult fantasies, the adult is not solely concerned with enhanced opportunity for growth and achievement. They are also concerned to keep the child under their watchful scrutiny to ensure protection and stability within an ever changing and increasingly dangerous world and, by so doing, to maintain control. We could argue that historically and with some considerable debris today, this sense of adult, particularly professional 'knowing' and control, emerges from a rather fixed understanding of the child. This is a construct of the child 'in need' of control and therefore in some way lacking, inadequate, with a tendency to stray and able to be subjected to a series of corrective experiences in order to return them to a steady and desirable growth pattern. In other words, within the adult world there seem to be 'mediated truths' around how a child should develop, behave and respond, and what a child should be experiencing and should become.

Subsequently, the identification of some children as not achieving their potential, perhaps because of environmental variables, appears to be being dealt with through the development of a wide range of government legislation that has led to a range of far reaching policies. This has resulted in a powerful restructuring of services, radically reshaping them and their attendant personnel. However, have these changes necessarily dislodged the notion of the 'root tree' by beginning to address authoritarian tendencies and regularity within services, or merely reaffirmed this as a central tenet? Instead, by identifying ineffective gardeners with ineffective tools, perhaps these changes are realizing a reconceptualized vision of services, but nevertheless working within the same conceptualization of the child. Undoubtedly, changes have appeared to be sudden, rapid and all-embracing, presenting a number of significant challenges for students, practitioners and tutors who are attempting to understand how the infrastructure of services and the changes in practices available for young children and their families will affect their lives.

The government makes the powerful case that through initiatives such as Sure Start Children's Centres and Full Extended Schools, systems will be more effective and practitioner relationships will be a central requirement of working together in the best interests of children. However, as demonstrated throughout this book, students in their classwork debate issues and concerns in multiprofessional contexts relating to the boundaries around many professional practices. It is as if the childcare services garden were heavily populated with gardeners, each with their own set of methods and practices for ensuring growth and a safe environment. Questions, such as 'how will the many practitioners understand which part of the garden or the child is their responsibility?' and 'whose words will weigh heaviest?', begin to explore the dynamics of multiprofessional working. But do these preoccupations remain within the restraints of the 'root tree' metaphor, denying a shift towards more creative constructions of the child swirling within rhizomatic activity?

In this book we have discussed how constructions of professional identity and status can often lead to the development of hierarchies of service that may undermine democratic and shared communication. This point raises concerns for the whole modernizing project referred to in the green paper *Every Child Matters* and suggests the need for a more deep-rooted examination of the ways that professional practitioners may relate to each other. A significant obstacle to service cooperation has been concerned with how practitioners appear to understand institutional and cultural dynamics required for improving communication and whether any barricades consisting of perceived difference and self-importance can be overcome. We ponder how the emergence of a shared language and integrated practices might begin to explore some of these dilemmas. However, we also wonder if we are still distracted by finding new ways to tender the same type of plantling rather than conceive of the plantling in new ways, upsetting all preconceptions that are brought to notions of growth (Brown and Jones, 2001: 179).

The Sure Start programmes, with integrated services and developing interagency collaboration, have worked to find very real ways to 'service' communities, by involving parents and widening participation in a range of endeavours. An example is a project based at Manchester Art Gallery, which involved parents, children and practitioners in a variety of creative experiences, exploring approaches to early years pedagogy in different contexts. This project has now developed into working more closely with parents to explore their own sense of creative expression and their use of the gallery as a context where their own learning can be a creative journey. Clearly, these could be seen as tokenistic and isolated experiences and, although parents and children were integral to the projects' evaluation, may be interpreted as predictable practices, where parents and children have things 'done to' them by professionals, rather than becoming part of a more fluid, rhizomatic journey.

Dominant white, middle class ideologies embedded within the 'root tree' pattern of development could be perceived to have influenced Sure Start's very geographical locations. Could a single way of understanding growth, a dominant view of conducive conditions for growth and the belief in particular types of intervention for what is thought to be 'hindered' or 'irregular' growth have been obscured by politically correct gestures to meet the needs of the community? Areas deemed 'socially deprived' or 'arid' in terms of their insufficient conditions for healthy growth and development are targeted for such programmes. Therefore, are families living in the vicinity of Sure Start programmes perceived as failing to furnish this normalizing construct of the 'root tree', whose plantling survival seems to be threatened by the destructive variables that abound, that is unless it is rescued?

Seeds for growth need soil, water, sunshine and so forth. If seeds are read as children, then we have a situation where things are 'done to' the child – in other words, the child is voiceless and uninvolved in their own development, a development that takes a singular form. However, Foucault reflects that resistance may play a significant part in relationships and can, in this instance, be related to a shift towards services recognizing the rhizomatic activities of the child/adult, professional/parent relationship: 'I think that resistance is part of the strategic relationship of which power consists. Resistance really always relies upon the situation against which it struggles' (1994: 168). How are children and families able to resist the all-enveloping scaffolding of reinvigorated services in the community? The first point of resistance is to raise questions around whose childhood is it anyway? Will children and their parents be unable to escape the monolithic, ubiquitous and confining ties of the elaborate framework that has been assembled around them with its high profile strategic objectives?

A second point of resistance is to explore how this framework constructs the child. If we can become sensitive to ways the child is positioned, it may enable us to begin to conceptually subvert the constructions of the child assumed by the framework's hierarchical structures. As mentioned within different chapters throughout the book (including, for example, Chapters 10 and 15), young children's development has historically been understood in many different ways and the services, provision and practices have evolved to accommodate those shifts. Within this conclusion it is suggested that development is perhaps best thought of as personal and structural, internal and external, continuous and discontinuous, open and bound, a rhizome that defies the regularity of linear growth. So, we contemplate how services can develop in ways that celebrate this forceful sense of complexity, whereby multiple conversations and sites of resistance are enabled in relation to the child contemplating 'who am I?' and 'who can I become?'

Perhaps Deleuze's and Guattari's (1987) positioning of the rhizome in polar opposition to the 'root tree' employs a dualism of models that allows us to move through a process making visible the situation against which resistance can struggle. An arborescent framework of services would pre-exist the individual, who is then integrated into it at an allotted place. Alternatively, services that are sensitive to rhizomatic activity would be without a centralized, hierarchical organization, allowing for the reopening of flows that otherwise are shut down. So, how do we perceive Sure Start programmes, for example, within this continuum, and how do we understand this notion of resistance? Resistance against what? By whom? We acknowledge that services need to be seen as constantly in the process of becoming, rather than as having arrived at, discernible points and hence are able to be categorized. The quantity, pace and ongoing changes within new centralized and government-led initiatives, which at the outset are characterized by an arborescent and hierarchical structure, seems to be an interesting point to consider within this context.

This top-down model seems to rely on the effectiveness of Sure Start and Full Extended Schools being able to develop a sense of meaningful relationships, not solely between each other but also importantly with families in the local communities. Families will be encouraged to access a range of services on one site and practitioners will be able to develop supportive and preventative programmes to reverse exclusionary stances by offering childcare and a range of courses such as those focusing on parenting skills.

However, it is the government that is taking the lead in identifying what counts as the 'needs of families'. In other words, these initiatives mentioned in the green paper have serious purposes to improve the potential of growth for both children and their families, but the way that growth is referred to is to reintroduce parents and carers in the community to seek paid work. Whilst this, it is claimed, can lead to a more inclusive society, self-exclusion from this strategy receives little sympathy. For some parents the policy espoused by *Every Child Matters* moves power from the family into the hands of professional practitioners, maintaining a framework of services that does indeed at the outset pre-exist the individual, who is then integrated into it at an allotted place. For practitioners and students alike, this approach may raise some uncomfortable questions about the purpose of intervention and whether surveillance is becoming a central, though rather understated, expectation which foregrounds all multiprofessional interaction and activity.

The long-term commitment to evolving longevity and 'grass roots' involvement of the community within all aspects of a programme's management, autonomy, development and aspirations may create the space and opportunities to resist the structures that initially dictated its purpose. Perhaps the passing of time will enable initiatives such as Sure Start to become bedded down into the fabric of local communities, for them to become integral to the ways communities operate, for services to capture and support the fragmentation of lived experiences and find new ways to nurture more meaningful connections. With time to develop, they may begin to become rhizomorphous, as Deleuze and Guattari suggest, to produce stems and filaments that seem to be roots, or better yet connect with them by penetrating the trunk, but put them to new uses. With time, services could begin to sprawl amongst the communities, wander like '. . . "couch grass", creating multiplicities of narratives and dimensions that proliferate in less predictable ways and towards unexpected places' (Piper and Garratt, 2004: 4).

One of these 'unexpected places' might be the short lifetime and eventual abolition of initiatives, which a recent article suggests is already a reality: '. . . one quite momentous change has gone relatively unnoticed: the government's much-lauded Sure Start programme has been abolished' (Glass, 2005: 2). So much has already been embedded within the Sure Start initiative, but time for further bedding down, reflection, transformation and a sense of ownership needs to be given in order to move beyond the constraints of the hierarchical structure from which it came.

When considering other 'unexpected places', we are not arguing for a polarized 'poor' or 'good' garden in relation to services, but rather how we think about growth and the child differently, how, when and to whom we can ask critical questions. The attractiveness of stability can lead services to become stuck, believing particular ways of doing things are 'successful', comfortable, safe, assured, but not necessarily creative. We have learned to read things in particular ways – for example, a well attended parenting class equals success, but consideration of who and why particular people are attending may give critical insights. 'Unexpected places' could bring a sense of flux and fluidity into the dynamics of what we are able to live with, whereby professionals become destabilized and positioned differently, opening the flow to a multiplicity of pathways and routes to more rhizomatic relationships. For example, Whalley *et al.* reflect upon an Early Excellence Centre which places a strong emphasis on the importance of including parents in devising and designing projects:

> . . . large numbers of parents were involved in conceptualizing the local targets and programmes of work . . . the key issue for early childhood educators . . . was to build a strong relationship with parents . . .
> (Whalley *et al.*, 2001: 7–9)

Perhaps here, those 'unexpected places' might be anticipated in the process of taking a more critical gaze upon taken-for-granted terms such as 'involved' and 'strong relationship'. The potential singularity of both could be reframed to encompass the multiple complexities of shifting and fluid relationships and the different ways they take form in the equally as fluid act of involvement. Rather than a pseudo-strength of relationship (which might be borne out of one talking, the other listening in the act of pseudo-involvement), the mobility of a rhizomatic journey – on levels that engage the personal and structural, the internal and external, that is continuous and discontinuous, open and bound – could open up pathways to resistance on multiple levels.

References

Beck, U. (1992) *Risk Society: Towards a New Modernity*. London: Sage.

Bourdieu, P. (1990) *The Logic of Practice*. Cambridge: Polity Press.

Brown, T. and Jones, L. (2001) *Action Research and Postmodernism: Congruence and Critique*. Buckingham: Open University Press.

Bruer, J. (1999) *The Myth of the First Three Years: A New Understanding of Early Brain Development and Lifelong Learning*. New York: Free Press.

Deleuze, G. and Guattari, F. (1987) A Thousand Plateaus: Capitalism and Schizophrenia.

Glass, N. (2005) Surely Some Mistake?, *Society Guardian*, 5th January: 2–3.

Lather, P. (1993) Fertile obsession: validity after post-structuralism, *The Sociological Quarterly*, 34(4): 673–693.

Lecerle, J-J. (1990) *The Violence of Language*. London: Routledge.

Morss, J. (1996) *Growing Critical: Alternatives to Development Psychology*. London: Routledge.

Penn, H. (2005) *Understanding Early Childhood: Issues and Controversies*. Maidenhead: Open University Press.

Piper, H. and Garratt, D. (2004) Identity and Citizenship: Some contradictions in practice, *British Journal of Educational Studies*, 52(3): 276–292.

Rabinow, P. (1994) *Michel Foucault Ethics – Essential Works of Foucault 1954–1984 Vol.1*. London: Penguin.

Shore, R. (1997) *Rethinking the Brain: New Insights into Early Development*. New York: Families and Work Institute.

Trinh, T. Minh-ha (1989) *Woman, Native, Other: Writing Postcoloniality and Feminism*. Bloomington IN: Indiana University Press.

Whalley, M. and the Pen Green Team (2001) *Involving Parents in their Children's Learning*. London: Sage.

Index

Related books from Open University Press
Purchase from www.openup.co.uk or order through your local bookseller

---

CRITICAL ISSUES IN EARLY CHILDHOOD EDUCATION

Nicola Yelland (ed)
Victoria University, Australia

This book is a valuable contribution to the creation of a more critical and theoretically diverse approach to early childhood policy and practice. Through many vivid examples and a varied cast-list of authors, both academics and practitioners, it shows the potential of this approach for pedagogical work in early childhood institutions and the education of the early childhood workforce.

> Professor Peter Moss, Institute of Education, University of London, UK

This book challenges long-established beliefs about early childhood education. It offers readers the opportunity to think about the aspects of their profession that are fundamental to providing effective and equitable educational opportunities for young children in the 21st century. Well-known contributors explore issues that are not only 'critical' in terms of being fundamental to early childhood education, but also 'critical' in that they present alternative ideas and use frameworks that are not traditional to the field. Organized in three parts, the book considers:

- Contemporary views of early childhood education and teaching
- The rethinking of early childhood practices
- The emergence of new technologies and multiliteracies

The chapters in the book focus on aspects of early childhood education that have for a long time been accepted as truisms, or have been too hard to deal with and thus often ignored. For example, they include a consideration of issues that range from examining play that might be sexual in focus or learning how to cope with traumatic events in young children's lives, to the ways in which popular culture and new literacies impact on what young children are interested in and how they can be engaged in learning with information and communications technology.

Essential reading for students in all early childhood studies programmes, as well as early childhood practitioners who want to engage in more reflective practices around their work.

Contributors
Yarrow Andrew, Mindy Blaise, Liz Brooker, Sheralyn Campbell, Gaile Cannella, Eileen Honan, Richard Johnson, Anna Kilderry, Jackie Marsh, Jeanette Rhedding-Jones, Leonie Rowan, Sharon Ryan, Jonathan Silin, Jennifer Sumsion, Daniel Walsh, Nicola Yelland

April 2005   208pp   0 335 21596 3 (Paperback)   £18.99
0 335 21597 1 (Hardback)   £60.00

UNDERSTANDING EARLY CHILDHOOD

Helen Penn

Understanding Early Childhood offers a broad and wide-ranging perspective on the ways in which we try to understand young children. It summarizes some of the current debates in child development and looks at other forms of understanding and the kinds of methods used to gain understanding. It explores personal memories of childhood; neuro-scientific and genetic interpretations of childhood; and cultural understandings. Drawing on research evidence from across the world, it includes chapters on history, health and child rights. The book concludes with an analysis of everyday practices in working with young children from across the world.

This book is key reading for early childhood students and practitioners.

Contents
Preface – Remembering Childhood – Researching Reality – Not Piaget Again – Genes, Neurons and Ancestors – The Other Side of the World – Past Present and Future – Children's Rights: A New Approach to Studying Childhood – Hoping for Health – Practice Makes No Difference – References

Contributors
Priscilla Alderson; Val Thurtle

c.192pp   0 335 21134 8 (Paperback)   0 335 21135 6 (Hardback)

SHAPING EARLY CHILDHOOD
LEARNERS, CURRICULUM AND CONTEXTS

Glenda Mac Naughton

This key textbook introduces students and practitioners to a wide range of different approaches to early childhood. It provides practical strategies for developing and implementing early learning experiences that promote excellence and equity for children. By examining different perspectives, the book helps early childhood practitioners to navigate their way through competing views, make informed choices, and be critically reflective in their work. In an accessible, lively and user-friendly way, it explores issues such as:

- What constitutes an appropriate early childhood curriculum
- How best to study and assess children
- Involving parents and children in early childhood learning

The book features a range of pedagogical devices to inspire early childhood workers to reflect critically on their work and the ideas underpinning it, including boxed definitions of key terms; ideas summary charts and ideas galleries; clarification exercises; case studies; further reading lists.

This essential textbook is ideal for students undertaking early childhood qualifications at degree level, Masters courses in early childhood education, and for practitioners who work with children from birth to eight in early childhood settings.

Contents
Foreword – Acknowledgements – Introduction – Part 1: Models of the learner – Reflecting on the learner – Models of the learner: Conforming to nature, conforming to culture – Models of the learner: reforming through interaction between nature and culture – Models of the learner: Transforming culture and nature – Models of the learner: Critical reflections – Part 2: Positions on the early childhood curriculum – Reflecting on the early childhood curriculum – Curriculum position: conforming to society – Curriculum position: reforming society – Curriculum position: transforming society – Curriculum positions: critical reflections – Part 3: Curriculum contexts – Reflecting on contexts – Curriculum contexts: parents and communities – Curriculum contexts: becoming an early childhood professional – Curriculum contexts: critical reflections – References – Index.

368pp   0 335 21106 2 (Paperback)